AF646180

LOOK EAST POLICY AND INDIA'S NORTH EAST

Polemics and Perspectives

ABOUT THE CENTRE

The *Centre for Alternative Discourse, Manipur*, which is run by Research Foundation Charitable Trust, a registered body, constituted under the Indian Trusts Act, 1882, and registered under Registration of Societies Act, 1908, publishes the journal 'Alternative Perspectives'. The *Centre for Alternative Discourse, Manipur* is an outcome of year long discussion and consultation among the academicians, intellectuals, social activists and scholars of the state with a view to promote a sensible, systematic and informed study on various issues in human society through the publication of an academic journal. The very inception of the idea of establishing a centre to promote constructive, insightful, critical inquiries into the existing material conditions and circumstances in the state, the region and the world, which has a direct or indirect bearing upon the lives of the people came from the recognition of a need to critique the economics, politics, history and culture of the realities surrounding our lives. The establishment of the *Centre for Alternative Discourse, Manipur* represents our understanding that we belong to a critical historical epoch.

About the Editor

Dr. Thingnam Kishan Singh is a senior faculty in English in Manipur University. He taught earlier at Shyam Lal College (Delhi University) and D.M. College of Arts, Imphal. He is the author of the book *Rethinking Colonialism* (Delhi and Kolkata: Worldview Publishers). Besides contributing regularly in several journals across the country he has been the editor of the quarterly journal *Alternative Perspectives* since 2005. He can be reached at th_kishan@yahoo.co.in

LOOK EAST POLICY AND INDIA'S NORTH EAST

Polemics and Perspectives

Edited by

Thingnam Kishan

Published for

Centre for Alternative Discourse, Manipur

by

CONCEPT PUBLISHING COMPANY, NEW DELHI-110059

Cataloging in Publication Data—DK
Courtesy: D.K. Agencies (P) Ltd. <docinfo@dkagencies.com>

Look east policy and India's north east : polemics and perspectives / edited by Thingnam Kishan Singh.
p. cm.
Contributed articles; previously published in Alternative frames, a journal.
Includes bibliographical references.
Includes index.
ISBN 13:'9788180694486
ISBN 10: 8180694488

1. India—Foreign relations—Southeast Asia. 2. Southeast Asia—Foreign relations—India. 3. India, Northeastern--Economic policy. 4. Manipur (India)—Economic policy. 5. India, Northeastern—Politics and government. I. Kishan Singh, Thingnam. II. Centre for Alternative Discourse, Manipur.

DDC 327.540 59 22

All rights reserved. No part of this work may be reproduced, stored in a retrieval system, or transmitted in any form or by any means, electronic, mechanical, photocopying, micro-filming recording or otherwise, without the prior written permission of the copyright owner and the publisher.

ISBN-13: 978-81-8069-448-6
ISBN-10: 81-8069-448-8

First Published 2009

© Centre for Alternative Discourse, Manipur

Published and Printed by
Ashok Kumar Mittal
Concept Publishing Company
A/15-16, Commercial Block, Mohan Garden
New Delhi-110059 (INDIA)

Phones : 25351460, 25351794
Fax : 091-11-25357103
Email : publishing@conceptpub.com

Preface

The present edited volume is an overall product of a series of articles published thematically in the first four issues of *Alternative Frames*, a quarterly journal which was subsequently rechristened as Alternative Perspectives following the granting of RNI—Title Clearance to it. The journal is a humble attempt to critically intervene into the debates generated from the impending India's Look East Policy. Apart from initiating a sustained academic engagement on the said issue, it also aims at providing critical and constructive evaluation of the existing conditions and circumstances keeping in view the socio-political, historical, cultural and material realities surrounding the region and the world.

The *Alternative Perspectives*, formerly known as *Alternative Frames*, as cited above intends to serve as an academic platform where the ever increasing researchers and intellectuals can reflect upon the deep-rooted socio-political and economic crises besetting the state and the region and also lead an insightful and objective investigation and interpretation of the social phenomena in their multiple aspects. The *Alternative Perspectives* is published by the Centre for Alternative Discourse, Manipur (CADM), which is run by Research Foundation Charitable Trust, a registered body, constituted under the Indian Trust Act, 1882, and registered under Registration of Societies Act, 1908. The Centre for Alternative Discourse, Manipur is an outcome of year-long discussion and consultation initiated by the academicians, intellectuals, scholars, thinkers and social activists of the state with the objective to promote a sensible, systematic and informed study on various issues confronting the North East Region through the publication of an academic journal. The very inception of the idea of establishing the centre came from the recognition of a need to critique the realities surrounding our social existence. The establishment of the Centre for Alternative Discourse, Manipur represents our understanding that we belong to a critical historical epoch. An acutely felt need to engage the emerging as well as persisting realities is crucial behind the genesis of the centre.

Beginning October 2005, the Centre for Alternative Discourse, Manipur has till date successfully published seven issues of Alternative Perspectives of which the first four issues constituting volume one were devoted to India's Look East Policy under different themes. However, taking due cognizance of the widespread appreciation and acknowledgment that we received from the academic community across the country for our humble initiatives, we at the CADM, deeply felt the need to produce the first volume of the published works in the book form. The present publication has also been necessitated by the steadily growing media publicity and the ever increasing public concerns that revolve round the much-hyped India's Look East Policy which was initiated in the early nineties in the immediate aftermath of India's economic liberalization. As news of India's Look East Policy is generating widespread interest in the region amongst different sections of society cutting across class, status and position, it has became increasingly significant to comprehend the policy in order to evolve an understanding of its impact on the people and their lives. The nature of its impact on the region needs to be properly scrutinized *vis-à-vis* the growing aspirations of the indigenous people.

Acknowledgements

The Centre for Alternative Discourse, Manipur is thankful to all the contributors, especially to those who have consistently contributed articles to *Alternative Perspectives* (earlier *Alternative Frames*), a quarterly journal, published by the Centre. The present exercise would have been difficult without the regular responses from researchers, scholars and activists, who have translated their thoughts and researches into writings for *Alternative Perspectives.*

The Centre is also thankful to the readers, whose critiques have immensely helped to arrive at constructive reviews and exchange of ideas. Without the mention of the subscribers, individuals and institutions, this acknowledgement would be incomplete.

The Centre is especially indebted to Laishram Nandalal, Premananda Hidam, Rajeev Kshetrimayum and Sanjeev Thingnam for their support in bringing out the issues of *Alternative Perspectives* on time.

We also take the opportunity to thank Homen Thangjam and A. Noni Meetei for re-reading the entire document and for their constructive suggestions without which the book would have been unsystematic. We also thank Yaiphabi Chanu Th for extending her help in editing some of the chapters.

Last but not the least, the Centre is thankful to Mr. A.K. Mittal, Concept Publishing Company, New Delhi for the publication of this volume.

Contents

SECTION 3
MANIPUR: CLOUDS OF UNCERTAINTIES—
REDEFINING FRONTIERS THROUGH LEP

SECTION 4
MYANMAR FACTOR AND THE GLOBAL DYNAMICS

The Contributors

Thingnam Kishan Singh is author of *Rethinking Colonialism* (World View Publication) was former Assistant Professor in the English Department, Manipur University.

Ajailiu Niumai, teaches Sociology at the School of Social Sciences, University of Hyderabad and was earlier involved with the Himalayan Policy Research Conference in the University of Winsconsin, Madison, USA.

Langpoklakpam Suraj, the author of *Movement for Democracy in Myanmar* (Akansha Publishing) is Lecturer of Political Science in D.M. College of Arts, Imphal and also Visiting Research Fellow at Thammasat University, Bangkok.

Konthoujam Indrakumar is a JRF scholar, working on Indo-ASEAN relations for his Ph.D. programme at the Department of Political Science, Manipur University.

Hidam Premananda is currently working on 'Governmentality' for his Ph.D. programme at the Department of Political Science, Delhi University.

Hanjabam Ishworchandra is a Research Scholar at the Department of Economics, Manipur University, where he is working on 'Rural Non-Farm Sectors of Manipur' for his Ph.D. programme.

Laishram Churchill, a Research Assistant with CADM.

Khuraijam Senate, a social activist, was earlier associated with the Documentation Section of People for Urban Knowledge and Action, Mumbai.

Thingnam Sanjeev, an archivist by training and earlier Research Assistant with the Oral History Division, Nehru Memorial Museum Library, New Delhi is currently working on Military History at the Jamia Millia Islamia University, Delhi.

Hanjabam Gyanendro, is Research Assistant at the Centre for Alternative Discourse, Manipur and Circulation Manager of the quarterly journal, '*Alternative Perspective*' based in Imphal.

Kangujam Sanatomba is a Ph.D. student currently working on his doctoral research programme on 'Comparative Insurgencies' at the Department of Political Science, Manipur University.

Introduction

The initiation of Look East Policy (LEP) by India in the early 1990s is a turning point in the quest for making a foray into the domain of South East Asia and East Asia. In 1991, the move to forge a greater economic and strategic tie with Association for South East Asian Nations (ASEAN) was initiated by Prime Minister Narasimha Rao. The significance and necessity of the LEP was generated by myriad by-product factors of Post-Cold war geo-political reconfiguration. It was indeed a foreign policy response of the Indian Government to the unfolding global power equations of the Post-Cold war era. Also, such developments provided the grounds for opening up of India's economy to global capitalism. LEP, in short, is a composite policy aimed at accomplishing greater economic and political tie with the countries of South and East Asia.

It is in this context, the present edited volume, 'Look East Policy and India's Northeast: Polemics and Perspectives', seeks to critically engage and question the basis and practice of the 'policy'. To be more specific, the whole issue of opening the 'Eastern Gate' of India pertinently brings in the question of North East India, whose physical location 'at least' cannot be downplayed if India has to reach out to the ASEAN countries, may be in terms of trade or strategic concerns. To put it more elaborately, the North East Region, which has been witnessing drastic changes due to the transformations at the global as well as regional level, needs a rigorous academic intervention to assess and evaluate the ideologies, attitudes and culture informing that condition. Much as the present realities in the North East represent an assorted picture of poverty, destitution, backwardness, underdevelopment, anxiety and unrest, the conspicuous lack of development has been projected as one of the overarching factors behind the picture. Prolonged debates from the development perspective have perhaps been part of the move to initiate an increasing awareness of the need to open up the North East for development. This may entail an effort on the part of the state to work on convergent factors *vis-à-vis* the onset of globalization and increasing economic liberalization. A significant move in this direction ultimately finds concrete manifestation in the form of India's LEP. Popular demands for structural transformations that can bring meaningful and substantial changes in the living conditions of the people in the North East remain an important issue in India's development discourse. With massive underdevelopment the region has witnessed a long drawn history of superficial development policies and programmes that failed to take into account the complex realities on the ground. Whether the lapses are on the part of the political leadership in the power corridors of New Delhi or the administrative machinery warped in its traditional elitist mould, people in the region still find their aspirations largely derided. Manipur as one of the states in the region which is unable to pull itself out of the problems arising from the inability to fulfil the growing aspirations of North East Region.

Located in a peripheral position, in both geographical and political terms, the contemporary history of Manipur along with the other states of the North East Region conspicuously failed to witness changes in the progressive sense. Perception and understanding of Manipur and the North East have been engaged from two vantage positions, operating more or less with similar dynamics. One reflects the bureaucratic position of the geo-strategic location of the region and its identification with the security/defence matrix of India. Geo-strategic concerns from the Indian national security point of view lead to the conceptualization of the failure of changes as an administrative or law and order problem. The other position, apparently liberal in its outlook, talks about developmental perspectives and failure to transform the economic backwardness of the region. As such, there is a compelling need to analyse and assess the production and consumption of these notions *vis-à-vis* the recent thrust to bring changes in Manipur and the North East through the LEP. The hype generated over this policy on the one hand raised expectations of widespread structural transformation in terms of paradigmatic change in the socio-economic landscape of Manipur and the North East. On the other hand, there has been widespread apprehension about negative impacts the policy is likely to produce. The present volume is primarily designed to present our critique of the Look East Policy from multiple dimensions.

The whole volume is divided into four units that contain fourteen essays. The pattern of arrangement of the essays into different sections has been done after close scrutiny of the various themes, which each essay seeks to focus. While an earnest effort has been undertaken to present a comprehensive understanding of the Look East Policy, readers will find special thrust being given to the North East and Manipur. This was felt highly essential as the North East is going to experience the impact of this policy in an unprecedented scale and magnitude in spite of the massive underdevelopment prevalent in the region. Different essays in this collection seek to assess and evaluate the Look East Policy of India from various angles.

The first essay in the collection by Thingnam Kishan entitled 'India's Look East Policy: Origins and Conceptualization' traces the advent of this policy to the phenomenon of economic liberalization in the country, which in turn was an inevitable consequence of the crises precipitated by the capitalist logic of development. Thingnam argues that the phenomenon of capital export or overseas investment that became the predominant feature in the creation of world economy along with the rise of imperialist politics amongst the industrially developed countries of the West continued even in the 'post-colonial' period. As India adopted the capitalist path of development, it was inevitable for its economy to face a series of crises precipitated by capitalism. It had no other choice but to succumb to World Bank and International Monetary Fund propelled 'economic liberalization'. Subsequently, India had to make conjunctive policies *vis-à-vis* the rapid march of globalization in the wake of the triumph of global capital. Look East Policy is thereby seen as part of global capital's move to integrate different economic zones of the world in its interests.

Konthoujam Indrakumar in the second essay 'India's Look East Policy: Shifting Alignments' argues that India's Look East Policy is rooted in its history, culture and size. He conducts a brief mapping of the multiple dimensions of relations between India and Southeast Asia. His main contention is that with the centre of gravity shifting towards the Asia-Pacific region, India's Look East Policy is designed to play a greater role in shaping the politics in the region in tune with its own national interest. There is no denying the fact that India's Look East Policy is a logical consequence of global capitalist project of structurally conditioning the developing countries into a 'free trade regime' to advance the interests of developed countries. The writer however states that the policy is also guided by India's politico-economic interests of asserting its place in shaping the new global order through strategic linkages with the countries of Southeast Asia and the Asia-Pacific region.

The third essay by Ajailiu Niumai titled 'Development and Discontentment Meet in the North East: Perspectives on India's Look East Policy', offers a critique of the development strategies in the North East region. Taking note of the excessive 'security' concerns that override economic and social development in the North East, the essay surveys the project's cruciality to the implementation of the Look East Policy. While assessing the nature of development institutions instrumental in formulating policies, Niumai contends the failure of the Indian state to involve the people of the region as an important factor behind the failure of development policies. Niumai also raises concerns about the rapidly changing demographic profile in the face of massive influx of immigrants from Bangladesh, Nepal and mainland Indian states like Bihar, Bengal, Uttar Pradesh, Orissa, Punjab and Rajasthan. It eventually became a major cause of discontentment in the region. Discontentment in turn makes it problematic for smooth implementation of development policies.

In his essay 'Imagining the North East through Look East Policy: Towards a contextual understanding' Konthoujam Indrakumar explores the conceptualization of the North East as a 'frontier periphery'. A British colonial legacy, the frontier concept perceives the region solely in terms of strategic importance. Except for the oil, tea and timber, the region's economic importance has never been seriously assessed. Konthoujam contends that the notion of 'frontier' is inextricably inter-twined with military notion, connoting an area that needs to be defended militarily. The very nature of integration of the region within the Indian fold in the post-British period is also another crucial factor for the persisting unrest in the region. Noting the possibilities of development of the North East region, Konthoujam argues that it equally entails dangers of blatant exploitation and erosion of the fragile economy of the region. Keeping in mind the present state of unpreparedness in all conceivable aspects, apprehensions of the region being transformed into a mere transit point find succinct expression.

The fifth essay entitled 'India's Look East Policy and North East: A Study on Environmental Impact' by Laishram Churchill explores the ecological and environmental implications in the North East *vis-à-vis* LEP. Laishram Churchill interrogates the basic assumptions behind large-scale development projects. He argues that development projects pursued in the interests of globalization hardly take into account the crucial ecological and environmental issues. Citing several instances where such projects sponsored by the metropolitan finance capital and multinational corporations wrecked havoc for environment, the essay foregrounds the need to place environment in its centrality. The essay raises strong concerns for the need to have an overall Environmental Impact Assessment (EIA) prior to the implementation of the LEP.

Sanjeev Thingnam, in the sixth essay entitled 'A Colonial Articulation of Manipur', underscores the historical framework of British colonial policy of creating a frontier zone in Manipur and the North East region. British colonial administration took note of the geo-strategic importance of the region in the backdrop of French expansionist threat emerging from Indo-China during the Eighteenth century. Perpetuation of this 'frontier' legacy virtually made the region being excluded from colonial development projects. Certain British officials proposed roads and rail networks to link the North East with mainland India, Burma and China as a requirement for economic and commercial exploitation. Historical investigation in the essays points to parallel and similarities in the present policy dimensions in the post British period. Thingnam argues that the historical trajectories of the British colonial period are revisited through a globalized LEP in the post-liberalization India.

Khuraijam Senate provides a comparative critique of the polemics of development at the global and local levels in the seventh essay 'Look East Policy and Manipur: Uncertain Trajectories'. Taking into account the underdeveloped nature of Manipur's socio-economic landscape, Khuraijam interrogates the basic premises of the LEP framed under the aegis of globalization. Post-liberalization India's efforts to integrate with Southeast Asian economy entailed formation of such a policy. Manipur as a late entrant to the realm of development finds itself in a perilous situation. The essay rigorously contests the logic of globalization propelled development policies in underdeveloped regions like the North East.

The eighth essay in the collection by Hanjabam Ishworchandra titled 'India's Look East Policy and Manipur Economy: A Critical Scrutiny' takes an incisive look into the prevailing economic issues to provide a picture of implications of India's LEP on the economy of Manipur. The essay foregrounds the feature of increasing tertiarization of Manipur's economy as a serious issue in the smooth implementation of development programmes. Hanjabam argues that de-industrialization is the current trend in the state. With serious economic crises prevailing, the essay asserts the failure of the Indo-Myanmar Border Trade as a crucial factor in assessing the role of LEP in Manipur. Industrial policies of the state formulated at various stages in conjunction with development policies devised in New Delhi have failed to address the realities on the ground. The essay reiterates the need for creation of substantial economic and industrial infrastructures to envisage a positive role for Manipur in the execution of the LEP.

Thingnam Kishan traces the history of underdevelopment of Manipur's economy to the insinuation of British colonial policies. The ninth essay 'Understanding Underdevelopment: Contextual Reading of India's Look East Policy and Manipur' by Thingnam foregrounds India's capitalist mode of development as an important factor in the underdevelopment of Manipur's economy in the post British phase. As a legacy, it persisted and worked effectively towards increasing peripheralization of the underdeveloped economies in the face of widespread regional imbalance and uneven development. Thingnam interrogates the basic assumptions behind the development framework projected in the LEP as the fragile economy of Manipur faces imminent threat from the sudden opening up of the state to the outside world.

Entitled 'Indo-Myanmar Relations in the Greater perspective of India's Look East Policy: Its Implication on Manipur', the tenth essay by Langpoklakpam Suraj foregrounds the importance of India-Myanmar relations in the smooth implementation of the LEP. Tracing the different phases of relationship between the two countries, the essay argues that India's overriding 'security' concerns have always played spoilsport in Manipur and the North East. Langpoklakpam points out the serious threat that the illicit drug trafficking poses in the region propelled by the massive narco trade between metropolitan Indian cities and Myanmar. Failure of the Border trade policy is a grim reminder of the nature of development projects in the region. Langpoklakpam stresses on the need for synchronization of India's Myanmar policy for meaningful contribution by Manipur in the LEP.

The following essay in the collection by Kangujam Sanatomba titled 'Trade, Security and Strategic Concerns: The Politics of India's Look East Policy' argues that trade and economic development serve as a mere pretext for intensifying militarization in India's bid to contain the insurgency movements in the North East. Pointing at the exclusive nature of the LEP where the peoples of the region were not allowed to participate in the formulation of the policy, Kangujam contends that it is firmly located within the British colonial framework of securing the region militarily as a frontier zone. The essay reveals the paradox of growing Indian support for the military rule in Myanmar, which became stark in its relentless opposition to the military regime in Pakistan. Kangujam anticipates the negative impact that the indigenous peoples of the North East have to bear in the wake of the impending Trans Asian Highways and Trans Asian Railways along with other projects like the Shwe Gas Pipeline. Stating that the peoples of the North East have nothing to export from India's LEP, Kangujam predicts that Indo-Myanmar region will witness extensive militarization because of India's overarching security concerns *vis-à-vis* the North East in its development policies.

In the twelfth essay 'Look East Policy: Its Gaze and Danger in the North East' by Hanjabam Gyanendro, a holistic understanding of the LEP is provided in terms of the rising trend of globalization. Rapid march of capital in almost every domain of life along with proliferation of consumerism is seen as a corollary of such a move like the LEP. The need to transform the geo-political space of the North East from being 'local' to the 'global' is part of the wave of consumerism that comes with the process of globalization. India's LEP is thereby seen by the writer as an adjunct to foreground the cultural invasion which is an important instrument of globalization.

In the last essay by Hidam Premananda titled ' India's Look East Policy and the Political: An Interrogation into the Survey of 'Global' in Manipur', the notion of fragmentation of subjected lives is discussed in terms of development policies like the LEP where the 'local' is ruptured by imposition of the 'global'. It offers a theoretical analysis of the incomprehensibility of experiences where decision making is detached from actual conditions. Extending the Focauldian concept of 'govenrmentality', Hidam surveys the nature of disjunction anticipated in a land like Manipur whose beleaguered history speaks volume for the marginalized existence experienced by the people for the last six odd decades. Hidam foregrounds the role of the state in subjectivising the lives of the people through structural transformation that actually fail to address realities on the ground.

India's LEP is thereby seen as an instrument for aggravating the disjunction in the material conditions of existence.

Every interested individual or group is expected to participate in this debate so that a meaningful consensus is reached on the much-publicized India's LEP. Any constructive suggestion and criticism for the present publication will be highly appreciated and necessary changes will be incorporated in the next edition.

Section 1
Trends and Background

1

India's Look East Policy: Origins and Conceptualization

THINGNAM KISHAN SINGH

The recent interest shown by India towards the South-East Asian region in terms of forging closer economic ties through what it calls the 'Look East Policy' signals the onset of a new trend in Asian politics. This will, no doubt, have a direct bearing on contemporary international affairs. It is an altogether different track that India has decided to tread, given its history of a conspicuous legacy of a westward orientation.

Contemporary Indian history, ever since it became an independent state after British departure from the subcontinent in 1947, exhibits a pervasive orientation that is westward. The East remained shut from the collective vision of India's decision makers as it adopted a policy of keeping aloof from South East Asian Politics. In spite of initial indications of developing ties with South-East Asian nations in the light of regional efforts like the Bandung Conference (1954) and subsequent attempts from the Non-Aligned Movement (NAM), India never really made serious efforts to look eastward. On the other hand, it maintained a marked distance from the Southeast Asian region. The dramatic turn in India's planning to take through its 'Look East Policy' (LEP) raises certain basic and fundamental questions. One of the most crucial questions would naturally revolve round the origin and conceptualization of this policy. An attempt to comprehend the factors and circumstances leading to the origin and conceptualization of this policy will necessarily entail a study of the historical forces—both political and economic—that shaped the contemporary world order.

Historicization of the contemporary world order is crucial in evolving any kind of understanding of a phenomenon conditioned by events and developments in contemporary human history. What actually compelled or prompted India to initiate drastically new measures that will have an overall bearing on its politico-economic policies need to be scrutinised. India's economic development in the post-independence period cannot be analysed separately from its pre-independence phase as certain tendencies and trends persist. The conspicuous note of capital export by the colonial powers during colonialism persisted in the post-independence period. Besides, the prevailing legacy of capitalist development in India responsible for precipitating the crises that underscored the logic to initiate World Bank-IMF style 'economic liberalization' serve as a crucial matrix for an examination of a policy like LEP. It is an accepted proposition that any policy does not emerge in a vacuum. Several material circumstances determine the framing and evolution of a policy and it is crucial to foreground the circumstances in a study of any kind of policy. The circumstances, in turn, may not actually be immediate and contingent ones as they very often underline the consequentiality of certain historical factor(s) or force(s) persisting over a period of time. To provide a frame of reference to understand the origins and conceptualization of India's LEP, it is necessary to foreground the history of capital export *vis-à-vis* development of the concept and practice of free trade. An assessment of the perpetuation of international division of labour and capital alongside the perpetuation of the division of the world between advanced economies and underdeveloped economies appears peremptory in a study of this kind.

A characteristic feature of the growth and development of modern capital is its fluidity. The role of capital moving across national boundaries towards the later half of the nineteenth century in industrial Europe can be a pertinent starting point for this analysis. The surplus of capital in the most advanced industrial countries of Europe led to the search for new profitable opportunities for accumulation overseas (Brown 1974: 171). The mobilization of capital in Europe intertwined inextricably with the foray into the non-European world through trade and plunder has been quite explicit. Engagement with the non-European world through outright plunders or through plunder disguised as trade was responsible for transfer of tremendous wealth to Europe (Baran

2001: 5). The onset of direct colonial intervention policies and exploitation led to a situation where the treasures captured outside Europe by undisguised looting enslavement and murder flowed back to the mother country and transformed into capital (Marx 1946: 826). Overseas operation with the free movement of capital, financial transactions and labour became a distinct feature in the latter half of the nineteenth century (Hobsbawn 1987: 39). The rapid expansion or scramble for colonies in the non-European world has been analysed by many scholars from this conjecture.

The blatant rise in overseas operations with foreign investment playing a dominant role in the economics of imperialism can be seen in the leading role played by British capital, closely followed by other European capital (Hobson 1938: 61-3). Exploitation of cheap land, labour and primary resources became the hallmark of these overseas operations through capital export.

Table 1.1: European Countries Foreign Investment Stock, 1854-1914

(US$ million)

Year	*Britain*	*France*	*Germany*	*Others*	*Total*
1854	1,100	—	—	—	1,100
1862	1,900	—	—	—	1,900
1874	5,000	1,000	—	—	6,000
1885	7,000	3,500	—	—	10,500
1900	11,000	5,600	1,450	4,000	22,050
1913	18,300	8,700	5,600	11,400	44,000

Source: Imlah (1958), Table 4; UN 1949.

The relation between colonial expansionism, capital export and new monopolistic practices was indeed a glaring feature of the late nineteenth century. Between 1815 and 1913, estimates of British foreign investment or capital export overseas reached around £4,000 million (Gallagher and Robinson 1953: 1-15). Imlah and Feis, too, confirm this (Table 1.2). At this juncture, it is pertinent to note that overseas investment did not necessarily accrue a corresponding return in terms of rate of profit. Increased foreign investment was supposed to carry the logic of a higher rate of return. However, it has been noted that the rate of profit on industrial capital at home was much higher, despite a steady decline after 1874.

The purpose of investing abroad in spite of lower returns was definitely part of the move towards the creation of a single global economy, which was a major fact of the nineteenth century. It was no secret that some foreign issues were made more attractive with the lower premium rates and the security provided by the government (Brown 1974: 177). The desire for security of income of the investors and the government's thrust towards an integrated world economy amongst the imperialist powers went hand in hand.

Table 1.2: Growth of UK and French capital export 1815–19

	UK Capital			*French Capital*	
	Absolute increase (£ million)	*Compound increase (%)*	*Average rate of return*	*Absolute increase (Franc billion)*	*Compound increase*
1815-1825	88	26	4.6	—	—
1826-1835	43	3.9	3.5	—	—
1836-1845	42	2.7	4.5	—	—
1846-1855	64	3	4.7	—	—
1856-1865	241	7	5	—	—
1866-1875	575	8	5.1	5-a	4
1876-1885	432	3.4	4.7	—	3
1886-1895	698	3.9	4.7	8-c	3.4
1896-1905	447	2	4.3	17-d	3.5
1906-1913	1,348	5.3	5	—	—

Source: Imlah (1958, Table 4); Feis (1930, pp. 23-4).

Note: (a) Rate of return is calculated from interest and dividends as a percentage of accumulated capital abroad in the middle of each period.
(b) 1869-80
(c) 1880-90
(d) 1890-1900
(e) 1900-17

The process of the integration of various economies into a world economy was accelerated as international trade in primary products grew enormously, supported all along by the overseas operation of European imperialist powers and the newly emerging industrial power of America. Inspite of Britain being the dominant economic power, the rapid movement towards a world economy in the face of increasing capital export saw intense competition with France, Germany, the USA, Belgium, the Netherlands, Switzerland and the rest; among them making up 56 per cent of the world's total overseas investments while Britain alone constituted 44 per cent (Pollard 1985: 492).

All these entailed a different equation for the primary producing undeveloped colonies as they were sucked into the vortex of the rapidly expanding world economy without any independent form of leverage. Political subservience logically translated into economic dependence on the metropolitan economies as the colonies were more or less tailored to produce what was profitable for the imperialist economies. Capital export basically contained the logic of the international division of labour and product as the colonies of Asia and erstwhile decolonized countries of Latin America were compelled to evolve into specialised producers of one or two primary products for export to the world market (Hobsbawn 1987: 64). Tin and rubber came from Malaya, coffee from Brazil, nitrates from Chile, meat from Uruguay, sugar and cigars from Cuba, copper from Chile, Peru, Zaire and Zambia, and gold and diamonds from South Africa. The association between capital exports and imperialist powers reveal an unscrupulous logic of infrastructural development to secure privileged markets and sources of raw materials. As much as infrastructural developments went into the undeveloped world, the integration of the world economy was getting more intensified.

Decolonization in the post-Second World War period did not altogether bring about any significant changes in the nature of economic relationship between the developed industrialised imperialist powers and the former colonies. The economic forces that operated before the onset of decolonization continued to operate albeit in an apparently different political order. It was not a dissimilar environment that was made visible as continuing economic dependence on the industrially developed powers, integration into powerful economic zones, economic infiltration through capital investment, loans, aid, unequal concession and finances directly controlled by the Western powers made the world economy operate with the same imperialist logic seen before (Wood 2003). Even after decolonization and the run down of the sterling balances with the advent of dollar convertibility, income still flowed into England from the former colonies. As investments remained more or less intact, capital export was still a predominant feature in the post-War phase.

Table 1.3: Direct Company Foreign Investment, USA and UK, 1929-1996

Area	USA Capital						UK Capital			
	Investment Stake				*Annual average investment flow*	*Annual average investment income*	*Investment stake*		*Annual average investment flow*	*Annual average investment income*
	1929	*1949*	*1959*	*1968*	*1960-64*	*1967-68*	*1960*	*1968*	*1964-69*	*1967-69*
Total (US$ billion)	8	11	30	65	3.5	5	12.6	19.7	1.2	2.3
By region (%)—a										
Europe	19	14.5	16	30	38	22	10	13.7	18.5	13
Canada/USA	25	31	33	33	30	18	24.5	23	19.5	23
Latin America	33	39	35	17	12	27	36.5 - c	30.3 - c	22.5 - c	30 - c
Other underdeveloped developed by Sterling—b	23	15.5	16	20	20	33	29	33	39.5	34
By sector (%)										
Manufacturing	24	33	32	41	50	26	32	36	41.5	28.5
Oil	15	29	33	29	20	46	28	25	21	44
Mining	16	10	10	8	10	13	—	—	—	—
Utilities	21	11	9	4	10	15	40 - d	39 - d	37.5 - d	27.5 – d
Others	24	17	16	18	10					

Source: (Brown 1974: 208-09).

Notes: (a) Regional distribution for investment excludes oil and finance,

(b) UK investment in sterling development areas includes Zimbabwe,

(c) UK capital figures are combined for Latin America and other underdeveloped,

(d) UK capital figures are combined for mining, utilities and others.

The post-War world economy also witnessed the rapid growth of transnational or multinational firms or corporations that increasingly replaced the financial groups as the accumulators of capital. In what has been termed as 'multinational synergy', transnational or overseas operations through movement of funds to minimize exchange losses, transfer pricing to minimize taxation, switching location or areas of operation to avert effects of labour disputes, production of components in countries at different levels of technology according to the cost of labour and capital became rampant (Brown 1974: 226). These firms own and manage economic units in different countries at the same time. These firms establish and operate production and distribution facilities overseas through foreign direct investment (FDI) (Rowthorn 1971). Capital export or overseas investments remain as predominant as ever in the world economy with the British and American firms leading in overseas investment and production.

Table 1.4: Expansion overseas 1957–65-a

	Exports	*Overseas*	*Overseas sales*
US	2	13	15
UK	12	20	32
France	6	1	7
Germany	14	2	16
Italy	24	5	30
Netherlands	27	17	43
Canada	33	13	46
Japan	17	2	20

Source: Rowthorn (197).

Note: (a) Percentage of sales increase accountad for by manufacturing firms.

It is interesting to note that arguments on international trade in favour of the developed industrialized world never really penetrate deep into the logic of capital's need of places for investment. The core issue of the motives behind foreign investment or capital export is always overlooked conveniently besides the reality of uneven trade. The politics behind capital export has always been inextricably intertwined with profit motives at the expense of undeveloped and underdeveloped economies. Prevalence of this legacy of extracting profit at the expense of the undeveloped and underdeveloped economies has been analysed in terms of persisting politics and practice of colonialism (Frank 1969a, 1969b; Griffin 1969; Mandel 1964; O'Connor 1970).

Table 1.5: Direct Investment Overseas (US$ billion)

	1957-60	*1961-64*	*1967*
USA	2.83	3.21	3.15
UK	0.51	0.67	0.74
Germany	0.12	0.22	0.25
Italy	0.06	0.17	0.23
Japan	0.05	0.09	0.12
Belgium	—	—	0.05
France	0.01	0.1	0.2
Netherlands	0.71	0.12	0.21
Canada	0.06	0.1	0.08

Source: IMF, OEC.

The phenomenon of creating 'enclaves of development' in the underdeveloped world to secure them in the world capitalist economy emerges as a distinct reality in the contemporary economic order. In spite of the apparent progress made by some of these countries in the field of industrialization, penetration of foreign capital remains a conspicuous reality (O'Connor 1970). Parallel to this legacy, the imbalance in international trade between the developed and the underdeveloped world still persists. The pattern of trade reveals that it is conducted basically between the developed countries accounting for 80 per cent of the total world import market. In addition, over 90 per cent of all industrial commodities originate in the developed countries thereby making the share of developing countries in exports of manufactured goods less than 10 per cent. (Rangarajan 1984: 130).

Parallel to these developments, the Anglo-American policy of creating a stable world economic order based on the Bretton Woods framework needs careful security *vis-à-vis* capital export and world trade. The Bretton Woods Conference in 1944 was the consequence of an Anglo-American desire to avoid the instability created by the destructive competitive depreciation and policies of the 1930s. A persisting anxiety of possible instability underlined the attempt to maintain economic stability through multilateral financial institutions. With the impact of the Great Depression and the Second World War, the aim was to evolve a framework in which governments would have considerable freedom to pursue national economic objectives, yet, the monetary order would be based on fixed exchange rates (Gilpin 1987: 131).

Table 1.6: Trade between Developed and Developing Area

	1950	*1958*	*1968*	*1973*	*1978*
1. *Terms of trade*					
Developed areas	97	98	100	98	92
Developing areas	109	105	98	107	135
Developing areas (less oil producing areas)	117	104	97	97	93
2. *Food and raw materials, excluding fuels*	50	88	125	143	—
Developed	66	88	117	115	—
Share of Developing Countries (%)	40	33	32	28	—
3. *Percentage share of manufactured goods in total exports of developing countries*					
	1950	11.7 %			
	1958	11.3 %			
	1973	25.5 %			
	1978	23.7 %			
4. *Exports of manufactures of developing countries share of*					
None-ferrous metals	—	62	45	29	18
Textiles, clothing	—	18	24	27	27

Source: L. Rangarajan.

The phenomenon of international finance which started with massive capital accumulation in England and other industrial economies subsequently resulting in the export of capital in the latter half of the nineteenth century eventually took a new turn in the post-Second World War era with the entry of the World Bank (WB), regional development banks like the Asian Development Bank (ADB) and the International Monetary Fund (IMF). A multilateral institution, the IMF perceives itself as the administrator of the global international monetary system, presiding over a specific system of rules in relation with fixed exchange rate regimes, influencing macroeconomic policies of dependent states. Within the framework of such conditionalities, it 'assists' states in the area of debt servicing through structural adjustment loans. Structural Adjustment Lending (SAL) introduced by the IMF in 1986 is closely linked with Structural Adjustment Programmes (SAP) introduced by the WB in 1980. It is pertinent to note that microeconomic projects initiated by the WB and subsequent 'aid' or 'loans with interests' necessarily apply conditionalities to draw the underdeveloped world deeper into the vortex of 'global capital' through the LPG model—liberalization, privatization and globalization. Working in tandem, these two institutions are responsible for major changes in the contemporary world economic order. Their strategy *vis-à-vis* the borrowing country has been described as 'you twist their right arm and we will twist their left arm' (Lobo 2004: 402). The stark logic of capital export can be seen in a World Bank commission report titled 'Partnership in Development':

> We have received the definite impression that most low-income countries would welcome a larger flow of foreign investment, sharing our belief that such flows would contribute to faster growth (Pearson 1969: 105).

Alongside the debt crisis and debt servicing *vis-à-vis* the WB and the IMF lendings, growing concerns of the less developed countries over uneven and unequal trade practices imposed through the World Trade Organization (WTO) significantly capture the metanarrative of imperialism that has prevailed ever since the beginning of the phenomenon of capital export. WTO conditionalities have further exacerbated the plight of the poor countries. Dumping of cheaply produced food grains from the developed countries to the poor countries is on the rise.

Flow of foreign investment or capital export subsume conditionalities ranging from massive cuts in social spending and abolition of price subsidies for essential commodities including food, water, fuel, energy, etc. A direct withdrawal of the state from its welfare activities like providing basic healthcare, education and other public services form the matrix of the conditionalities. Another significant aspect of foreign investment in the less developed countries is that most of the investments tend to be portfolio investments.

Structural adjustment policies and the rapid march of the global economy to integrate the whole world by rigorously promoting market forces alongside the debt problems, generated through dubious and unequal economic and trade practices, the collapse of the Soviet Union and the receding of the international socialist tide eventually led many less developed countries (LDCs) to initiate (or succumb to) economic reform measures. Hailed by the industrialised capitalist economies, the WB and IMF as the only way out of the quagmire of poverty, debt and backwardness, economic reforms or liberalization in the LDCs primarily entailed the opening up of their markets, reduction in tariff barriers, removal of restrictions on quantitative imports, abolition of protective mechanism in both agriculture and industry and liberalization of their capital or finance markets.

Apologists of economic liberalization in India trace its origins with the Congress Government's recognition of the country's economic malaise in the 1980s—the declining growth rate over three decades, the high cost structure of industry and its falling productivity, the decline of Indian exports and loss of competitiveness, etc. A sudden need to accelerate reform measures with drastic changes was precipitated by the severe macroeconomic crisis of 1991—the balance of payment problem, the Gulf War, inflation, etc. (Shand 1999; Joshi and Little 1996)—thereby leading to a massive 'liberalization' programme in 1991. The much-vaunted economic liberalization, however, did reveal a host of other factors intertwined with the logic of capital export. All along the history of post-independence India's development, the imperialist pressures for a relatively autonomous course of capitalist industrialization have been noted (Patnaik 1999: 174-93). Mention can be made of the World Bank's attempts to force India to allow operations of oil multinational corporations and to open the fertilizer industry to multinational capital, the sustained campaign against industrialization led by America and the advanced capitalist countries and the persistent efforts to reinforce international division of labour by forcing India to abandon the Second Five Year Plan's ambitious industrialization programme. The World Bank mooted, all along, thrust and confinement in the agriculture sector with increased investment. Efforts to stall India's industrialization lost steam due to sustained support by Soviet Union's technological and financial back up. This led to a perceptible change in the attitude of the advanced capitalist countries and multilateral aid agencies. A more sophisticated strategy eventually suggested the necessity of industrialization in a 'liberal' environment. This 'liberal environment' purportedly meant the removal of protective barriers to the entry of foreign capital and technology, and replacement of domestic state owned industries by private or multinational corporations and their capital. The primary motive was to facilitate easy and massive entry of foreign capital and products in the domestic market. Liberalization to allow market forces to operate freely was vaunted as the key to growth and development along with the need to unshackle private enterprise from state control.

Besides, the role of India's own policies of economic development needs careful scrutiny in the attempt to understand the emerging changes. Like any other country in the wake of decolonization in the post-War era, the options available for economic development were either the socialist path or the capitalist path. With the exception of a semblance of the socialist model *vis-à-vis* the establishment of state owned industries and state investment and the formulation of a centrally planned economy, India's economic development was on the capitalist path. The failure of the Indian State to discard the legacy of colonial development, the capitalist mode of production, in 'decolonized' India was meant to safeguard the interests of metropolitan capital, which in turn allied with the indigenous capitalist classes.

Table 1.7: Incremental Gross Capital-Output ratio (at 1970-71 prices)

Plan	*Period*	*Capital/output ratio*
First Plan	1951-52 to 1955-56	3.2
Second Plan	1956-57 to 1960-61	4.1
Third Plan	1961-62 to 1965-66	5.4
Annual Plan	1966-67 to 1968-69	4.9
Fourth Plan	1969-70 to 1973-74	5.7
Fifth Plan	1974-75 to 1978-79	3.9

Sources: Sixth Five Year Plan (1980-85).

Over the years, it has become clear that the Indian state as an engine of capitalist development subservient to the interest of metropolitan capital and the indigenous capitalist class has evolved complex strategies for achieving growth of capitalism (Bhambri 1988: 6). The mobilization of large resources for investment and the resultant high capital-output ratio reveal the logic of capitalist contradictions.

Another important aspect of capitalist development in India is the long-standing land concentration in the hands of the landlords whose transformation to a capitalist landowning class was facilitated by different policies pursued by the Indian State. In spite of the much-hyped land reforms carried out under the aegis of government policies, the structure of land concentration remained unchanged (Patnaik 1999: 180). A complete distortion of land ownership is visible with small and marginal farmers who constitute over 70 per cent of the landowners operating in barely 24 per cent of the land.

Table 1.8: Distribution of Land Holding in India in Selected Year

Size of holding	*Percent of operational holdings*			
	1976-77	*1980-81*	*1985-86*	*1990-91*
Less than 1 Ha	54.6	56.4	57.8	59
Small 1.0-2.0 Ha	18.1	18.1	18.4	19
Semi-Medium 2.0-4.0 Ha	14.3	14	13.6	13.2
Medium 4.0-10.0 Ha	10	9.1	8.2	7.2
Large 10.-0 and above	3	2.4	2	1.6

Sources: Agricultural Statistics at a Glance, 1996, Directorate of Economics and Statistics, Ministry of Agriculture; Agriculture Research Data Book, ICAR, Krishi Bhavan, New Delhi.

With no radical land distribution, the distribution of operational holding thus constitutes to be very unequal with a small number of relatively large holdings accounting for nearly 60 per cent of total land (*Economic and Political Weekly* 1981: 77). Other factors which contributed significantly to the phenomenon of economic 'liberalization' in India are enumerated as follows:

(a) State investment in the expansion of domestic market and production structure envisaged in the Bombay Plan to serve the interest of the leading monopoly capitalists,
(b) Deficit financing,
(c) Support for World Bank propelled 'liberalization' by a set of newly emerging industrial houses in their attempts to break the existing monopoly in the domestic market and the collaboration with metropolitan capital.

The logical consequence of openness in trade and capital inflows with a shift towards an export oriented economy as the model of growth and development make it imperative for India to frame policies that are conjunctive. Economic policies to suit the various demands of the newly emerging equations *vis-à-vis* the triumph of global capital and the rise of American uni-polarism in the post Cold War era signal the beginning of path breaking shifts. Thus, the capitalist crisis that precipitates the severe economic crises consequently compelled India to rethink and redefine its economic equations. Post-independent India's economic history being a capitalist led economy geared towards the interest of its capitalist class, comprising of leading industrial houses and feudal landlords turned capitalist agriculturists, it had no other option but to sway to the tunes of the IMF and the WB as the only possible way out of the capitalist precipitated crisis. The political economy of the emerging configurations reveals a frantic quest for new ventures in the field of trade and foreign policies. Complementary policies in line with the emerging changes are thereby projected as inevitable and logical. On the economic front, the need to work in tandem with the global market and global trading patterns induces paradigmatic shifts evident in the rapid move towards a WTO framework.

Parallel to this movement was the simultaneously felt need to integrate and consolidate India's trade *vis-à-vis* the rise and proliferation of the practice of managed trade, regionalism and regional trading blocs. Trade creation and trade diversion as a rising trend in the backdrop of regional blocs propelled India to visualise conjunctive operations. A conspicuous need to rethink and redefine the political-economy of India's geo-political strategies in line with the emerging economic and political configurations necessitated India to look beyond SAARC. It has been a much debated and accepted reality that SAARC cannot further India's economic interest. Its movement has been relatively slow because of the persisting differences between the three major constituents—India, Pakistan and Bangladesh; differences have been markedly political in nature rather than economic. In spite of the economic potential it holds (Raghavan 1995), SAARC has failed to make any significant headway primarily on account of political differences between the three big players.

The need to envisage new openings led India to undertake a paradigmatic shift by looking eastwards. A move towards closer ties with Southeast Asia becomes the focal point. The political economy of this shift can be analysed in terms of the prevailing global economic trends, political environment, geo-strategic needs and internal/domestic stability (Kapila 2005). 'Look East Policy'—a policy that aims to forge closer ties with Southeast Asia—was formulated during the tenure of Narasimha Rao as Prime Minister. There has been a continuous effort ever since to move closer to the Southeast Asian countries. Substantive efforts towards closer political, economic and military ties underscore the logic of India's LEP. The increasing level of political and military interface between India and Vietnam, Cambodia, Indonesia, Thailand and Myanmar in the recent years as parts of India's LEP signals a broader regional engagement. On the economic front, trading and development oriented ventures like the BIMST-EC (Bangladesh, India, and Myanmar, Sri Lanka, Thailand—Economic Cooperation) and Mekong Ganga Project have gained prominence. Free trade between the countries of this Bay of Bengal grouping and other Southeast Asian countries figure prominently in India's LEP. Facilitation of these projects entails the sponsorship of the World Bank as plans for the 1,360 km. trans-Asian highway to link India, Myanmar and Thailand in the first phase and with Indo-China in the second phase are on the card. This trans-Asian highway will, in due course of time, be part of a much larger trans-Eurasian highway linking South Asia, Southeast Asia, China with Europe. India's LEP can, therefore, be analysed and assessed in terms of the circumstances compelling India to look towards a framework of integration with Southeast Asia.

Emerging trends in the post-Cold War era indicate a sustained attempt to move closer towards the United States as India finds itself increasingly pressurized both at the regional and international level. Rising Chinese power—political and economic—evident in the enormous influence exercised in Southeast Asia and Pakistan convinced India of the need to forge alliance with the United States. A mutually beneficial frame evolved as the United States needs a strategic partner in the region to check China. Maintaining ties with Pakistan, India and ASEAN in the bid to contain China remain imperative for American strategic interests. On the internal domestic front, India's relative success in containing the conflict in Kashmir and the failure to make SAARC a success can be seen as circumstantial factors in framing the LEP. Closer ties with Myanmar and other Southeast Asian countries are needed to contain conflict in its Northeastern region. These political objectives are conjunctively supplemented by the economic imperative of integration with ASEAN economy *vis-à-vis* the interests of global capital. It is not surprising that India's attempt to integrate with ASEAN economy finds patronage and support from the World Bank and the IMF. Subserving the interests of metropolitan capital, which has already made significant inroads in the Indian economy along with the interests of the indigenous capitalist coterie, the LEP is set to serve varied politico-economic interests. As part of the invigorated march of global capital *vis-à-vis* a global economy integrating different economic zones into its vortex, Indian resistance to this grand design virtually finds no articulation or space in the aftermath of economic 'liberalization'. It, however, remains crucial for India to extract as much leverage as possible within the framework of the LEP, which is an instrument to further the goals of metropolitan capital. A comprehensive reading of the LEP will necessary comprise a holistic assessment of the varied interests ranging from the economies of metropolitan and local capital to the intricate political and strategic configurations.

REFERENCES

Baran, Paul A. 2001. 'Extracts from the political Economy of Growth', in Peter J Cain and Mark Harrison (eds.), *Imperialism: Critical Concepts in Historical Studies—Vol. II,* London & New York: Routledge.

Bhambri, C.P. 1988. *Politics in India 1947-1987*. New Delhi: Vikas.

Brown, Michael Barrat (1974). *The Economics of Imperialism.* Harmondsworth: Penguin Books.

Economic and Political Weekly 1981. Bombay, September.

Feis, H. 1930. *Europe, The World's Banker 1870-1914*. New Haven: Yale University Press.

Frank, Andre Gunder 1969a. *Capitalism and Underdevelopment in Latin America.* New York: Monthly Review Press.

____ 1969b. *Latin America: Underdevelopment or Revolution*. New York: Monthly Review Press.

Gallagher, J. and R.E. Robinson 1953. 'The Imperialism of Free Trade 1815-1914'. *Economic History Review, 2nd Series, VI. (1-15).*

Gilpin, Robert 1987. *The Political Economy of International Relations.* Princeton, NJ: Princeton University Press.

Griffin, Keith 1969. *Underdevelopment in Spanish America*. London: Allen & Unwin.

Hobsbawn, Eric 1987. *The Age of Empire: 1875-1914*. London: Abacus.

Hobson, J.A. 1938. *Imperialism: A Study*. London: Allen & Unwin, First published in 1902.

Imlah, A.H. 1958. *Economic Elements in the Pax Britannica*. Harvard: Harvard University Press.

Joshi, Vijay and I.M.D. Little 1996. *India's Economic Reforms*. Delhi: Oxford University Press.

Kapila, Subash 2005. 'India's Foreign Policy Challenges 2005: A Perspective Analysis' <www.saag.org>

Lobo, Radhica 2004. *Southeast Asia Crisis: An Economic Analysis*. New Delhi: Serials publications.

Mandel, E. 1964. 'After Imperialism?' *New Left Review*. No. 25, May-June.

Marx, Karl. 1946. *Capital Vol. I.* London: Allen & Unwin.

O'Connor, J. 1970. 'The Meaning of Economic Imperialism', in RI Rhodes (ed.), *Imperialism and Underdevelopment: A Reader*. New York: Monthly Review Press.

Patnaik, Prabhat 1999. *Whatever Happened to Imperialism and Other Essays*. Delhi: Tulika.

Pearson, LB and *et al.* 1969. *Partners in Development*. New York: Praeger.

Pollard, Sidney 1985. 'Capital Exports 1870-1914: Harmful or Beneficial?' *Economic History Review*. XXXVIII.

Raghavan, S.N. 1995. *Regional Economic Cooperation among SAARC Countries*. New Delhi: Institute of Economic Growth.

Rangaranjan, L. 1984. 'The Politics of International Trade', in Susan Strange (ed.), *Paths to International Political Economy*. London: George Allen & Unwin.

Rowthorn, R. 1971. *International Big Business 1957-67*. Cambridge: Cambridge University Press.

Shand, Ric (ed.) 1999. *Economic Liberalization in South Asia*. Delhi: Macmillan.

United Nations 1949. *International capital Movements in the Inter-War Years*. New York: UN.

Wood, Ellen Meikins 2003. *The Empire of Capital*. New Delhi: Left World Books.

2

Mapping India's Look East Policy: Shifting Alignments

KONTHOUJAM INDRAKUMAR

Why does India 'Look East'? Or what made India adopt the Look East Policy (LEP) in the aftermath of the Cold War? This type of questions sound simple but requires a complex multi-faceted explanation in order to provide satisfactory answers. In fact, the genealogy of the policy is rooted in India's size, culture, civilization and several mutations taking place at the global, regional and domestic political and economic levels; the significant ones are the end of Cold War and consequently India's adoption of a more overt capitalist market economy. As the phrase Look East Policy itself suggests, it signifies India's desire for greater competition with and containment of China, and engagement and integration with Southeast Asia and ultimately with Asia-Pacific region. The Policy is guided by a myriad of inter-related national interests. It is not simply guided by trade as the prime motive but overall politico-economic interests of a burgeoning India *vis-à-vis* emerging geo-political configuration. India's LEP is a major foreign policy shift, in fact, a 'paradigm shift', which has brought changes in India's orientation *vis-à-vis* China and Southeast Asia. Till recently India's foreign policy has been Pakistan-centric in particular and subcontinental specific in general. Thus, for the first time India has decided to come out of the 'sub-continental Cold War situation' and take up a proactive role in the region. In this context, it can be argued that India's LEP is not just a passive response to the changing geo-politics of Southeast Asia in the post Cold War era, but a proactive initiation on its part *vis-à-vis* changing geo-political equations at the global and regional level. Furthermore, it can be argued that the policy shift is an attempt to assert India's role and power in collaboration with the advanced capitalist countries to establish its place commensurate with its size and civilization in the changing global power equation.

India's willingness and desire to exercise the role of a major power in shaping world politics can be traced back to the early phase of its foreign policy. Nehru, the architect of modern India, projected Indian culture, history and civilization, etc. as a basis in its pursuit for a place in world affairs. Prior to India's independence in 1947, he expressed the desire to participate in world affairs—with an independent foreign policy—as a free nation and not as a satellite. A careful study of this expression made in 1946 reveals the main objectives of India's foreign policy that revolves around the preservation of India's territorial integrity and freedom of policy and promotion of international peace. With these objectives in view, India under Nehru's leadership adopted the policy of Non-alignment in the prevailing Cold War between two super powers having two contradictory ideologies in the backdrop of mutual distrust, hatred, suspicion, military alliances, stiff arms race and competition for global domination. It was against this backdrop of bloc-politics that Nehru adopted Non-alignment as a foreign policy alternative to find a space for third world countries of Asia, Africa and Latin America (ASAFLA). It was conceived with the hope that these countries could have an effective voice and influence in global politics. To be more precise, Non-alignment had three major features such as:

(a) To abstain from entering into military alliances with any of the superpowers in particular or with any country either of the Western or of the Eastern blocs in general,
(b) To take foreign policy decision in accordance with one's own judgement and merit of the issue, and
(c) To maintain friendly relations with all countries, whether they belong to military blocs or not (Appadorai & Rajan 1985: 34-35).

India's exposition of an independent approach to foreign policy was manifested in the position it took on significant world issues. For instance, India condemned British and French invasion of Suez

(1956), Soviet interference in Hungary (1956) and Korean crisis (1950). Unlike many third world contemporaries, India always played or wanted to play an active part in global politics by raising its voice, extending help in bringing and restoring peace and order when called upon to do so. Sending of peace keeping force to Gaza strip (1956) and in the Congo (1961) in response to UN Secretary Generals appeal are glaring testimonies to the fact that India always habours the ambition of playing a major role in shaping world order commensurate with its size, culture and civilization. In fact, India always projected itself to be the leader of Third World Countries until she suffered a major defeat in the 1962 Sino-India War.

India's foreign policy basically aims to promote 'multiple centers' of powers with each power having capacity to shape and effect desired result within its 'Sphere of Influence.' Citing the nature of India's foreign policy, an analyst wrote that India's foreign policy rests on an expansive vision of the country's destiny; till date, India lacked the resources that could turn vision into reality (Cohen 2002: 34). It was further asserted that both Nehru and his successors believed that India was a great state and would produce leaders who would act wisely and teach the rest of the world (Cohen 2002: 38). Truly, the worldview of India's political elite was founded on a tendency to play the role of global teachers as well as leaders. Although successive generations differ with Nehru in terms of mode of economic production and distribution, they share his vision of India's role in the global configuration of power. They all valued the greatness of India's civilization, and far and wide influence of Indian culture. So India's LEP can be regarded as a reassertion within the space provided by cultural and civilizational bonds coupled with the factors of convergence between India and Southeast Asia in the post Cold War global geo-political equation. It is, therefore, not surprising that successive ruling parties endorsed the policy of 'multilateralism' as one of the main foreign policy objectives. The present ruling coalition of United Progressive Alliance (UPA) in New Delhi in its Common Minimum Programme endorsed the idea of 'multilateralism'. Therefore, any foreign policy decision taken in connection with a region must be studied and analyzed against the backdrop of broader foreign policy objectives of India.

The presence of unfavourable politico-economic realities during the Cold War period seriously hampered India in its pursuit for a rightful place within the comity of nations. However there has been drastic changes occurring at domestic and global levels since the end of Cold War. India can now assert its power and role with more weight, effectiveness and vigour in shaping regional geo-political environment conducive to its national economic and security interests than ever before due to the unfolding factors of convergence with more advanced countries of Southeast Asia and Pacific region. Among the more favourable factors that will help India sustain the momentum of its Look East strategy is India's resilient economy with capitalist market orientation having high dose of neo-liberal ideology and (its) emerging military capability accentuated by the nuclearization of its defence system. A close look at the following data will indicate India's rising power status. According to the World Bank's World Development Report (1999-2000), India's economy is gigantic in terms of overall gross national product. It ranks eleventh in the world, with a total figure of US$ 421 billion, compared with China's US$ 929 billion, and Japan's whooping US$ 4,090 billion, the world's second largest economy. In terms of military expenditure, India is among the top dozen highest states. India ranks 12th in this regard in 1999-2000 with spending figures at about US$ 14 billion even though it is far lesser than China (US$ 40 billion), Japan (US$ 37 billion). Russia (US$ 54 billion) and USA (US$ 250 billion). Above all, India now possesses nuclear weapons and has joined the 'nuclear club of five'. With a relatively better economic structure and advanced military technology and prowess, which it lacked earlier, India is in a much better position to play a major role in shaping global or regional order in its advantage.

Indo-ASEAN in the Cold War: A Clash of Interests

India's LEP involves the development of a comprehensive cooperation in various sectors particularly economic and political with the countries of Southeast Asia and Asia-Pacific region. It is not possible to elaborate on the bilateral relations with each of the country comprising Association of South East Asian Nations (ASEAN) within the scope of this paper. However, the study of emerging Indo-ASEAN relations in the post Cold War period will certainly reveal the changing bilateral relations as well. The burgeoning Indo-ASEAN relations in various aspects must be seen in the backdrop of unfolding regional dynamics of Southeast Asia. India and countries of Southeast Asia are geographically, culturally and strategically linked. It is needless to emphasis the importance of Southeast Asia in the defence and security of India. Next to South Asia, Southeast Asia constitutes the vital security parameter of India because of their geographical location. A close look at the Atlas will indicate the strategic position of Southeast Asia. To be more precise the region is located between the Indian and Pacific Oceans, and some of the countries of Southeast Asia have boundaries with India and China, two of the major powers of Asia. Besides the economic and strategic imperatives, there are close cultural and civilizational bonds between India and Southeast Asia. India has exerted a great cultural influence on East and Southeast Asia. Nomenclature of Indianised kingdoms such as Khmer, Sailendra, Funan, Sri Vijaya, Angkor etc. (Jaffrelot 2003) narrates the deep cultural ties rooted in the historical past. Indian cultural influence can still be witnessed by the popularity of Ramayana in Southeast Asia. Due to its widespread cultural ties, it is not uncommon with certain Indian political-cultural thinkers to perceive Southeast Asia as 'Greater India' or *Akhand Bharat*. Therefore, it is not surprising that independent India under Nehru's leadership tried to forge a good rapport not only with Southeast Asia but also with other countries of Asia.

In spite of many similar factors like geographical proximity, ancient cultural and economic ties and a shared colonial heritage the synergy between India and countries of Southeast Asia did not developed to the expected level due to the onset of Cold War in the post Second World War period. In fact, the Cold War, which was characterized by deep hatred, mistrust, suspicion, enmity, arms race and competition for global domination between erstwhile Soviet-led Eastern bloc and United States led Western bloc, made relationships between India and Southeast Asia problematic and restricted one. The Cold War politics shaped the nature and pattern of relationship between India and ASEAN. During the period there were fundamental differences in economic ideology, political outlook and security assumptions between India and ASEAN countries. India's pro-Soviet tilt and adoption of a closed market or system of mixed economy characterised by quantitative restrictions on import and tariffs restrictions posed problems for ASEAN *vis-à-vis* its overtly market oriented economy and signing of US led military alliance SEATO (South East Asia Treaty Organization). India regarded ASEAN as West's Trojan horse and stooges of Western imperialism. Moreover, India's signing of the 'Treaty of Friendship' with the Soviet Union in 1971 and India's closer ties with Vietnam, after Chinese invasion of the latter in February 1979 against its (Vietnam's) military intervention in Cambodia to overthrow pro-Beijing Pol Pot's regime, were perceived by ASEAN member states as a threat to their security. The spectre of Cold War haunted Indo-ASEAN bilateral relations. But the most decisive factor that accentuated Indo-ASEAN differences was the American containment policy of Soviet expansionism in Southeast Asia. It affected the entire region. Extensive US military intervention in the South Vietnam after France withdrew as a result of Geneva Conference of 1954 was based on Eisenhower's logic of 'Domino theory' and this perhaps was the greatest flaw in American foreign policy *vis-à-vis* Southeast Asia. The basic logic of 'Domino theory' is that if a country falls to the communist bloc, it would start a chain reaction knocking others, in its turn, like a row of dominoes. The political and psychological impact of American pullout would be felt throughout the area, if not in other regions as well. Moreover to American leaders the 17th Parallel dividing North Vietnam from South Vietnam represented a frontier between the free world and communist world (Spanier 1989: 163). South Vietnam, therefore, was to be saved from the invasion of North Vietnam by any possible means. Thus, the emergence of Cold War in the post Second World War period and Nehruvian India's pro-Soviet politico-economic tilt were the main stumbling blocks in India's relation with most countries of Southeast Asia and Asia-Pacific region.

Politico-Economic Determinants

In order to have a substantive understanding of the content and purpose of the so called 'Look East Policy', there is a need to have retrospective look at the multiple geo-economics and geo-political factors operating in the late 1980s and early 90s of the 20th century at the global, regional and domestic levels. Foreign policy decision is determined by various factors prevailing at particular periods. The factors that made India rethink and redefine its relations with Southeast Asia and Asia-Pacific is based on the transformations in the global geo-political equations in the post Cold War era.

Disintegration of Soviet Union had serious implications not only for India's politico-economic conditions but also for its foreign policy. The disintegration meant loss of a time-tested friend and ally who supported India at various issues, be it Kashmir, Goa or Indo-Pak wars, the United Nations and other international fora. Erstwhile Soviet Union was the biggest source of investment and financial help for India's economic development through centralised planning. Collapse and disintegration of Soviet Union meant loss of market for Indian goods. In the aftermath of the Cold War both India and Russia faced serious politico-economic crises. Radical transformations and reorientation in the foreign economic and political policies became inevitable in the post Cold War Russia and India. The point of convergence that existed between India and Soviet Union during the cold war period disappeared. India's policy of Non-alignment became redundant to Russia's geo-strategic interest due to the emergence of a uni-polar world order. Suddenly the ties between Moscow and the Third World Countries ruptured. Almost overnight, the countries of the Third World became for Moscow 'distant foreign countries' (Varma 1999: 181). As the Russian economy during this period became bankrupt, it began to look towards the West for her economic regeneration. Unlike erstwhile Soviet Union, the Successor State, Russia's foreign policy objective at this stage became West centric. The re-prioritization, readjustment and redefining of interests among Russia's ruling circle had produced all time low Indo-Russian relation in the early part of the post Cold War period.

During this period, Indian side of the story went parallel to Russia. It desperately needed to fill up the politico-economic 'vacuum' created by the disintegration of Soviet Union. Faced with a serious balance of payment crisis as its foreign exchange reserve reached an all time low of US$ 1 billion only. It became impossible to avoid the tremendous pressure exerted by the Bretton Woods institutions—World Bank and the International Monetary Fund (IMF)—to liberalize India's market and economy in order to get access to much needed loans to save the economy from collapsing or going bankrupt. Indian economy during the period was on the verge of bankruptcy. There was an external debt crisis and a severe crisis of 'balance of payment'. The external debt crisis hung like the 'Sword of Damocles' over the fate of the fragile economy (Nayar 2002). There was a sudden realization that governments can and do become insolvent even if countries go bankrupt. In the context of Indian economic reforms, which is associated with massive liberalization and privatization of its economy and market, it has been observed that there can be no doubt about the response being driven—even to the extent of being dictated—by the crisis. It was not at all a planned process. The fact that Indian economic reforms in 1991 were the result of deep economic crises, accentuated by drastic transformations in the international world order cannot be denied. India's debt in dollar terms nearly quadrupled during the 1980s from approximately US$ 20 billion in 1980 to nearly US$ 82 billion in 1990; debt to banks and private individuals increased more than 10 times from just under US$ 2 billion to more than US$ 22 billion (Chandrasekhar and Ghosh 2004: 11).

With the collapse of bi-polarity, India's role as a leader of Third World Countries diminishes and a kind of inferiority complex emerged in India's ruling circle *vis-à-vis* Southeast Asia and East Asian economic development. For many decades, India thought it was far ahead of all the countries of Southeast Asia but the superior performance of 'ASEAN Tigers' (Malaysia, Singapore, Thailand and Indonesia) came as a rude shock to India inflicting great damage to its image and international status. With the liberalization and privatization of its economy, India seems determined to emulate the 'ASEAN Tigers' model. It is pertinent to mention that India's LEP is not a coincidental phenomenon but a logical outcome of neo-liberal economic reforms. India too was entrapped to follow suit of the advanced capitalist countries' strategy to convert the entire globe into a single integrated market. Collapse of the socialist order at this stage not only meant the collapse of the Eastern bloc and disintegration of the Soviet Union, but also the triumph of capitalism and reinforcement of the idea that there is no alternative to capitalism: capitalism is the only alternative. Such high sounding idea was manifested in Fakuyama's book *The End of History,* which was written against the backdrop of the erstwhile Soviet Union's disintegration. In the absence of any countervailing force to the march of global capital, it became easier to carry out the capitalist countries' agenda of transforming and restructuring global economy along capitalist lines through the IMF and the World Bank. In response to the crisis situation and the tremendous pressure of the financial institutions, the government set in motion a process of macro and micro economic reforms, as done by several developing countries in Latin America and Sub-Sahara Africa to the debt crisis in 1980s. Ever since India adopted 'market economy' with drastic reductions in trade barriers and privatization, the main barrier between India and most countries of Southeast Asia in particular and Asia-Pacific region in general became obsolete.

The end of the Cold War was followed by the outbreak of the Gulf War in 1991. It made India realize that it cannot always rely on the Gulf region for sources of its ever-increasing energy demands and requirements. In order to prevent energy shortage in future, India began searching for other alternative sources of energy. It started looking eastward for a viable alternative source of energy along with other strategic purposes in mind. It is India's internal economic compulsions along with the geo-strategic implications of the Asia-Pacific region to India's geo-political interests that compelled her to initiate the LEP under Prime Minister Narasimha Rao's stewardship. The policy is a product of the realization on the part of India's ruling clique that global geo-politics has shifted from Europe to the Asia-Pacific region due its geo-strategic and geo-economic implications in the emerging post cold war global environment it is the economy that determine the status of a nation in the global power equation.

As the phrase LEP itself suggests, ASEAN will occupy a central position in India's strategy to advance its political, economic and security interests in Southeast Asia in particular and the Asia-Pacific region in general. New Delhi's perception of the 'East' in the phrase Look East Policy is not confined to the ASEAN with its 10 members, but ultimately aims at incorporating the Asia-Pacific region. It is clearly evident in Prime Minister Manmohan Singh's inaugural address to the Third Indo-ASEAN Business Summit in New Delhi held in October 2004. He used the term 'arc of advantage' for Asia-Pacific zone which spans from the Himalayas to the Pacific Ocean, proposed to be linked by efficient road, rail, air and shipping services (quoted in editorial, *The Hindu*, December 4, 2004). However, an immediate objective of the policy is to promote Indo-ASEAN relations from summit level partner to ASEAN+4 status through various bilateral and multilateral engagements with the members of the ASEAN and ultimately to have a strong foothold in the Asia-Pacific region. This region is vital to India's economic and political security because of its geo-political and geo-economic implications. Economically, the pacific impulse is fast overtaking the Atlantic impulse. The total income of the Asia-pacific community would rival the European Union's. In terms of trade it would be bigger than the North American Free Trade Agreement comprising the United States, Canada and Mexico and its combined foreign exchange reserves would be greater than those of the European Union and NAFTA (*The Hindu* ibid.). For a newly open economy like India Asia-Pacific region present an enormous growth opportunity. Even though Japan is India's second largest individual trade partner, accounting for 5.3 per cent of India's total trade, India is yet to find a strong foothold in the Asia-Pacific Economic Community (APEC) and the present LEP is deemed to be a major booster in this respect.

India's Look East and ASEAN: Emerging Convergence

Any sensible country having potentialities to play a major role in shaping world politics or at least regional politics cannot afford to ignore the Association of Southeast Asian Nations (ASEAN). This is particularly true for India due to its geographical, economic, cultural and strategic linkages with the Southeast Asian region. ASEAN had witnessed different facets of Cold War politics involving two superpowers, the USA and erstwhile Soviet Union, due to its geo-strategic importance that depends on two key elements—location and economic potential (Banerjee 1988: 1280). Besides the geo-politics of Southeast Asia, the geo-economic significance of the region cannot be ignored. Southeast Asia is the source of many of the world's primary products like rubber, tin, copper, coconut, timber, rice and spices. The discovery of oil and gas in large quantities has added to its economic potential. It can, therefore, be safely assumed that creation of good rapport with ASEAN occupies a pivotal position in India's Look East strategy.

Before studying Indo-ASEAN relations in detail, it may not be out of context to mention in brief the history of the formation, objectives and nature of ASEAN in order to grab the true nature of Indo-ASEAN relations. The five non-communist member countries, namely, Indonesia, Malaysia, Philippines, Singapore and Thailand, established the Association of Southeast Asian Nations (ASEAN), on August 8, 1967 in Bangkok. Subsequently, Brunei Darussalam joined on January 8, 1984, Vietnam on July 28, 1995, Laos and Myanmar on July 23, 1997 and Cambodia on 30 April 1999. Thus the founding members' dream of a unified ASEAN including all the countries of Southeast Asia was fulfilled on April

30, 1999 with Cambodia joining as the last member country with the end of the Cold War signalling the emergence of sheer similar perceptions in economic and security matters among the member countries as logical fallout of post cold war politics in the region. ASEAN has become a cohesive and well-developed regional organization having multi-faceted objectives. In the present era of capitalist market economy, ASEAN, a vibrant regional growth zone, occupies a vital 'economic space' to any country pursuing the neo-liberal free market economy. A close look at the main statistics of the ASEAN substantiates the above point. It has a population of about 500 million, a total area of 4.5 million square kilometres, a combined gross domestic product of US$ 737 billion and a total trade of US$ 720 billion making ASEAN one of the most vibrant growth zones in the world.

The ASEAN declaration of August 18, 1967, states the following as its objectives:

- to accelerate economic growth, social progress and cultural development in the region through joint endeavours in the spirit of equality and partnership in order to strengthen the foundation for a prosperous and peaceful community of Southeast Asian nations,
- to promote regional peace and stability through mutual respect for justice and the rule of law in the relationship among countries in the region and adherence to the principles of the United Nations Charter.

A close scrutiny of the aims and objectives of ASEAN reveals the fact that though overtly guided by socio-economic and cultural aspects, covertly ASEAN is equally guided by political objectives of countering the Communist regime in Indo-China (Vietnam, Laos and Cambodia). It also seeks to prevent intra-regional domination by any Southeast Asian country. In fact objectives such as 'regional peace and stability,' 'respect for justice and rule of law' and 'adherence to the principles of the United Nations Charter' are political stands and conditionalities of ASEAN upon any country willing to have economic and political rapport with the pro-capitalist ASEAN. Moreover, its perception on the security of the region was greatly determined by fear of Communism as a political and economic doctrine, which contradicted liberal democratic and economic principles. So, any country harbouring dreams for having political relations must accept the above principles. Behind this covert political agenda, newborn ASEAN was presented as a sub-regional grouping for economic, social and cultural cooperation to provide a safety valve to the already instable political condition created by the intense rivalry between the two superpowers.

Security concerns and political motives always figured prominently among the founders of ASEAN. Former Indonesian Foreign Minister Ali Alatas, a key figure in ASEAN diplomacy, underlined the close connection between ASEAN and politics ever since its inception. He pointed out the conspicuous convergence among the five original members *vis-à-vis* a common political outlook and shared convictions on national priority objects. A compelling need to find means and ways to secure these objectives in the evolving strategic environment of East Asia led to the formation of ASEAN. Hence, it will be misleading and politically naïve to presume ASEAN simply as a socio-economic and cultural organization bereft of political ambitions. Politically speaking, ASEAN can be considered as a tool in expanding and exporting capitalism across the continent.

The emerging convergence between ASEAN and India underscores the logic of the former's increasing influence—political, economic and strategic—and the latter's need to forge new alliances amidst the rapidly changing global configurations of power politics. As ASEAN grows in strength and size, incorporating India's next-door neighbour Myanmar; it has to make efforts to engage this growing regional bloc. ASEAN is central to India's LEP in the entire Asia-Pacific region. The policy not just aims at establishing trade relations with the countries of ASEAN; it is a multi-pronged approach to establish strategic links with many individual countries and evolve economic bonds with the region. India's LEP adopts a three-pronged approach. First, it is an attempt to renew political contacts with the ASEAN partners; second, it aims to increase economic interaction (trade, investment, science and technology, tourism etc.) and third, it seeks to forge defence links with ASEAN partners as a means to enhance political and strategic interests and understanding (Visvam 1997). With these objectives in view India under Prime Minister Narasimha Rao supported by his erstwhile lieutenant Finance Minister, Manmohan Singh, initiated a conscious effort in 1991 to forge economic and strategic ties with ASEAN.

Under this effort, Narasimha Rao made a series of visits to the ASEAN countries stretching from Singapore and Malaysia to Thailand and Vietnam and established what ASEAN leaders called 'instant personal chemistry'. His efforts paid off in 1992 with India becoming a sectoral dialogue partner of ASEAN and full dialogue partner in December 1995. The sectoral dialogue partnership was to promote trade, investment and tourism relations, while dialogue partnership had broader agenda for cooperation in various fields. It includes security, political, economic and cultural areas of cooperation. The successive governments of the United Front under H.D. Deve Gowda and I.K. Gujral sustained the momentum gained during Rao's government. National Democratic Alliance-led coalition government under A.B. Vajpayee and the presently United Progressive Alliance under Manmohan Singh rigorously pursued massive economic reforms under the liberalization regime to create a conducive atmosphere for free trade with ASEAN.

The consistent and sustained efforts made by successive governments to integrate India's economy with Southeast Asian countries bore fruits in 1996 as India became a member of ASEAN Regional Forum which aims at confidence building, conflict resolution and preventive diplomacy in order to create a stable political environment to ensure free trade in the region. The defining moment in Indo-ASEAN relation came when Indo-ASEAN relation was elevated to summit level in November 2001. Till then, three Indo-ASEAN summits have been held: first, at Phnom Penh (Cambodia) in November 2002, second, at Bali (Indonesia) in October 2003 and third, at Vientiane (Laos) in November 2004. The burgeoning Indo-ASEAN ties indicate the absence of differences in political, economic and security perceptions present during the Cold War period.

Economic Dimension

The economic cooperation involving free flows of capital, commodities, investment and functional cooperation between India and countries of Southeast Asia and Asia-Pacific region in various sectors constitute one of the main dimensions of India's LEP. Over the years, India's economic relations with ASEAN have improved significantly. Trade between India and ASEAN stood at US$ 2.5 billion in 1993-94, US$ 6 billion in 1996-97; the figure reached

US$ 7.8 billion in 2001-02 and crossed US$ 10 billion in the year 2003 and promises to increase to US$ 50 by 2007. India's trade with the ASEAN is likely to increase manifold once the ASEAN Free Trade Agreement (FTA), which is planned to enforce fully by 2010, is materialized. Momentous increase in the trade volume with ASEAN is indicative of India's sustained economic reforms. Thus, Indo-ASEAN relations are blooming and will continue to do so depending on India's unflagging economic liberalization and privatization. In short, the more India embarks upon 'market capitalism', the more intense will be its relation with ASEAN. The two-way trade constitutes about 6 per cent of India's total trade. While trade with other countries of ASEAN is on the rise, India's principal ASEAN trading partners are Indonesia, Singapore, and Malaysia. India's exports to ASEAN grew by 37.9 per cent in 2002-03 and the value stood at US$ 4.65 billion. Imports from ASEAN stood at US$ 4.8 billion in 2002-03. The main items imports consist of artificial resins, vegetable oils, electronic goods news print, natural rubber, pears and precious stones, wood and woods products, coal, fertilizers, organic chemicals, metaliferous ores, etc. The main items of Indian export to ASEAN comprise oil meals, gems and jewellery, meat and meat preparations, cotton yarn, fabrics, cosmetics, engineering goods, transport equipment, machinery and instruments, electronic goods, pharmaceutical drugs, chemicals, sugar, wheat, spices etc. Rapid increase in individual ASEAN countries trade with India can be ascertained from Table 2.1.

Table 2.1: Indian Trading Ties with ASEAN Countries: 2002-03

(Figures in US$ millions)

Country	*Export*	*Import*	*Total*
Singapore	1,434	1,445	2,880
Malaysia	753	1,477	2,230
Indonesia	833	1,392	2,225
Thailand	717	23	739
Philippines	476	125	600
Vietnam	340	29	369
Myanmar	76	339	414
Combodia	20	1	21
Laos	2	0	3
Brunei	4	0	5
Total	**4,654**	**4,831**	**9,486**

Source: Commerce Ministry of India.

From Table 2.1, it can be seen that trade with some of the less developed countries of ASEAN particularly Cambodia, Laos, Myanmar and Vietnam (CLMV) is very low compared to their size, economic volume and potentiality. Many hopes are pinned on the Mekong-Ganga Cooperation, which involves India and five ASEAN countries of CLMV and Thailand. Another important feature of Indo-ASEAN economic cooperation is the increased flows of Foreign Direct Investment (FDI) in various sectors. India's economic liberalization is the single most important factor in this regard. Countries of ASEAN, especially, Indonesia, Malaysia, Singapore and Thailand have become major sources of FDI flows into India. From 1992-2003, ASEAN accounted for about 3.55 per cent of the total FDI inflow into India. Sectorwise, power and oil refinery, telecom, electrical equipment, and Information Technology has received the largest share of ASEAN investment. Now pharmaceuticals, biotechnology and infotech are turning out to be promising areas for ASEAN investments. Functional cooperation in various sectors between India and ASEAN is another vital aspect of economic cooperation between two entities. Currently India is closely collaborating with ASEAN countries in many fields such as trade and investment, science and technology, tourism, human resource development, transport and infrastructure. Since India is a recognized IT power, ASEAN expects to harvest benefits in this sector. As Lakshmana Chetty maintains that visits of Secretary-General of ASEAN, Rodolfo Severino, Prime Minister, Goh Chok Tong, Shinawatra and Mahathir and President Megawati to Bangalore, Silicon Valley of India and the Hi-Tech City (Hyderabad), clearly demonstrated the eagerness of the Southeast Asian countries to exploit India's expertise in the field of IT. Ninety-four ASEAN candidates were imparted advanced software techniques at NIIT (India) in 2000. An ASEAN-India Digital Archive (AIDA) project is also being set up. In 2000-02, NIIT and APTECH opened eight IT schools in the Philippines. The Vietnamese FPT Company has entered into joint ventures with APTECH and opened training centres for Vietnamese experts.

In the field of human resources development, India has offered hundred seats in various training courses at reputed Indian institutions. Under the Indian Technical and Economic Cooperation (ITEC) programme India has been offering scholarships every year to various Southeast Asian Countries—Laos 30, Cambodia 40,

Indonesia 63, and Vietnam 110—for pursuing short term and medium term training in a plethora of fields. In biotechnology, cooperation includes projects in plant and animal biotechnology and establishment of an ASEAN-India Bio-informatics Network. Given the progress made by India in medical research, there is ample scope of cooperation in tropical medicine and the surveillance and control of communicable diseases with ASEAN. As the Foreign Minister of Vietnam Nguyen Dy Nien, has pointed out, Southeast Asian Countries needed India's cooperation in eradicating diseases like tuberculosis, cholera, diarrhea, dengue, hemorrhage fever Japanese encephalitis leptospirosis and malaria.

Tourism is another industry, which can blossom fully and benefit both India and ASEAN due to their cultural connectivity and bonds in the historical past. Malaysia, Singapore and Thailand have been the favourite destination of Indian tourists. Now the CLMV countries (Cambodia, Laos, Myanmar and Vietnam) are making conscious effort to attract Indian tourists. The extension of land corridor from India to Myanmar going upto Hanoi and the direct flights between India and Cambodia and extending the flights between Delhi and Bangkok to Phnom Penh and Siem Reap, the seat of Angkor Vat, are seen as real boosters to the tourism industry.

A logical consequence of the LEP is the construction and development of trade routes besides the sea routes where bulk of Indo-ASEAN trade is carried out. India is now exploring land routes from New Delhi to Hanoi, through construction of railways and highways. Tamu-Kalewa-Moreh road has been constructed and direct trade and transit facilities have been increased with the ASEAN. A very important component of economic dimension in India's LEP is inter-regional groupings having immense political and economic implications such as BIST-EC (later on BIMST-EC) and the Mekong-Ganga Cooperation (MGC). The idea of a inter-regional grouping was first mooted by Thailand at a ministerial meeting in Bangkok in June 1997 which was attended by India, Sri Lanka, Bangladesh and Thailand to foster a free trade regime with the three contiguous countries around the Bay of Bengal. Myanmar was included as a member of the grouping in December 1997 thereby changing the acronym into BIMST-EC from BIST-EC. The purpose of the grouping is to take advantage of synergies of land and maritime contiguity and to strengthen relations between South Asia and Southeast Asia. This will help India, to a great extent, in fostering good neighbourly relations with Bangladesh and Sri Lanka through cooperation in various sectors, which Gujral Doctrine (named after former PM of India I.K. Gujral) 1996 had envisioned. BIMST-EC, with the inclusion of Nepal and Bhutan recently, can provide an alternative to SAARC—which is besieged with Indo-Pak rivalry—for economic cooperation. With relatively better economic performance, rising power and status in global arena, India is now in a much better position to win the confidence of its smaller South Asian neighbours in providing progress, stability and security in the region. In fact, India can emerge as a centre of gravity for the countries of South Asia and isolate Pakistan in economic and political matters concerning South Asia through BIMST-EC (Bangladesh, India, Myanmar, Sri Lanka, Thailand Economic Cooperation). The broader economic objective of BIMST-EC is to have a free trade agreement (FTA) among the member countries by 2017. India and Thailand have finalized the modalities for implementing the first phase of the free trade agreement in the Bangkok summit of BIMST-EC. It entails reduction of tariffs on eighty-two (82) agreed items under the fast track or Early Harvest scheme in a span of three years. If it is successfully implemented the two countries will have a fully free trade regime by 2010. The logical collorary of a FTA is to have physical interconnectivity through road and rail links among the member countries. In this respect BIMST-EC transport corridor, which is under construction (*The Hindu* September 24, 2005) once completed will make operation of free trade regime possible. The 1,360 kms. long trilateral connectivity project announced in Yangon, Myanmar in April 2002, will connect Moreh in Manipur to Mae Sot town in Northern Thailand through Bagan in central Myanmar. This trilateral Indo-Myanmar-Thailand Highway will eventually become part of the Trans-Asian Highway, mooted by the World Bank, connecting Indo-China region (Vietnam, Laos and Cambodia) with India.

The Mekong-Ganga Cooperation (MGC) launched in Vientiane in November 2000 comprising India and five riparian states of Mekong, namely Cambodia, Laos, Myanmar, Thailand and Vietnam is another important component in India's strategy to evolve a comprehensive relation with the Southeast Asian Nations. The key areas of cooperation will include culture, human resource development, transport and communication. Even though it is in its infant stage, MGC can be considered parallel to the Greater Mekong Cooperation between Yunan Province of China and five riparian states of Mekong. Since MGC and BIMST-EC involve the countries of South Asia and Southeast Asia, they can serve as a bridge between the SAARC and ASEAN and will ultimately help in converting SAARC and ASEAN into a unified free trade zone.

Strategic Dimension

It will be incomplete if one limits India's LEP to economic considerations only without taking into account the strategic dimensions of the policy because two are inextricable parts of India's LEP. Indeed world geo-politics has shifted from Europe to the Asia-Pacific region. For obvious reasons, the 21st century belongs to this region in general and Southeast Asia in particular. The end of the Cold War saw the emergence of a new security dynamics in the Asia-Pacific region. In the unfolding post Cold War environment some previous threats have disappeared or become latent and other threats appear or become manifest. Dissolution of the contentious issues of Cambodia and integration of Myanmar and Vietnam into the ASEAN fold made Southeast Asia a stable region and ASEAN a well-knit regional organization. However, Chinese continental and maritime expansion during the last decade has created a 'perceived Chinese threat' founded on substantive evidence both within India and Southeast Asia. The Chinese expansion and US military presence in the area may create a Cold War situation in the region. Chinese occupation of the disputed Spratly groups of islands and Paracels islands is a testimony to the fact that China wanted to turn South China Sea into a virtual Chinese lake making it its exclusive domain. China's action has raised many eyebrows among the leaders of ASEAN and India.

What will be India's role in the emerging security matrix of the region? How can India fully exploit the factors of convergence *vis-à-vis* ASEAN to advance and sustain its national interests? Liberalization of India's economy and end of the Cold War dismantled the 'psychological wall' dividing India and most countries of Southeast Asia. Subsequently, there has been an unprecedented convergence in defence and security perceptions between India and ASEAN. Southeast Asian countries, in the post Cold War period, cannot afford to ignore India in terms of its growing military prowess *vis-à-vis* the arms race with Pakistan, which ultimately led to the nuclearization of its military in May 1998. It is increasingly felt that India's military strength can no longer be ignored in the emerging balance of power structure in Asia. Changing configurations ensured India's role as a balancing power in the region. Southeast Asian nations began looking forward to India's balancing capability. India's strategic interests to check Chinese influence and dominance in the region in the eventual reduction of the presence of superpowers coincided strikingly with similar thinking within the Southeast Asian community (Naidu 2004: 338). In this context, India's LEP can be seen as a well-coordinated strategy to exploit these 'converging factors' and advance its strategic interests in the region. For ASEAN, India with its increasing military and technological prowess and post-liberalization economic reforms can pose a credible balance against Chinese expansionism and for that matter against any major power intended to dominate the Southeast Asia.

Indian strategic concerns always found China's maritime expansion and inroad into the Indian Ocean through Myanmar a cause of worry. The collapse of Soviet Union and China's normalization of relations with the successor state Russia, withdrawal of US military from the region with the dismantling of Clark and Subic Bay bases in Philippines and withdrawal of erstwhile Soviet forces from Camranh Bay in Vietnam left a 'power vacuum' in the region. It instantly paved the way for Chinese maritime and diplomatic expansion. China has always asserted that Indian Ocean is not India's ocean. India's phobia of Chinese maritime expansion into the Indian Ocean is accentuated by the latter's naval capability. In terms of operational ability, Chinese navy ranks third in the world after the United States and Russia. Indian apprehension of China's contemplated move to develop a three-aircraft across this ocean carry bulk of its overseas trade. Its geo-strategic significance led analysts comment that whoever controls the Indian Ocean will dominate Asia. This ocean is key to the seven seas. In the 21st century destiny of the world will be decided on its waters.

Its strategic importance compelled the imperial powers, in the past, to tussle among each other to control and dominate the Ocean. A brief historical detour reveals its importance since the discovery of the sea route to India by the Portuguese. They established a 'Thalassocracy' (a naval empire) within Indian Ocean, lasting for about a century. Their monopoly in the ocean was challenged and destroyed by the Dutch and the English. The struggle amongst Dutch, French and English powers for the domination of trade in Indian Ocean led to the British subjugation of the Indian sub-continent starting with the coastline and littoral states thereby making Indian Ocean into a 'virtual British lake' for nearly one and half century. It enabled Britain to defend her overseas colonies from her arc rivals. When world politics was sharply divided into two blocs during the Cold War period, the Indian Ocean once again became the playground of super power politics, particularly between USSR and USA with the marginal Chinese presence. Its geographical position and tremendous natural resources have enhanced strategic importance. The strategic significance of India Ocean has increased due to its geo-economic importance. In its bed, it harbours minerals vital to the security and well being of any State. With the fast depletion of vital fossil based mineral resources on land, oceans are becoming the 'centre of gravity' for most of the major powers in their quest for mineral resources. The energy crisis of 1973 (popularly known as oil crisis in the Gulf region) had given momentum to oil explorations in the sea and ocean beds. Moreover, oceans contain vast potential of food, hydrocarbon and mineral resources. In this context, India Ocean, which covers about 20 per cent of the world's total ocean area, is no exception. It is rich in various kinds of natural resources of vital importance. For instance Asia has the highest known offshore petroleum reserves. The continental margins from India to Korea are reported to be among the most promising areas of oil reserve in the world (Agarwal 2000: 21).

Indian Ocean is sandwiched between the Atlantic and Pacific Oceans in the west and east respectively ensuring easy routes for transportation to the Pacific Coast countries in the east and to the Mediterranean and Atlantic Ocean region in the west. As mentioned earlier this ocean is the key to the seven seas. From the Arabian Sea vessels can sail up to the Black Sea and the Sea of Azor in the Soviet Union through the Red Sea, the Suez Canal, the Mediterranean Sea, the Aegean Sea, the Strait of Dardanelles, the Sea of Marmara and the Strait of Bosphorus and again up to the Atlantic Ocean through the Mediterranean Sea and the Gibraltar Strait.

In the east, ships can sail from the Bay of Bengal to the countries of Pacific Ocean and South China Sea through a number of straits like the Malacca Strait, Sundra Strait, and Ombai Strait, and the

Timor sea. Most of the oil from the Persian Gulf area—where 62 per cent of world's known oil reserves are located—is being shipped across the Indian Ocean into the Red Sea towards the Suez or around the Cape of Good Hope to Europe and America and through the grand Oceanic trunk road to the strait of Malacca towards Japan and China. A major part is shipped to points on the Indian Ocean itself, i.e. to India, Australia and Singapore. Besides, this ocean is also the thoroughfare for the transportation of other vital commodities like tin, rubber, foodstuff and minerals (Agarwal 2000: 19). It can be observed that Indian Ocean along with its strategic straits will be an arena for contest among the major powers in the present era of neo-liberal capitalism and globalization to ensure free flow of multilateral trade.

India along with Southeast Asian Nations perceives a common interest in protecting the vital sea-lines of communication and transportation in the Ocean. Commenting on the geo-strategic importance of the Indian Ocean on the security of littoral states analysts observe that if any of the naval powers (primarily the superpowers in this respect) tries to place impediments to maritime transportation *anywhere* in the Indian ocean, at the exit entry-point (such as the Cape) or elsewhere, all the countries in the area would be immediately involved. Nations of the two other oceans, geographically more decentralized, will not react in a similar manner. If something like the Cuban missiles crisis arises in the neighbourhood of the Marmuz Strait or the Cape, with embargo of oil or other material commodities, it would immediately set many countries aflame (Vali 1976: 40). It is also true of the Malacca Strait, a vital choke point where more than 40 per cent of the world's oil and over 60,000 ships pass annually which is more than double the number that traverse the Suez and treble that of the Panama Canal. Any maritime power that controls this strait can exercise tremendous power in the politics of South and Southeast Asia and the Pacific region.

The implication of strategic position of the Indian Ocean on the security of its littoral states has compelled China to develop strategic ties in different aspects. It is trying to open up an alternative route to the India by establishing navigation facilities in Myanmar controlled islands in the Bay of Bengal. Moreover, it is also working on road and rail constructions in Myanmar. Panelists in a 1994 seminar in Beijing pointed out the importance of a transport route from Yunan to Rangoon in the event of a blockade of sea-lines. China is helping Myanmar in expanding the latter's naval facilities at Great Coco island, the site of a major signals intelligence facility near India's strategically important Andaman and Nicobar islands (Gopal 2003: 146). Pointing out the overlapping contradictory interests between India and China *vis-à-vis* Myanmar, a commentator observed that for China, Myanmar is an important component of its strategy to prevent its encirclement by the US and its allies and to secure vital naval routes to oil supplies in the Middle East. For New Delhi, Chinese influence in Burma is a threat to India's plans for naval dominance in the Bay of Bengal and strategic influence in South East Asia (Kumara 2005). India's deep concern for increasing Chinese influence in Southeast Asia and Asia-Pacific is reflected in Defence Minister Pranab Mukherjee's concluding Address at the IDSA's 7th Asian Security Conference. Speaking at the conference he foregrounded the shift towards the Asia Pacific in terms of economy. He asserted that the region is witnessing a realignment of geo-strategic equations. Among the most significant developments are the rise of China and the political dimensions of its increasing regional economic engagement. Not only is China growing as an economic power in the region, but also it is also keen to ensure that the geo-political environment will enable its growth and consolidation (Mukherjee 2005). India's LEP aims at engaging China and other major powers in different aspects of economic and strategic matters both at bilateral and multilateral regional security forum like ASEAN Regional Forum and to prevent domination of Southeast Asia by any major power, especially, China. As the Defence Minister pointed out, India's strategic perspective *vis-à-vis* East Asia is based on two fundamental principles:

> First, the maintenance of equitable strategic balance and prevention of regional rivalries from destabilising the region.
>
> Second and more importantly, India would like to engage all players both bilaterally and collectively through institutions like the ASEAN Regional Forum (Mukherjee 2005).

India's LEP will enable India in facing non-conventional security challenges such as energy security, security of the sea-lines of communication and transport, rising incidence of sea piracy, terrorism, natural disasters, illicit trafficking of WMD (Weapon of Mass Destruction) and narco crimes. Unlike conventional threats, non-conventional threats are trans-border in character and require a common front among the nations to deal with such threats. One important area of great concern is the rising incidence of sea piracy and terrorism in the Malacca Strait, the last year 40 sailors were kidnapped—four were killed and about US$ 1 million was paid in ransom, substantiate the point. In order to ensure the security of this strategic trade route Malaysia, Thailand, Singapore and Indonesia have launched joint security-initiative known as the 'Eyes in the Sky' project to protect the global trade route of Malacca Straits with 'combined air-patrols'. The project is now part of a wider 'Malacca Straits Security Initiative' (*The Hindu,* September 25, 2005). Former Indian Prime Minister Atal Bihari Vajpayee's signing of two broad agreements for comprehensive economic cooperation and combating terrorism with ASEAN during the Second Indo-ASEAN Summit in Bali, October 2003, is a manifestation of increasing strategic ties with Southeast Asia. The budding Indo-ASEAN strategic relation is manifested in the signing of ASEAN-India Partnership for Peace, Progress and Shared Prosperity on November 30, 2004 during the 3rd Indo-ASEAN Summit. The agreement acknowledging ASEAN-India cooperation essential for promoting peace, stability, development prosperity in Asia and the world endorses, among other things, to jointly address the common challenges to the comprehensive political and economic security including food, human and energy security. It seeks understanding in combating the menace of international terrorism and other transnational crimes such as trafficking in drug and arms, environmental crimes, sea piracy and money laundering through effective institutional linkages and programmes of cooperation giving priority to information exchange and capacity building.

However, India will not have easy sailing of its LEP because several other major powers such as China, Russia, Japan and most importantly the USA have stakes in the region. There is possibility of becoming Asia-Pacific region into a contested space among the major powers more especially between China and USA due to former's economic and strategic expansion challenging the America's, what Andrew Bacevich, a conservative-turned-realist American called, 'project of global imperium'. Foreign Minister Li Zhaoxing in a run up to UN's 60th anniversary related summit in New York, September 14 and 16, 2005, identified multilateralism for the 'harmonious development of international relations' whereas American main thrust is to sustain unilaterlism through shifting alignments. In a major policy shift of the US and India, the two country signed 'New framework for the Indo-US defence relationship' during India's Defence Minister's visit to America in July 2005. The framework, among other things, includes 'to collaborate in multinational operation', 'expand collaboration relating to missile defence' and 'assist in building worldwide capacity to conduct successful peacekeeping operation'. The implications of such pact must be seen against the geo-political development in Asia-Pacific region in the post-cold war period. The Indo-US framework for defence relationship is part of the US grand strategy to get itself embedded in the politics of Asia-Pacific region. The signing of the India-US 10-year defence pact and subsequently India's decision to vote against Iran at crucial meeting of the Board of Governors of the International Atomic Energy Agency on September 24, 2005 is indicative of India's pro-US shift in its foreign policy. The decision is evidenced of the Manmohan Singh Government's shameful willingness to abandon the independence of Indian foreign policy for the sake of strengthening its 'strategic partnership' with the United State (Editorial, *The Hindu*, September 26, 2005). Secondly, India's LEP also signifies a shift in India's economic policy from a state guided to neo-liberal market economy. Henceforth, drastic disinvestments in PSUs (Public Sector Undertakings), massive privatization and opening of domestic market in order to attract foreign companies and foreign direct investment in various sectors of the economy will be the major thrust of India's foreign economic policy.

REFERENCES

Agarwal, Amita 2000. *Indian Ocean and World Peace*. New Delhi: Kanishka Publishers and Distributors.

Appadorai, A. *et. al.* 1985. *India's Foreign Policy and Relations*. New Delhi: South Asian Publishers Ltd.

Association of Southeast Asian Nations <http//www.aseansec.org>

Banerjee, D. 1988. '"External Powers" Interests and Role in Southeast Asia'. *Strategic Analysis*. February.

BIMST-EC Summit: A Milestone Towards Pan-Asian Regional Cooperation'. *India News Online*. <http://news.indiamart.com/news-analysis/bimst-ec-summit-a mi-7074.html>

Chandrasekhar, C.P. and Jayanti Ghosh 2004. *The Market That Failed: Neoliberal Economic Reforms in India*. New Delhi: Left Word Books.

Cohen, Stephen P. 2002. *Emerging Power India*. New Delhi: Oxford University Press.

Defence Minister Pranab Mukherjee's concluding address 2005 at the *IDSA's* 7th *Asian Security Conference*. January 29.

Gopal, S. 2003. 'South East Asia and Major Powers'. *Dialogue*. Vol. 5, No. 1. July-September.

Jaffrelot, Christopher 2003. 'India's Look East Policy: An Asianist Strategy in Perspective'. *India Review*. Vol. 2, No. 1 April. London: Frank Cass.

Kumara, Sarath 2005. 'Burma Visits Highlights India's "Look East" Strategy'. 6 April <http://www.wsws.org/articles/2005/Apr.2005/indi-a06.shtml>.

Naidu, G.V.C. 2004. 'Whether the Look East Policy: India and Southeast Asia'. *Strategic Analysis*, Vol. 28, No. 2. April-June. New Delhi: IDSA.

Nayyar, Deepak 2002. 'Economic Development and Political Democracy', in Rakesh Mohan (ed.) *Facets of the Indian Economy*. New Delhi: Oxford University Press.

Singh, Swaran 1995. 'China's Aircraft Carrier Programme'. *Maritime International*. Vol. 1, No. 10. October.

Spanier, John 1989. *American Foreign Policy since World War II*. New Delhi: Tata McGraw Hill publishing Company United.

Strategic Digest 2005. Vol. 34. No. 5 May. New Delhi, IDSA.

The Hindu 2004. Editorial. December 4.

Vali, Ferenc A. 1976. *Politics of the Indian Ocean Region*. New York: The Free Press, a Division of Macmillan Publishing Co. Inc.

Varma, Shanta N. 1999. *Foreign Policy Dynamics Moscow and India*. New Delhi: Deep & Deep Publications Pvt. Ltd.

Visvam, S. 1997. *World Focus*. Vol. 18, No. 6. June.

Section 2
The North East Perceived Threat

3

Development and Discontent Meet in the North East: Perspective on India's Look East Policy

AJAILIU NIUMAI

Development as an issue remains central in studies on different aspects of human society. It assumes a much more potentially challenging arena particularly in regions where stark poverty and associated backwardness persist. Economic, social and political issues are inextricably intertwined with development policies and programmes as the larger interests of the masses always appear to be placed on the margins in contemporary development discourses. The essay seeks to underline the significance of trade relations and increased social mobility both within and across the nations of South Asia and Southeast Asia as factors that can enhance an overall economic integration of the region. It also tries to examine the debates on the matrix of relationship between development and discontent in the North East involving cross-border movement and social mobility. Different equations emerging out of the changing scenario finds reflections in India's attitude towards the region. This essay attempts to examine the nature of the debates on development and discontent *vis-à-vis* the policies and strategies of the Indian government.

Introduction

North East India is a land locked region with only one narrow strip linking with the rest of India. Presently, the region comprises eight states viz. Manipur, Assam, Meghalaya, Arunachal Pradesh,

Mizoram, Tripura, Nagaland and Sikkim. The area covers a landmass of around 2,62,500 sq. kms., wherein 98 per cent of its border is shared with the neighbouring countries of Bhutan, Bangladesh, China and Myanmar. According to the Census of India, 2001, the region has a population of around 39 million, which constitute, approximately, 3.8 per cent of India's total population. Rich natural resources of the region have not been utilized properly to enhance the process of development (Dutt and Nag 1997: 33). However, in the recent years, the Indian government apparently speaks of the need to develop the region. The government claims to take keen interest in developing the region at par with other states of the country.

Strategies have been framed to remove poverty and provide basic minimum services. The North East regional development concerns are tackled through the state five year plans and those of the Union Minister and central agencies. Funds are also allocated through the Northeastern Council (NEC). The Union Government with the objective of streamlining the strategy of development in an effective way has established Ministry of Development of Northeastern Region. The major agenda of the government is to provide special assistance to upgrade and expand infrastructure. Besides, it also attempts to strengthen and facilitate professional support to the NEC. In spite of these moves in recent times, the region still finds it immensely difficult to initiate any substantial development measures owing to the virtual absence of economic and industrial infrastructure. As a result of absence in structural transformations in the infrastructural base the development programmes fail to make any positive headway.

The political leadership in New Delhi urged the NEC to focus on the crucial issues of development and security asserting that it is in a good position to synergise developmental goals and efforts with security needs. Development of human resources available in Northeastern region needs to be taken up on the highest priority. Simultaneously, the marketing chain has to be developed because value addition at primary local level will enhance income at the family level and provide financial security and a sense of psychological satisfaction. However, it needs to be noted that security needs appear to supersede development concerns. India's security phobia has always been a dampener on different development initiatives in the region.

Look East Policy: Dramatics

What will be the impact of India's Look East Policy (LEP)? This Policy of the Government of India facilitates promising opportunities and challenges for the future of the Northeastern region. The North East is a part of the Indo-Burma biodiversity hot spot, marked by prevalence of innumerable exotic species of flora and fauna. Economic contribution of the North East also includes tea and rice. Undoubtedly, the North East would emerge as a producing and exporting region in South Asia if the policy would be properly implemented. Time will tell us if this policy would bear fruit in a desirable manner. LEP aims to take full advantage of the geographical location of the North East. Markets of the Association of South East Asia Nations (ASEAN) provide big opportunities for India's trade and the North East may take advantage particularly in areas horticulture, floriculture and medicinal herbs. Affinity in the cultural background will make the region's products acceptable once the connectivity gets improved. Potential sectors in this regard are Information Technology (IT), tourism, minerals, gas, oil downstream industries, education and health services, etc. Development analysis in mainland India thinks that the collective wisdom of the NEC will be instrumental in taking a holistic view at the regional level and catalyze the implementation of government policies in liaison with the concerned ministries. NEC should attempt to engage the people in profitable and creative endeavours, so that they continue to prosper and thus lead the region on the road to progress, peace and prosperity.

Indian development analysts suggest that India and ASEAN countries could adopt 'cooperative security' as a means to make the vision a reality. Security related cooperation between India and the ASEAN is perceived essential for peace, stability and prosperity of the wider Asia-Pacific region. One of the fundamental steps towards realising 'North East Vision-2002' is for India to enter into a free trade agreement with the ASEAN. It is essential to make substantial development in the Northeastern region in order to accomplish its potential as the springboard for such a vision.

A committee has been appointed by the chairman of the NEC to draw up a blueprint for formulation of comprehensive time bound road map for speedy socio-economic upliftment of the North East. In the view of the policy makers in New Delhi, 'North East Vision

2020' document is being prepared, taking into account the heightened consciousness of the people in the region, their aspirations needs and sensitivities. It would encompass all the key sectors of the economy and the vast resource potential of the region. A major initiative to seek international cooperation for development of the Northeastern region has also been undertaken. Under this initiative, five core sectors were identified for preparing the Vision Documents in order to facilitate externally aided projects (EAPs). They include 'Integrated Road Project', 'Urban Development Project', 'Trade and Investment Creation Initiative', 'Water Resource Development' and 'Integrated Energy Project'. The 'Urban Development Project' and the 'Integrated Road Project' have already been started with the technical assistance grant from the Asian Development Bank (ADB) of US$ 2.08 million. Consultants have started the work and the blueprints are expected to be ready soon. ADB has indicated a backup loan of US$ 400 million and US$ 200 million, respectively for these projects. While other projects are in the process of discussion with multilateral agencies, an agreement has been signed with ADB for Trade and Investment Creation Initiative during the year 2004-05. This initiative is likely to result in a large number of EAPs in the Northeastern region enhancing resource flow to the region substantially. This will also bring institutional reform as well as modern project management technology in various sectors (*Yojana* 2005: 64). However, it remains to be seen whether these projects will ever see the light of the day in the face of several instances in the past where infrastructural projects remains non-starters. Regular announcements of grant packages for development in the North East have remained a hallmark in New Delhi's power corridors. Routine announcements and associated hype in the mainstream media always remain sore point for people in the region with virtual absence of any significant change on the ground. More than six decades into India's centralized planning, the region has failed to witness any substantial measure for economic and industrial infrastructure.

With regard to tourism, the Northeastern region has limited facilities and services, which need to be re-framed in order to change the existing organization structure. One of the main reasons that hinder the tourists to visit the Northeastern region is the Inner Line Regulation, which prohibits entry of any outsider to the area without permits. Another constraint is due to the Restricted Area

Permit for a foreigner, which was implemented by the Central Government of India since 1958. The tourism sector can also enhance social integration between North East India and South Asia if the existing Acts are lifted up and infrastructure improvements are arranged. Besides the existing air link between Guwahati and Bangkok, several such ventures need to develop with the neighbouring countries following the LEP. Moreover, tourism is an industry that also requires infrastructural development. It is not just the facilities regarding transport that need to be looked into but there are hordes of other associated areas. Roads, hospitality related infrastructures like hotels, restaurants, recreation centres, theme parks, gardens, shopping malls, health care centres, holiday resorts, tourist assistance centres and highly improved banking services are necessary for a good tourist industry. Acute lack of adequate support structures and the absence of tourism based infrastructure in the North East point towards the impracticality of pushing forward tourism as an industry at the moment. Only when ground conditions are fulfilled tourism in the North East can thrive. It would be futile to imagine tourism as a development alternative in the sheer absence of adequate infrastructure.

Analysts found India emerging on the 'wrong side' at the end of the cold war, isolated and without partnerships of consequence (Grare and Matto, 2001). In their view, the LEP is a quest for definitions and certainties in the context of post-Cold War Asian security, where the balance or distribution of power appears to be to China's decided advantage, emphasizing the vulnerability of lesser regional states, and is an attempt to make India attractive both as a major regional power and a destination for investment.

At such a juncture, it is important to point out that while formulating this policy, the Government of India did not consult the people of the North East who will get most affected. Besides, the pros and cons of this policy need to be carefully examined before implementing it. The crux of the matter is that, gaining support and faith from the public has to be the cornerstone of this policy. Shahin (2003) argued that the slow pace of economic reforms and lack of better integration of its foreign and trade policies has made many analysts skeptical whether India will be able to effectively sustain its LEP, despite all the hype associated with the Indian Prime Minister's annual trips to the region.

North East: Business Hub of South Asia

It is important to raise the question whether the Northeastern states can build a sustainable trade relation with the neighbouring countries such as Bangladesh, Bhutan, Myanmar and China unimpeded by barriers successfully. Change in India's economic policies since 1991 in the aftermath of economic 'liberalization' had a positive affect on Indo-ASEAN relations. However the perception that India was a difficult place to do business still persisted. The political instability in the country for sometime was matter of serious concern for the observers in ASEAN. However, views about India have been changing in the last few years. India's success in Information Technology has been acknowledged. India and ASEAN have started downplaying the negatives and playing up the positives in their relations.

There has been a debate about the possibility of allowing the North East to become the hub of business centre in South Asia because of its strategic geographical location. Trade relations (both legal and illegal) through Moreh town (one of the business centre in Manipur) and Tamu town (Myanmar) have enhanced economic integration to a certain extent. However, an in-depth research has to be carried out to examine the trends of integration that prevail as a result of trade relations. If the North East is developed as a business hub of South Asia and Southeast Asia, backed by required infrastructure, India stands to benefit immensely.

The North East as a major manufacturing and redistribution hub will materialize if policy makers give more efforts in facilitating better connectivity between the region and ASEAN countries keeping into account the creation of productive base in the region. Currently, ASEAN has much more to offer to India than India has to offer to ASEAN. Hence, the matrix of relationship is perceived to be mutually beneficial in largely economic terms (Sheereen: 2005). Historically, the North East has been a major world trade route, facilitating an alternative silk route to China in earlier times. Since 6th July, 2006, India and China have open Nathu La pass for entry and exit of people, means of transport and trade engagement in the border areas. The infrastructure for border trade in the Indian side has already been set up with over 9.5 acres at Sheratang at an altitude of nearly 13,500 feet in east Sikkim district (*The Hindu*: June 14, 2006). Hence, increased social mobility through the re-opening up of the trade via Nathu La Pass will enhance the opening up of an additional point on each side for border trade. It may have a tremendous impact in view of the immense potential to generate a whole range of benefit to the North East. Moreover, India may have a chance to emerge as the main supplier of intermediate products for the Chinese manufacturing units. Even in the primary sector, trade route can facilitate major opportunities for accessing third markets and help the sub regional markets that connect Bangladesh, Myanmar and Bhutan. If the border trade relation is legalized and institutionalized, the illegal trade practices which have intrinsic links with illegal migrants and cross border crimes like drug trafficking may get minimized considerably. Re-opening of the trade routes along Indo-China border would promote social integration of the North East and Southeast Asia.

On the other hand, if the recent dialogue of the Government of India with the military junta of Myanmar for a sea link materializes project between Kolkota and the Sitwe port—it would benefit both the North East and the countries of ASEAN. India's Foreign Secretary Shyam Saran (*The Hindu*, March 8, 2006) emphasized that the economy and viability of projects in North East would improve with the development of a multi-modal project for reviving shipping links from the ancient port of Sitwe to Kolkata and Chennai on one side and use of river and highway to enter into Mizoram on the other.

Security has been the major issue in dealing with North East. However, in such a time like this, India have to shed sensitive security and trade fears in order to engage in initiatives to create a matrix of relationships with ASEAN through the Northeastern region, Interestingly, the Government of China has expressed willingness to re-open the old Stillwell Road built in the 1940s during the Second World War. The road links Kunming (capital of China's Yunan province) to Ledo (Assam) through Myitkyina (Myanmar). Here, the question is how much the North East would in particular and India in general benefit from the re-opening of the old Stillwell Road? Perhaps, the restoration of this old route may enhance communication and promote the Northeastern region to rise as the main business centre for trade with ASEAN. But, it is futile to draw an optimistic picture at this juncture.

To a certain extent, the restoration of this route may also facilitate social mobilitv both within and across the nations of South Asia.

Hypothetically, it is possible to assert that social mobility will promote social integration of the North East and Southeast Asia and the re-opening of this road may help in enhancing an overall economic integration of the region. It may also mean employment generation in the region. At present, India has a road project to connect the North East region to Thailand through Myanmar and a railway system to link Manipur with Yangon. The Government of Thailand is keen to facilitate the re-opening of this old road as it has a free trade agreement with India.

Disconnectment and Its Impact

Innumerable problems such as ethnic conflicts, unemployment, poverty, HIV/AIDS, insurgency, massive influx of illegal immigrants from Bangladesh and Nepal and outsiders from mainland India are significant indicators of discontentment in the North East. Over the years, there has been great influx of Bangladeshi and Nepali migrants and immigrants from mainland states like Bihar, Uttar Pradesh, Bengal, Orissa, Punjab and Rajasthan into the region. India has failed to tackle this crucial problem generating immense doubt and discontent in the region, the dilemma generated by the cross-border movement by diplomatic bilateral measures based on a dialogue of trust and cooperation.

A combination of an agreement and a bilateral understanding accountable for supervising the cross-border movement of people can address this sensitive issue. There should be a serious attempt to check the rapid erosion of the demographic profile in the North East. Massive influx both from the neighbouring countries and mainland India should be checked and the outsiders deported. The need of the hour is also to address the aspirations of the people of the region sincerely and focus on development programmes through substantial infrastructure building. These sensitive issues need to be examined and thoroughly studied in a collective manner by the intelligentsia, social activists, NGOs and the Government taking into confidence the people of the region.

Since the 1962 Chinese invasion, the North East came into focus but a false and over-hyped sense of security has been overarching in dealing with the region. In spite of the establishment of the NEC to address the developmental issues pertaining to the region. But, the question arises as to why this important institution is also burdened with security concerns. Recently, the Indian government gave constitutional statutory status to the NEC to handle the planning and development of the region in consonance with the LEP. How will this institution utilize its new power accorded to them to minimize discontentment in the region? It is obvious that people in the region will be keenly watching their performance.

The Indian Prime Minister, Manmohan Singh recently constituted a committee to examine issues of discontentment in the North East. Two recommendations made by this committee have found consent with some changes in the power corridors of New Delhi. Firstly, the Northeastern Development Finance Corporation (NEDFI) was re-organised as a specialized financial institution with an outlay of US$ 0.2 million. Secondly, the North East Industrial Policy of 1997 was adopted wherein several concessions and subsidies from the Central Government for industries in the Northeastern region were declared. Significant declarations include Excise Duty and Income Tax exemption for various specified industries in particular areas, Capital Investment Subsidy and Transport Subsidy, besides, a Department of Non-lapsable Central Pool or Resources activities in the North East. The region has remained underdeveloped despite the numerous schemes because of the structural lapses inherent in India's development approach. Lopsided polices devoid of sincerity and linkage with ground realities has been instrumental in pushing the region further towards underdevelopment.

Conclusion

It is not feasible to assess development issues unless structural transformation takes place on the ground. Poor Infrastructure in the region needs to be critically examine and the policy-makers should emphasized strongly on strengthening the Northeastern region rather than look across the international boarder for integration. There should be a serious move to remove regional disparities and imbalances in the countries before looking beyond the borders. Economic development of the Northeastern region depends on the local community who inhabits the area rather than on the surplus of natural resources available there. The people of this region need to be considered as the basic resources for development and prime mover of economy. Development model should be made into regional specific. The development models used in mainland India cannot be imposed in this region as it is important to study the region from a sociological perspective taking into consideration there costume, culture, tradition and ethnic complexities.

Development strategy of the region lies on mutual understanding of different states. Economy of the North East should be treated as a single economy with free inter-state flow of commodities. Instead of pumping money in the region, the government needs to bring concrete solutions. Unless, the government has a genuine commitment to solve the problems, discontentment will continue to grow. The government should identify important actors in the region for meaningful participation at the policy making and implementation. Demands of various ethnic groups need to be carefully examined because in an area facing discontentment, neither integration nor development can take place.

REFERENCES

Dutt, G.K. and Nag 1997. 'Development of Infrastructure for Science and Technology Input in North-Eastern India', in Dutta Ray (ed.) *North East India 2000 AD Perspective for Futurology*. New Delhi: Deep and Deep Publication.

Gare, Frederic and Mattoo, Amitabh 2001..*Indian and ASEAN: The Politics of India's Look East Policy*. New Delhi: Manohar.

Shahin, Sultan 2003. 'India's Look East Policy Pays off'. *Asia Times*. October 11.

Sheereen, Zeba 2005. 'Regionalism and Economic Opportunities for India-SAARG or ASEAN'. *Third Concept*. April. New Delhi.

Sridharan, Kripa 2003. 'India's Look East Policy: View from Southeast-Asea'. December 22.

The Hindu 2006. March 8.

The Hindu 2006. June 14.

Yojana 2005. December, New Delhi.

4

Imagining the North East through Look East Policy: Towards a Contextual Understanding

KONTHOUJAM INDRAKUMAR

The North East Region (NER) which immediately conjures a picture of being a land of violence and insurgencies in the popular imagination of both the minds of both the mainland intellectuals and the common citizens is contrasted by the untold story of long years of deprivation, underdevelopment, neglect and negation of every fundamental rights including the rights to life and liberty on its part. The penetrating eyes of every responsible citizen of this country is yet to see the deep rooted sense of secular culture, polity, sensibility to reason and love and a care for peace and prosperity that form the 'other reality and face' of this region. The long years of failed process of development which is manifested in the economic landscape marked by the regional inequalities, burgeoning problem of educated unemployment coupled with shrinking economic opportunity, low per capita income of the region—(12,918 as per NSDP) from the National average of 17,823 (at the current prices of 2001-02)—and ever increasing migration influx which pose a serious politico-economic and cultural problem with several dimensions. The failed process of State and Nation making is also reflected in the existence of armed opposition groups contesting the very legitimacy of the notion of a union called India. The region is poor and underdeveloped in spite of an abundance of rich natural flora and fauna, mineral and the forest resources. To be more precise Assam, a relatively resourceful state, rich in tea (accounting 50% of total tea produced in the country), oil (producing 5 million tons of crude oil annually), natural gas (producing 3,740 million cubic metres annually) is still underdeveloped. The region is also rich in *eri, muga* and mulberry types of silk and fruits such as pineapple, banana, orange, papaya and guava. It is also rich in other valuable mineral resources like limestone, coal and uranium (found abundantly in Meghalaya). Moreover the region possesses about 300 varieties of medicinal plants and herbs (Prasain 2004) and wild orchids of 400 species. It is seen as a rare phenomenon in terms of being a bio-diversity hotspot. Moreover, it has enormous power resource with a potential upto the tune of 70,000 MW, which is about 30 per cent of the total requirement of the country (Sunil 2004); yet the region remains in the dark as far as developmental work is concerned. In terms of strategic location the NER is a *sui generis,* that is, a class in itself. The NER, which occupies an area of 2,62,264, square km. (nearly 8% of the total area of India) with a population of 3,98,35,585 (accounting for 3.88% of the country's total population as per 2001 census), lies in the confluence of South and Southeast Asia having international boundaries with Bhutan (650 km.), China (1,000 km.), Myanmar (1,450 km.) and Bangladesh (1640 km.). It can be safely described as a gateway to Southeast Asia from the Indian perspective and a gateway to South Asia from ASEAN's perspective. The present essay aims to assess the politico-economic landscape of the region in order to locate the present crises in economy and polity in its specific historical and social context.

The North East: A 'Frontier Periphery'

The NER, which represents a distinct framework in India in terms of its different culture, nationalities, languages, race and state of economic development is posed to become a major trading route between the South and South East Asia as a result of India's Look East Policy. Its strategic position within the defence parameter of India has remained a vital preoccupation in the formulation of policies concerning the region. The region covering an area of 255,083 sq. km. has 4825 km. of international border with Bangladesh, Bhutan, China and Myanmar and thereby occupies a central position in India's strategic calculation *vis-à-vis* its defence matrix. The strategic importance of the region is embedded in its geo-political location. The approximate borderline and the length between the states and the neighbouring countries are—Assam-Bhutan 500 km., Arunachal Pradesh-Myanmar 525 km., Bangladesh-Assam 200 km., Manipur-Myanmar 425 km., Mizoram-Bangladesh 275 km., Tripura-Bangladesh 625 km., Meghalaya-Bangladesh 400 km. Besides the region is connected with the rest of India through the narrow Siliguri Corridor (known as the chicken neck) with a breadth of just 20 km., has added to its strategic dimension in the Indian security analysis. In terms of its location the region can be safely described as the 'underbelly' of India's security. A persisting concept of being a frontier inherited from the British colonial legacy continues to dominate the construction of a perception towards the region by the ruling class of postcolonial Indian State. The perception is rooted in the colonial belief that a frontier region needs to be militarily defended. The Indian ruling class's perception *vis-à-vis* the region was characterized by lack of knowledge about its distinct political, cultural and historical identities. In short, the North East has long been considered as an anthropologists' paradise for their research works, far removed from its existence as a distinct political and economic entity; hence the region has remained aloof from the 'Developmental Sphere' of the Indian state.

The 'Frontier' concept held by the Indian ruling class is derived from the British colonial legacy and an associated perception of non-economic importance of the region. It connotes only strategic importance in the defence configuration. Moreover, it is due to geo-political considerations that for all practical purposes the whole region is looked upon as a single unit (Kotwal 2000). A popular assertion among mainstream analysts of the region categorically speaks of the oil and tea produced in Assam being undoubtedly important for India; but as far as the other areas of the North East are concerned, economically India has little to gain from them (quoted in Srikanth 2005: 30). As such for the Indian State it is not economic considerations but political and strategic compulsions that force it to hold on to the North East. While the geographical fact of North East forming India's political border cannot be denied the very notion of 'frontier' had serious flaws in the construction of an inclusive Indian nationhood. Firstly, the notion of 'frontier' implies a military connotation—an area that needs to be defended militarily—resulting in the extensive miniaturization and institutionalization of state violence in the region through draconian legislations like the Armed Forces (Special Powers) Act, 1958 (AFSPA) that was subsequently amended in 1972 for application in the entire region.

The imposition of the AFSPA, a British colonial heritage, in the North Eastern part of 'independent' India was justified by the world's largest democracy in the name of preventing unwanted political mayhem created by the armed struggle of the Naga National Council (NNC) under the leadership of Angami Zapu Phizo. Secondly, it ignores the region as a distinct political and cultural entity, which needs to be accommodated within India through a democratic process of dialogue. The history of the integration of this region within the Indian fold and subsequent political evolution of states narrates the story of acute lack of democracy in the integration process. The territorial dimension of the region was given more importance over distinct political and cultural aspects of the peoples of this region in subsequent policies of the Indian State towards the region. Besides the overarching historical reasons, rise of national liberation movements (advanced by the insurgents) and proliferation of the armed opposition and resistance lend testimony to the reality of deep rooted sense of deprivation both in the economic and political aspects—frustration, insecurity and a sense of 'otherness' from the rest of India among the peoples of the region. Consequently the very 'legitimacy' of the notion of India as a nation-state is contested right from the birth of India in the North East. The long geographical isolation, lack of political connectivity in the past historical memory, racial and cultural distinctiveness of the peoples of North East India (NEI) resulted in the formation of a distinct and exclusive identity of the region from the rest of India. Moreover, failure of the 'Pan Indian Anti Colonial' struggle against the British colonial subjugation to reach the region—except in the Brahmaputra and the Surma valleys where Gandhiji's political movement touched marginally—has contributed immensely to the existence of an exclusive identity of the North East. The historical isolation of the North East is manifested in the lack of reference to the region in the geographical and political discourse of Ancient and Medieval India.

Lack of historical connectivity, distant geographical location, proximity and affinities with Southeast Asia, existence of Assam, Manipur and Tripura as 'sovereign political' entities in the political history of respective states and the British policy of non interference in the socio-cultural lives of the states except in certain administrative matters contributed significantly in the preservation of socio-cultural distinctiveness from the rest of India. Hence, a natural deep-rooted sense of 'otherness' among political communities of the region persists. The very perception of otherness is substantiated by the unimaginative and blunderous politico-economic responses of the Indian State *vis-à-vis* the crises in the region. Failure to understand the political history and cultural uniqueness of this 'deprived and burning periphery' on the part of the newly emerged Indian ruling class led to serious 'democratic deficiency' in the process of integration of Manipur, Tripura (both princely states at the time British withdrawal), Naga Hills (Nagaland) and the Lushai hills (Mizoram). The unfolding complex and volatile political realities resulting from the 'lapse of British Paramountcy' and the subsequent partition of the subcontinent conditioned the very psyche of newly emerging ruling class of India. Therefore, the incorporation of Indian states had to take place in a hasty manner in 'two phases—a skilful combination of baits and threats of mass pressure' (Sarkar 1985: 451).

It is not within the scope of the essay to foreground the details of the 'integration process of Indian sates, suffice it to say that there was absence of proper democratic dialogue, patience, respect for democratic institutions along with a failure to address the fear, anxieties and aspiration of political communities of hitherto independent states on the part of the ruling class while negotiating for a common Indian nationhood. This deprivation of democracy in the contested process of merger, not surprisingly, led to unwanted political and social dislocation in the region.

Casualty to Democracy

Not surprisingly the first casualty to democracy occurred when India failed to recognize the first democratically elected Manipur Legislative Assembly (under the Manipur Constitution Act, 1947) by full adult franchise under a constitutional monarchy. A sense of bitterness pervades the inclusion of this ancient Asiatic kingdom. The bitter irony, as Manipuris see it, is that independent India, which proclaimed its dedication to democracy, wilfully refused to recognize the democratically elected government of its tiny neighbour and instead persisted in dealing with the former feudal ruler, who himself repeatedly protested that he had surrendered his power to the elected Assembly. Furthermore, Manipur was not a petty state surrounded by Indian Territory, but a border state more akin to Sikkim and Kashmir. It is a difficult to deny the force of these arguments, and to resist the conclusion that the Union Government, in its eagerness to maximize its borders, simply annexed Manipur (Parrat 2005: 120).

The peripheral position of the region in the consciousness of India's ruling class was slightly disturbed by the armed struggle of the Naga National Council under A.Z. Phizo. The NNC was determined to secure the right to self-determination, because its leaders, particularly A.Z. Phizo, were convinced that Nagas were never Indians and will never be so and in a few years Naga Hills became India's first major theatre of insurgency. In a broader sense, it also posed for the first time the most sustained challenge to the demonstrative territoriality of the post-colonial Indian State in the North East (Bhaumik 1998: 313).

The outbreak of Sino-Indian War in 1962 also sparked the consciousness among India's ruling class about the region's strategic significance. However the dawn of a new consciousness was marked by the flawed response of the Indian State towards the armed struggle of the Nagas. Application of the draconian AFSPA that confers extraordinary powers to the Army and other Paramilitary forcers operating in the 'disturbed areas' of the North East was a conspicuous political exercise in the history of 'independent' India. Even more significant was the colonial legacy of the act that can be traced to the 1942 Armed Forces (Special Powers) Ordinance of the British Imperial Government originally intended to enable the colonial apparatus to suppress the 'quit India' movement launched by the Indian National Congress during the Second World War. The revival and application of this draconian Act in a part of independent India was justified and meant to prevent loot, arson, and extortion of the Naga rebels. The Act was subsequently amended in 1972 to cover the whole of the North East. In fact, the whole region is virtually subject to an undeclared state of emergency. Therefore, the very contradictions in Indian democracy are revealed in the application of an act with a colonial heritage within its territory in order to tackle a handful of rebels. Besides, the manner under which the act of 1958 was passed in the Parliament of India clearly depicts the plight and helplessness of small units in a majoritarian polity. Although the Act bears serious implications upon the liberties and rights of individual citizens as well as state governments, the Indian Parliament with minimum discussion—barely three hours in the Lok Sabha and four in the Rajya Sabha—passed the Act in spite of opposition from some of its members. Assuring the Parliament, Pant, the then Home Minister of India declared that AFSPA was a short-term measure to deal with the specific and united situation of the Naga threat and would soon be lifted (Paratt 2005: 151).

What was intensely shocking and alienating for the peoples of the North East are the more draconian provisions of the Act than Linlithgow's Armed Forces (Special Powers) Ordinance, 1942. Comparison of the 1942 colonial Act and 1958 independent India's Act, shows that the 1958 Act goes much further than the 1942 British legislation. It replaced the term 'emergency' with 'disturbed' areas. Originally the particular state government concerned could only declare the status of a disturbed area, but in 1972 this power was also given to the Central Government. Equally important was the fact that whereas the 1942 Act gave the special powers granted by the Act only to those with the military rank of captain and above, the 1972 amendment extended this to 'any commissioned officer, warrant officer, non-commissioned officer, or any equivalent ranks—in other words to anyone but the humblest private (Parrat 2005: 150). Thus the military response of the Indian state to a political movement, which was deeply rooted in the construction of 'otherness', can be seen as a serious flaw that eventually led to the violation of human rights and subjugation of the people. It also bred various forms of discontent.

The institutionalization of state violence through AFSPA under the pretext of countering a handful of Naga rebels in so early a stage of India's independence was pretentious and the justifications given by the Union Government were not convincing enough for the people of this region. To the 'deprived periphery' AFSPA amounts to an illogical discrimination amongst the citizens of 'free' India in putting an entire people into a second-class category. To surmise the arguments, a contested process of incorporation of the region within India, application of AFSPA and subsequent rampant human rights violations and economic underdevelopment of the region against the backdrop of a prevailing sense of 'otherness' both in historical and cultural terms from the rest of India produced conditions for alienation and a 'failed process of nation making' and state building. These factors have contributed significantly in the emergence of a discourse on 'internal colonialism' within the politico-economic frame of India among the intellectuals of the region. In fact a perusal of New Delhi's response and attitude towards the region, especially in the first three decades of Indian independence, is a story of relative deprivation both in economic and political terms, resulting from the cultural political and economic peripheral status in the perception of the ruling class in New Delhi. The 'frontier periphery' notion is substantially reflected in Nehru's now famous 'leaving Assam to her-fate' comment during the 1962 Sino-Indian War (Bhaumik 1998: 317). It was not only regarded as evidence of Delhi's lack of commitment to the region but also serves as the testimonial evidence of the 'frontier periphery' status of the NER. It was only from 1970s that the Indian ruling class compelled by the strategic position of the region in the overall geo-politics of South and Southeast Asia—a fact exposed by the 1962 Sino-India War and the1971 Indo-Pakistan War, and the emergence of various armed opposition groups accompanied by sporadic peoples' movement against the State-led to some introspective studies to understand the region in its true essence. The granting of statehood to Manipur, Meghalaya and Tripura in 1972 according to the North-Eastern Areas (Reorganization) Act passed by the Parliament, in 1971 and establishment of the North Eastern Council as an instrument of regional planning in 1972 by the Central Government (Kumar 1996: 76) can be seen as attempts towards a newer way of looking at NER. The Council aims at two broad objective of bringing balanced development in economic aspect and reviewing from time to time of measures taken by the constituent states for the maintenance of security and law and order. However, it fails in both the aspects despite more than 30 years its of existence.

Paradox of 'A Weak–Strong' State

The peripheral status of the region in the political domain is. also manifested in the economic domain where the project of industrialization and gradual agrarian modernization initiated elsewhere in newly independent India did not take place. It has been rigorously argued that the nature of the Indian state comes as a paradox among the peoples of the North East in the sense that it came as a very strong state in the political domain whereas in the economic domain it remains immensely insignificant. A perusal of the contemporary economic history of the region reveals the fact that the ruling clique in New Delhi, by and large, sustained and continued the British policy of exploiting the raw material, especially tea, oil and timber from Assam to serve the interests of metropolitan capitalists. Even after half a century of India's independence the NER still remains a 'dependent periphery'. The British deliberately did not develop the necessary infrastructures for indigenous economic development. As a result development of modern industries, transport, banking and other aspects of capitalist growth did not take place during the British rule (Pukhon 2003: 27). Thus the colonial interlude arrested the growth of indigenous capital formation and accumulation.

The end of British rule and the partition of the subcontinent had tremendous economic and political implications in the region. It not only disturbed free flow of traditional trade but also reduced the region into a typical 'landlocked region' leaving just 20 km. (approx) as connecting point with the rest of India. The region with marginal political space and representation was fully dependent on the Indian state for its economic development. The stark logic of underdevelopment is laid bare as dependency persists. Failure of the Indian State to take up measures towards the development of the region compels the perpetuation of dependency. It has been widely accepted that New Delhi failed to encompass the region within its development sphere.

The composition of the ruling clique coupled with limited political space and representation in the overall policy-making resulted in the acute deprivation in the allocation and construction of necessary industries for economic growth and development. This limited representation in a 'majoritarian democracy' leads to marginalization. The states of the NER, including Sikkim, have a total of merely 24 MPs in a huge Parliament of 545. In terms of percentage it constitutes only 4.58 of the total MPs. It is obvious that these 24 MPs, divided by race, ethnicity, nationality and party ideologies and affiliation are hardly in a position to influence the decision of the majority (Nag 2005: 49). Not surprisingly the initial efforts of industrialization and modernization in the early as well as subsequent stages of the modernization project were concentrated in mainland India and did not take root in the region. It will be worthwhile to mention that Nehru's plan of modernization and the 'green revolution' that were meant to provide a radical transformation in the Indian industry and agriculture hardly reached the NER. The disadvantages of being a landlocked region resulting from the partition of the subcontinent have remained intact and there seem to be no serious effort to turn the situation reversed. The partition led to the disruption of the long existing trade links and infrastructure that the North East was accustomed to. The alternative trade routes and infrastructures that were developed in the post partition period have remained for long a makeshift arrangement as it were. A large part of the North East is yet to have railheads. The existing railway networks only serve to exploit the commercial interests of the colonial power. It is yet to be restructured for even growth. The net effect has been that people pay higher prices for their purchase originating in the rest of the country (Sarma 2001: 298). The features of British colonial policy of making the region a producer of raw materials and the market for the finished products still remain the dominant characteristic of the economy of NER.

The perpetuation and sustenance of such features led to the emergence of the North East as a 'colonial hinterland' (Misra 1980). A look at the following data reveals the low per capita deposit and a low per capita advance in all the seven states of NER as compare to all India average.

Table 4.1: Per capita deposit and per capita advance for North East states (in INR) as on December 31, 1981 for all the schedule commercial banks of NE

State	*Per capita deposit*	*Per capita advance*
Assam	222.3	96.48
Manipur	143.86	51.38
Meghalaya	412.93	33.28
Nagaland	315.45	109.28
Tripura	214.89	41.86
Arunachal Pradesh	214.82	32.24
Mizoram	224.94	42.59
N.E. India	229.95	94.78
All India	**648.02**	**444.51**

Source: Phukon (2003:28).

The deposits and advances include those concerning public sector enterprises and corporations. Moreover the reduction of Assam, a relatively better state in the North East, into one of the most backward states of India, is a clear manifestation of the logic behind the working of a 'peripheral economy' serving the metropolitan capitalists interests.

The relatively better position of Assam in terms of PCI not only diminished in the late 1950s, but also started declining since 1960s. The case is applicable to all the states of NER with the exception of Arunachal Pradesh, which has a relatively higher PCI from the rest of India. Another major dimension of underdevelopment of the NER is the failure to replace the intermediary classes of British colonial interlude as key economic player. The contemporary economic reality of the region is characterised by the fact that '*marwaris*' and other non-indigenous inhabitants are holding and controlling its economy. Along with foreign as well as domestic immigrants they play the role of a 'parasite class' in the regional economy in the sense that they consume and siphon off huge amount of wealth in the form of profit accrued from business and as labour wages. The problem of influx of migration both internal (domestic) and external (foreign) has serious implication in the economy of the region besides being a major threat to indigenous culture, tradition and polity. They occupy a large part of the 'economic space' in the region and consume as well as siphon off capital from the region.

Table 4.2: Per capita income (PCI) of Assam and India at constant (1980-81) prices in IN

Year	*Assam*	*All India*	*Gap between Assam & rest of All India*
1950–51	1173	1127	(+) 46
1960–61	1140	1350	(-) 210
1970–71	1221	1520	(-) 299
1980–81	1284	1630	(-) 346
1990–91	1544	2222	(-) 678
1994–95	1602	2449	(-) 847

Source: Phukon (2005: 529).

Migration of outsiders in large numbers into the North East is another crucial area in terms of its economic equations. The gravity can be seen from the assessment of Imtiaz Ahmad, a prominent Bangladeshi scholar, who estimated the number of people crossing illegally to India between 1961-71 at 1.72 million and another half a million between 1971-81. He says that not less than 6 lakh people crossed over Assam alone between1981-91. According to Hazarika's estimate based on semi-government data and official statistics from Bangladesh as well as material available in India, the number of Bangladeshis who are now in India could be anything between 12 to 15 million (Agarwal 2005: 111). In addition to external migration, there are problems of internal migration especially from U.P., Bihar and Bengal. These migrants form a large part of the labour force in the region's economy. From the region's perspective the migrants pose serious socio-political and economic problems. There are genuine reasons to be wary of immigrants on the part of the indigenous populace. The classic example being Tripura where the immigrants Bengalis from Bangladesh and Bengal have reduced indigenous Tripuris to a minority. This looming threat among the peoples of the NER finds expression in the fear of becoming 'strangers in their own land, and beggars in their own economy'. The problem of immigration is bound to magnify in the near future as the momentum of trade among BIMST-EC countries and Indo-ASEAN increases. The peripheral nature of the region's economy is manifested in the dependency of NER for most its essential commodities and economic, i.e. few modern industries in the midst of traditional industries with little or no interactions between the two. Existence of enclave type of industrial sector, which is manifested in the absence of backward and towards linkage industries, for example, tea, plantations require a wide variety of inputs such as fertilizers, chappals, umbrellas, small tools, and soon. None of this backward linkage-based industry, though economically viable, was set up in the region. Instead, the industry depended on supplies from outside the region. Similarly the oil industry had been hesitant for long to develop refineries, and a petrochemical complex, which could have led to developing many downstream industries in the region.

Despite the fact that region harbours abundance of prime resources like oil, timber, tea, gas, limestone, water and forests wealth there are few paper mills, cement plants, plywood industries, rubber and plastics, spinning mills, jute mills, chemical industries etc. in most of the states of NER excepting Assam. For instance there are 177 such industries as on March 31, 1998 of which 128 are in Assam alone (Agarwal 2005: 116). The net result is the draining of huge sum of money in buying products originating elsewhere of India. The flooding of NE market with foreign goods and goods of Indian origin clearly indicate the extent of dependent status of this resources rich region of India. The Shukla Commission estimated that about Rs. 2,500 crore worth of consumables are imported from outside the region every year. For instance Assam imports 74 per cent of its milk products, 94 per cent of its eggs and 98 per cent of its meat requirement from outside. Even though the region has abundant water resources; it imports half its first requirements from outside. In addition, the credit deposit notion being very low in the region, the banking sector transfers something like Rs. 5,000 crore from this region to other regions for investment (Ahmed and Biswas 2004: 56). The above data indicates that the NEC had failed to generate local forces of production because of its highly bureaucratic and technological approach it its pursuit for finding regional policies for the region. As a result it failed to create human capacity formation for a balance development in the region (Rafiul and Biswas 2004: 55).

Locating 'NER' within India's LEP

It is clear that the North East India lack in many respects the infrastructure to generate vibrant economic growth. In fact the region is handicapped by the absence of industrial and infrastructural base for a competitive market economy, which the policy of India's Look East has brought to its doorstep. The opening up of free trade areas between South Asia, India and ASEAN countries serve to connect the region with the global free trade regime in its search for markets and profits. The moot question is, are we, the people of NER, prepared to compete with the advanced industrialised countries? In this context it will be crucial to mention that the policy of 'Look East' initiated by India in the post-Cold War period signalled a different reorientation towards the perception of South East Asia and the emerging global economic and political realities. The present Look East Policy when implemented fully has the capacity to change the face of Asian including the Indian economy for better or worse. India's serious pursuit to build deeper economic and political relations with the South East Asian nations specially Thailand,

Singapore, Malaysia and Indonesia finds expression in its adoption of market economy. Therefore, the opening up of India's economy and market to the countries of Southeast Asian and East Asia and subsequent integration of its economy with global market economy constitute the cornerstone of Look East Policy (LEP). Since India's LEP is a result of pressures exerted by the global as well as domestic capitalists, the policy is an integral part of the capitalist project at the global scale or at least a single regional market for free trade. The Indian Prime Minister's assurance to be pragmatic and flexible while negotiating FTAs accord with the Association of South East Asian Nations and the call for creation of Pan-Asian FTAs in the recent India-ASEAN summit at Kuala Lumpur (December 11-14) are pointers to the fact that 'emergence of a pan-Asian Free Trade Regime (PAFTR)' is just a matter of time. The setting up of the East Asia Summit (EAS) on December 14, 2005 at Kuala Lumpur as a forum for dialogue on 'broad strategic, political and economic issues' of common interest and concern to promote peace, stability and economic prosperity in East Asia is a crucial step to carry the LEP forward.

The heads of the government from 16 countries—10 from the ASEAN and India, China, South Korea, Japan and Australia and New Zealand—signed the Kuala Lumpur Declaration. The Declaration stated, among other things, on fostering strategic dialogue and promoting co-operation, in political and security issues, promoting development, financial stability, energy security, economic integration and growth. The EAS, therefore, is bound to play a significant role in the construction and shaping of political-economic reality in the near future. Success of Indo-ASEAN free trade areas and South Asian Free Trade Areas (SAFTA) are perceived to bring widespread changes in the politico-economic context of the South and Southeast Asia. India's Look East Policy is an integral part of the global or at least Pan-Asian economic integration fuelled by the insatiable search for profit and market of the major MNCs and advanced capitalist countries. This region will certainly experience, to use the phrase of the Indian Prime Minister, 'a seamless web of trade and ties'. Within this 'seamless web of trade and ties' the North East Region (NER) forms the weakest link because of its relative deprivation in the infrastructural and industrial development in the primary, secondary and tertiary sectors. The absence of a white paper on the overall economic policy of the region in connection with ongoing Look East Policy makes it all the more difficult to assess the prospects of the region *vis-à-vis* LEP. However, from the present infrastructural and industrial backwardness, one can only visualize that the NER has become a part of the global free trade regime and will remain a periphery due to its inadequate industrial and infrastructural base necessary for any competitive economy. More than a decade after the initiation of India's LEP, there has been no serious introspective effort on the part of the State to change the infrastructural structure of the region. However, the present efforts in connection with LEP to make the NER a 'transit point' with no serious attempt to enhance the productive forces of the region for its economic regeneration and development undermines the utility of the policy. The Central Government's ongoing project of constructing a new rail link between Jiribam-Imphal-Moreh (Manipur) at a cost of around INR 2,900 crore and further linking it to Tamu-Kalay-Segji at a cost of around INR 1339 crore and Cabinet Committee on Economic Affairs' (CCEA) clearance on the proposal to augment the road network in the North-East at a cost of INR12,100 crore which also includes the connection of the capitals of Nagaland, Meghalaya and Sikkim with the East-West corridor (*Hindu* 24 September, 2005) gives fillip to the above argument. It may not be wrong to say that, looking at the present state of preparedness, even though potentials are there, is little prospect but immense implications. Therefore, the logic of free trade as an engine of growth and development needs careful introspection.

The NER of India, no doubt, has become a part and parcel of India's policy of forging greater political and economic integration with Southeast and East Asia. Intensity of the policy of looking east is defined by the proposed agreement on Free Trade Areas and the creation of East Asia Summit. Besides, the Japan-ESCAP initiative of connecting the entire Asian countries through 'Asian Highways' programmes starting from Tokyo up to Istanbul, the capital of Turkey clearly demonstrate emergence of a pan Asian free trade area within a specific time frame. As such the very process of globalization of free trade and market economy defines the present global order with profit making through competition as its cornerstone. The structure of India's LEP is characterised by free flows of capital, commodities, financial fluidity, de-territorialization of national politico-economic frontiers and increasing geographical mobility.

It is in this context that one has to locate the North East and its economy and possible repercussions that free trade might bring to this region.

REFERENCES

Agarwal, A.K. 2005. 'Structural Change in The Regional Economy: Trends and Implication', in C. Joshua Thomas (ed.) *Polity & Economy: Agenda for Contemporary North East India*. New Delhi: Regency Publication.

Ahmed, Rafiul and Prasenjit Biswas 2004. *Political Economy of Underdevelopment of North-East India*. New Delhi: Akansha Publishing House.

Bhaumik, Subir 1998. 'North-East India: The Evolution of A Post-Colonial Region', in Partha Chatterjee (ed). *Wages of Freedom: Fifty Years of the Indian Nation-State*. Oxford: Oxford University Press.

Japan-ESCAP CO-operation Fund: *Development of the Asian Highway*.

Kotwal, Dinesh 2000. 'Instability Parameters in North East India'. *Strategic Analysis*. April. Vol. XXIV, No. 1. New Delhi: IDSA.

Kumar, B.B. 1996. *Re-organization of North-East India (Facts and Documents)*. New Delhi: Omsons.

Kumar, Sunil 2004. 'Potential of Export From North-East to South East Asia'. Paper presented on the National Seminar on *Promotion of Border Trade Between India's North East and Myanmar: Problems and Prospects*. Imphal: November 8-9.

Nag, Sajal 2005. 'Politics of Tangents: Small States in Large Indian Democracy', in Joshua Thomas (ed). *Polity & Economy: Agenda for Contemporary North East India*. New Delhi: Regency Publication.

Paratt, John 2005. *Wounded Land: Politics and Identity in Modern Manipur*. New Delhi: Mittal Publication.

Phukon, Girin 2003. *Ethnicization of Politics in North-East India*. New Delhi: South Asian Publishers.

Prasain, G.P. 2004. 'Indo-Myanmar Development Co-operation: Implications for North East India'. Paper presented on *National Seminar on Promotion of Border Trade Between India's North East and Myanmar: Problems and Prospects*. Imphal: 8-9th November.

Srikanth, H. 2005. 'Insurgency and Counter-Insurgency: Agenda for Peace in India's North-East', in C. Joshua Thomas (ed). *Polity & Economy: Agenda for Contemporary North East India*. New Delhi: Regency Publications.

Surma, Atul 2001. 'Economic Development of the North Eastern States in the Context of Globalization'. *Strategic Analysis*. Vol. XXV. No. 2. New Delhi: IDSA.

The Hindu 2005. December 15.

The Hindu 2005. September 24.

5

India's LEP and the North East: A Study on Environmental Impact

LAISHRAM CHURCHILL

An initial attempt to understand the possible effects of India's Look East Policy (LEP) on the environmental framework of the North East would necessarily include an assessment of the existing environmental scenario of the region. The region's ecological system has been widely discussed in terms of extreme fragility. Onset of urbanization in the last few decades witnessed a massive onslaught on this fragile ecological system. It has been a picture of dismay as widespread destruction of the environment continues to persist in spite of feeble attempts to check this growing menace. The march of modernisation in the virtual absence of complimentary industrial measures along with the inability to adopt and generate modern means of sustainable development in the region contribute to the problem which has assumed colossal proportions. Primitive means of farming which includes the infamous 'slash and burn' or shifting cultivation and large scale lumbering in the absence of any significant development in the secondary or tertiary sector led to a massive onslaught on the environmental framework in the region. In the backdrop of this grim scenario the recent move of the Indian State to open up the region in terms of physical connectivity with the outside world through its much hyped LEP needs a detailed scrutiny *vis-à-vis* the prevailing picture of underdevelopment and the degenerated environmental framework. To begin with for the seven sisters of North East region, India's LEP is accompanied by a plethora of questions. It may indeed become a quagmire of problems, a 'Pandora's Box' full of prospects of disaster other than possible routes of development. We are not only tempted but also compelled to open it. If we are not adept in opening the box, there may not be even hope left with us. Thus, India's LEP is a 'Pandora's Box' full of hope and fear, prospect and apprehension, unprecedented progress and disaster. If such is the case with LEP, it is necessary to prepare ourselves for the much prophesised opening of the 'Eastern Gate'. But the moot question is the means and ways to prepare ourselves so that India's LEP does not become a damp squib for the North East region.

Socio-Economic Situation

It is worth mentioning that India's Northeastern region lags far behind other states of the country in every conceivable field of development. Moreover, its neighbours across the border—the countries of South East and East Asian countries—have forged quite ahead, taking their dignified places among nations of the world. Before going into the details of the reasons responsible for going in reverse gear as far as development and progress of the region is concerned, let us have a glance at the current state of affairs as a prelude to our answer for the reasons. Massive underdevelopment and wilful neglect of the region by the country's policy makers have generated a debased social existence in the region where the prevailing social scenario is marked by pervasive corruption, nepotism and favouritism. Such a trend has penetrated every sphere of our lives. Planning in its true sense is non-existent in this region with successive governments in New Delhi ignoring the plight of the region. In the absence of planning, problems spring up and become multiplied with every passing year. Such careless 'dispensation of duties' by those at the helm of affairs (the elite ruling class), their hedonistic life style and the ever-widening schism between 'plenty haves' and 'extreme have-nots' have filled the atmosphere of the region with unrest and tension rather than peace and development. We see bubbles of the impending anger and unrest craving for a total 'change of order' in the region. A full-blown eruption is only a matter of time. Many have squarely blamed both the Central Government and the state governments to be equally responsible for such a mishap and for the *fait accompli* undertaken by them in connivance with the regional leaders. With the exception of the government employees and the few influential contractors, the whole populace of the region is reeling under poverty. There is no infrastructural development, no income generating institutions and no room for self-employment. In fact, it resembles a third world within the fast developing country of India. All the symptoms of underdevelopment and all the syndromes of civil unrest are quite evident in the region. It is quite interesting to note that many attribute our underdevelopment to insurgency while many are of the opinion that insurgency is the outcome of underdevelopment. Leaving aside the question of which is responsible for which, peoples' suffering has reached a historical landmark which is well beyond the threshold of tolerance. The criticality of the situation needs to be noted in the light of the emerging dynamics generated by the hyped LEP.

India's LEP and the North East

It has been discussed widely that India's LEP is not without implications for the North East region. It is coming with a bag full of prospects and problems. However, the general reaction of the people to India's LEP is one of high hopes. People are hopeful that it will be the turning point in the economic history of the North East. People of some states are openly lamenting and complaining that the proposed trans-Asian Highway does not pass through their states directly. The Assamese are preparing themselves to make Gauhati the hub of the trade; the Nagas are preparing themselves with the establishment of International Trade Centre along its border with Myanmar. In Manipur too, there is widespread jubilation that the prophecy of *Nongpok Thong Hangba* (opening of the Eastern Door) is coming true. Such an enthusiastic response by the peoples of the region *vis-à-vis* India's LEP can be explained by the notion that the horizon of trade and commerce would be expanded at an unprecedented rate and free interactions with the nations of culturally similar South East Asia will become an eventual possibility. Through LEP, they hope to witness an era of economic regeneration and prosperity. But all these are only a few bright spots in the vast expanse of a huge dark backdrop.

Once this trade and commerce through the proposed trans-Asian Highway become operational, the flood-gate of cultural imperialism, economic imperialism, Indianization and globalization will sweep over the whole region. At this juncture it is pertinent to note that India is a huge country with a population of over one billion, the majority being constituted by a racially different people in comparison with the indigenous inhabitants of the North East. The indigenous populace of the region is highly sensitive to their ethnicity and distinct cultural patterns. As seen in the persisting conflicts in the region, any threat to their tradition, culture, economy or polity will lead to conflicts of multiple dimensions. But how can we cope or resist the impending juggernaut of cultural imperialism, economic imperialism, Indianization and globalization? Can people's civil movements preserve our ethnicity and uniqueness? Even as the answers to these questions are beyond the domain of this paper it is crucial to underline the implications posed by these problems. The aim of this paper is to focus on the possible impact of the LEP on the fragile environmental framework of the North East.

LEP and Environment

It is quite evident that there will be a great environmental change following India's LEP. Environmental degradation and deterioration will be an area of least concern to the Union Government. Environment *per se* is nobody's exclusive property; so to say environment knows no nationality. No physical boundary or no political boundary can safeguard or preserve an environment by the sole effort of any particular region or country. It necessitates a concerted effort from the global community. However, it is imperative for all of us to preserve our immediate surrounding environment at our best level. As economic considerations play a pivotal role in India's LEP economic gain will remain the primary motive of trade through the proposed trans-Asian Highway. Herein lies the necessity of dealing with 'environmental economics' to project a critical outline of the impending effects. In most cases, economic progress through modernization and industrialization of any country is counteracted upon by environmental degradation. This phenomenon of economic upliftment and environmental degradation was observed in many western European countries in the late 19th and 20th centuries. There is another case of environmental degradation with little or no economic progress. We can see such cases in many countries of Asia, Africa and Latin America (ASAFLA). The realization of the enormous harm caused by the environmental degeneration has resulted in the compelling drive amongst Europeans to enact a clear-cut Environmental policy followed by strict implementation. Unfortunately peoples of the Third World countries are willingly or unwillingly following the path abandoned by the Europeans in the post-Second World War period. The pattern can be easily discerned when we observe the two contrasting facts—the forest areas are steadily increasing in many European countries while the same is rapidly decreasing in most countries of ASAFLA. What we need is a visionary Environmental policy for the countries of the Third World that will be conducive in maintaining the global environment for posterity.

Deterrents to Environmental Policy

Even though most of the countries have their own environmental policies, their actual implementations are quite unsatisfactory and need detailed introspection. The policy advice advanced by environmental economists does not find a sympathetic ear. It may be because of irresponsible legislators and administrators. But then incorporation of environmental issues in the process of national planning is crucial to the development process. Obviously in all the policies and programmes of every government of the developing countries, improving people's living standards and pushing above the poverty line to meet basic needs is the first priority. It is the immediate necessity and the first and the foremost duty of these governments. The inertia of existing planning process involving both institution and individual is a problem in several developing countries. Environmental objectives do not always match with national priorities, and can in some cases conflict with these. Planning horizons are usually of a short term nature while many of the environmental impacts requiring corrective actions extend over the longer term, thus aggravating the problem of incorporating environmental considerations into mainstream planning processes (Kumar: 143).

As environment protection takes a backseat in most cases, there is a need to generate awareness and consciousness among the public and the policy makers at large. It needs to be specifically pointed out that the issue of environment should not be sacrificed for short-term development projects, which in the long run will have an adverse effect on the ecological balance in the area. Myopic and populist projects without a sustainable basis have led to large-scale destruction of environment in many Third World countries. Internal limitations to formulation and implementation of environmental policies in developing countries remain as constraints in environmental protection. On top of this, external factors in the field of environment degradation and destruction come mainly from foreign investors and multinational companies (MNCs). Many national and international programmes that are basically exploitative in nature are cloaked in the morally respectable rhetoric of welfare and development projects or schemes.

Although the flow of private commercial capital (of MNCs) may contribute to development, their volume and their geographical or sectoral distribution are principally determined by commercial considerations, divorced from any concern to assist developing countries (Dinwiddy 1973: 17). It has been a glaring truth that these private investors are always indifferent to the negative environmental impacts brought about by their commercial ventures. In their basic motive underlined by maximization of profit they fail to secure the environmental interests. Both these internal and external factors remain strong deterrents to implementation of a clear-cut Environmental policy in the developing countries. Where there is considerable presence of MNCs and foreign investors, the policy orientation and preferences of the governments are influenced by these MNCs and foreign investors are known to be guided by their own profit-oriented interests. MNCs and foreign investors with huge capital are highly influential and powerful enough to bring about even change of regimes (in some cases) to promote and maintain their pursuit of commercial gain. As such they frequently act contrary to democratic ethics.

Fluidity of modern capital in the hands of MNCs has been a distressing factor that impedes the formulation of any concrete policy with national interests at the forefront. International investors may act as a constraint on democratic institutions when capital moves in and out of countries in volatile ways. It has been widely seen that when investors force policy makers in developing countries to raise interest rates in order to follow trends in the advanced countries, developing countries cannot adopt counter cyclical policies in periods of shock for fear of provoking capital flight (Kumar 2003: 20). These external factors remain a formidable challenge to meaningful formulation and implementation of a sound environmental policy in the developing or underdeveloped countries.

National Planning and Environmental Policy

Incorporation of environmental policy in the overall planning of a country requires addressing those conflicts which growth can pose to sustainability. Viewing the quantitative and qualitative sides of growth together puts the spotlight on a balanced growth of three sets of assets—human, physical and natural capital—rather than an almost exclusive focus on promoting accumulation of physical capital. There is a strong need for broadening the policy framework to include an agenda addressing human, social and environmentally sustainable development (Kumar 2008: 18). These three sets of assets are non-exclusive and must be treated as a system of inter-connected and inter-dependent components. Huge accumulations of anyone of these three assets without corresponding development of the other assets will not be feasible. Even if it is possible, it will prove counter-productive in the overall development of a nation. It is crucial to understand the extent to which the Government of India will be willing to encompass these three assets in the development planning of the country. To find out which capital asset is given more importance is necessary in the light of the trends seen in the country so far. It is obviously growth in physical capital that tops the priority list while development of natural capital is almost wholly neglected. These can be discerned from the latest survey report of the Political and Economics Risk Consultancy Ltd. (PERC). As the report clearly indicates, India's physical and social environment is the worst in Asia. A clear picture of the government's failure to incorporate environmental interests is provided by the report. In the backdrop of such an attitude of the Union Government there is little hope for growth in natural capital.

Substantial improvement in the living standard of the people of the North East region needs infrastructural and resource development so as to enable the people of the region take full advantage of India's LEP. This ought to be executed under a long-term national and state planning with due consideration given to sustainability and environmental preservation. As far as the region is concerned, its environmental conditions are quite dismal. With massive destruction of the forest cover due to extensive unchecked lumbering followed by the acute absence of modern techniques of farming which in turn leads to the highly degenerative practices of farming and over-reliancé on agriculture contribute to the widespread environmental mess in the region. There is no proper waste disposal system in the urban centre; its sanitary systems are extremely poor and unhygienic. There is wanton destruction of natural resources under the patronage of the governments pursuing populist lopsided policies. Lack of proper environmental policies, halfhearted implementation and many socio-economic conditions are the various factors responsible for the sorry state of environment in the region.

Poverty and Environmental Degradation Nexus

To understand the socio-economic conditions acting as deterrents to conservation and protection of the environment, we need to study the nexus between poverty and environmental degradation. The popular poverty-environment degradation relationship states that it is poverty, which causes environmental degradation in the developing countries. Acute poverty and the virtual absence of alternative modes of securing livelihood followed by backwardness in the field of education and awareness of environmental issues contribute substantially to the rapid degeneration of environment. Environmentalists have tried to explain this nexus through the following assessment:

R1: Poverty – Environmental Degradation

A counter argument to R1 relationship is the view that it is not poverty but a combination of greed, power and the wealth that causes environmental degradation in many developing countries. Thus,

R2: Power, Wealth and Greed – Environmental Degradation

The third possible relationship (R3) looks at the links between market and the institutional failure with environmental degradation respectively. Hence,

R3 (a): Institutional Failure – Environmental Degradation

R3 (b): Market Failure – Environmental Degradation

The fourth and the final possible relationship R4 which may follow either from R1, R2 or R3(a) and R3(b) is the notion that environmental degradation is the major factor causing indigenous poverty:

R 4: Environmental Degradation – Poverty (Kumar 2003: 295).

Environmental Degradation as a result of poverty, i.e. R1 is observed extensively in the North East region. Jhumming, shifting cultivation, drainage of liquid and solid waste into rivers, improper disposal and treatment of solid wastes lead to environmental degradation. R2 does not account much for environmental degradation in the North East except the state of Assam. During the British colonial period large areas of forest were cleared for tea plantation. Without any consideration or proper study of the fragile ecological system widespread deforestation for the purpose of establishing large tea plantations created adverse effects on the environmental set-up. Such development greatly affected the ecology and bio-diversity.

At present, R3 and R4 don't account for much in the North Eastern region. However, once India's LEP becomes operational, it is highly probable that all the four relations R1, R2, R3 and R4 will take active roles in the overall degradation of the region's environment. Large-scale deforestation for plantation works, enhanced logging for construction works, large dams for irrigation and power generation, growth of multiple urban trade centres and complimentary pollution activities are all in the pipeline. Unfortunately, in all such activities, the respective state governments as well as the Union Government will, willingly or unwillingly, remain collaborators. Even if the governments are against these activities and stand to enforce a sound environmental policy, they will be under enormous pressure from those internal as well as external factors discussed above. On the other hand, the people as well as the governments will be highly tempted and motivated to favour the MNCs and private investors as a result of the acute poverty and absence of employment opportunities.

In the context of the North East region, incorporation of environment policy in the National Planning calls on the part of the people to do away with jhumming and shifting cultivation and develop provisions for alternative means. State intervention is crucial in this area as stringent policies needs to be backed by effective implementation and the securing of alternative means of livelihood for the affected people. Till now, deforestation by logging, large-scale tea plantation, practice of jhum and shifting cultivation are the main causes of environmental degradation. Here, it is interesting to note that against all these activities, environmental policies of the states did not and couldn't stand a chance for effective implementation. Logging has led to rapid decline in forest areas of the region. As per the 1989 forest survey report only 34.47 per cent of forest area is under dense forest cover, ranging from 13.5 per cent in Meghalaya to 65 per cent in Arunachal Pradesh. Open forest cover means higher degree of soil erosion leading to siltation in Barak and Brahmaputra, the two important rivers in the North East, indicating the effect of deforestation.

The catchment areas of the Brahmaputra, the Barak and its tributaries have also shown signs of soil erosion. Rainfall in the region has been below the average since 1990. Average temperature is continuously on the rise and there is scarcity of water. Associated with this is the problem of filthy water, soil degradation, global warming, sewage problem, polluted air, endangered species etc. leading to poverty (Pandey: 65). Despite the realization of the extent of land degradation caused by jhum and shifting cultivation in the North East, we are unable to forego these practices. In the region, jhum and shifting cultivation is done purely for subsistence. Until and unless the respective states do not provide alternative means for subsistence and growth, the unwanted practices of jhum and shifting cultivation will remain inevitable. It will ultimately sound our death knell sooner or later. If we look into the first three principles of National Environmental Policy (2004), certain core areas are addressed:

(1) Human beings are at the centre of the sustainable development concerns,
(2) Right to development, and
(3) Environmental protection is an integral part of the development process.

It is clear that the concern for development assets is overriding. Again the section on causes and impacts of 'Key Environmental

Challenges' in the draft policy begins with the assertion that the key environmental challenges that the country faces relate to the nexus of environmental degradation with poverty in many dimensions, and economic growth. Putting these entire together one cannot help but say that the preamble, objectives and the principles laid down by the draft of National Environmental policy 2004 are for a national policy for sustainable development and not for a national environmental policy. With such a dismal and unsuitable NEP (2004), conservation and protection of environment is still a far cry in the country. The draft NEP cites the Govindarajan Committee as having identified environment and forest clearances as being the largest cause of delays in development project. It is astounding that the NEP takes this as gospel truth, completely ignoring that development projects are in fact the largest source of environmental destruction (Kothari 2004).

The large scale dams such as the Aswan dam in Egypt, the Akosombo dam in Ghana, and the various dams suggested in the Colombo Plan for the Mekong basin offer another example of large scale project justified in the name of development which has been conceived with very little concerns for the larger environmental and ecological effects that they produce. The Aswan dam, for example, while more than doubling Egypt's irrigated farm land, also greatly reduced the fisheries in the eastern end of the Mediterranean (the rich nutrients which formerly fed the fish now producing a rapid silting behind the dam and a profusion of plant growth in lake Nasser). The Akosombo dam has created many similar environmental problems. In addition there were disruptions caused by the flooding of a number of tribal lands. The human cost of displacement and the accompanying social rupture have never been put in focus in the entire gamut of these large-scale projects.

On the other hand, how far can the investors go to subvert the process of law in order to implement their projects can be discerned from the case study of Engelhard Highland Pvt. Ltd. Engelhard Inc, a US based MNC in collaboration with Highland Pvt. Ltd. of India began to construct a pigment manufacturing unit in Kadandale in 1996. The location was sensitive as it was the source of Shanbavi River whose downstream is known as Mulki. It was highly sensitive in terms of the forest areas and the adjoining hill villages in the foothills of Western Ghats. Without sharing any project information, including even statutory authorities and the local panchayat, the factory construction began. When local communities raised concerns that the facility is being illegally developed and would pollute their main source of drinking water, the local MLA sought to dismiss this by issuing a 'clearance' which he claimed was provided to the project by an 'Environmental Clearance Committee' that he had constituted. Ironically the Committee included senior faculty members of the Karnataka Regional Engineering College and a former Additional Secretary of the Karnataka Department of Ecology and Environment and according to their report the project would have no adverse consequences on people's health or environment. Such questionable processes initiated by an elected representative instead of drawing attention of the statutory authorities who were repeatedly approached by the local communities for relief, the KSPCB (Karnataka State Pollution Control Board) accorded the project a *post facto* 'No Objection Certificate'.

Closer home, the Union Minister of Heavy Industries in connivance with the state governments of Manipur and Mizoram is pushing for the Tipaimukh High Dam at the tri-junction of Assam, Manipur and Mizoram against the very vocal and evident objections to the project raised by the people of the states for the last two decades. Till date all official attempts made by numerous non-governmental organizations and civil organizations protesting against the project have hardly created serious ripples in the elite circle of policy makers. No serious attempts have been made to get authentic copies of the Environmental Impact Assessment (EIA) and Environmental Management Plan (EMP). Repeated pleas by the people have been ignored by NEEPCO as they claim that the Environmental Impact Assessment has been completed and clearance from the concerned authorities taken well in advance. Taking into account the level of intransparency involved in this project, it has been concluded that no independent and thorough EIA or EMP as per the National Statutory Norms applicable to such projects have been conducted so far.

The question here is what prompts and impels such callousness on the part of the authority concerning various environmental and other impacts associated with such projects? One obvious answer is the lure of monetary gain in the name of modernization, viz. electrification, infrastructural development etc. Another factor contributing to this misadventure in the context of the region is the lack of farsightedness and concern for the people on the part of the state authorities even when they are fully conscious of the ill impacts of such projects in the long run.

Till now, all these misadventures and *faux pas* are our own making, more precisely of our political leaders. However, once the grand design of India's LEP is materialized and the free trade regime operationalised through the corridor which is wholly provided by the region, it is quite obvious that power generation and transport infrastructural development along with inherent urban centres would become a matter of great importance. Hence, the urgency, which they have begun in right earnest, should be noted carefully. By then, many MNCs and foreign investors would lead the way in pushing for big dams meant for power generation which are already endorsed by our state authorities. A certain level of haphazard urbanization, infrastructure development in terms of enhancing physical connectivity and a certain degree of industrialization is expected from the impending India's LEP. India's LEP is a well calculated move to merge itself with the Asia Free Trade Zone (AFTA) which includes the economically affluent South East Asian countries and further more it is a strategy to venture into the huge potential area of ASEAN-Pacific region. Development of infrastructure and construction of urban centres would be executed with much zeal and enthusiasm to facilitate smooth flow of trade and commerce. The North East would be at the receiving end as such developmental works are executed in most cases with the least concern for environmental degradation. The introduction of major infrastructural programmes in the form of canals, railways and roads in 19th century India by the British government was expected to benefit both the people of India and the investors in England. However, the impact of their imported technologies, concepts and the institutions was, of course, quite different from what was expected. There were two serious effects. First, because the canal and railroads were designed with little concern for proper drainage, some 4000 to 5000 square miles of agricultural land was lost to salinity not long after the conception of the projects. Second, while irrigation did increase production, it did so primarily for the spring export crops at the expense of autumn crops of millet and pulses upon which most of the population depended.

With the construction of Trans-Asian Highway-I which is already under progress and the North East region being located almost in the middle of the Highway, the region occupies a very critical position in the overall perspective and strategy of India's LEP. The region, which has always existed in the periphery of Indian geo-political set up, is now emerging as a vital link to ASEAN and to countries of the Asian-Pacific region. Of the various impacts expected to accompany such a grand project, we are at present dealing with environmental impacts leaving aside other equally consequential impacts to avoid overlapping with other topics. An unprecedented modernization is on the anvil following India's LEP and the Trans-Asian Highway. For such a large-scale modernization, roadways, railways, power generation, urban centres, drastic changes in the agricultural and land use patterns can be predicted with certainty.

(a) Physical Resources
  (1) Adequacy of basic data
  (2) Surface water quantities
  (3) Surface water quality
  (4) Ground water
  (5) Soils
  (6) Geology/Seismology
  (7) Watershed erosion
  (8) Downstream erosion
  (9) Climate
(b) Ecological Resources
  (1) Fisheries
  (2) Aquatic biology
  (3) Wildlife
  (4) Forest and watershed
  (5) Reservoir ecology
(c) Human use values
  (1) Water supply
  (2) Aquaculture
  (3) Navigation
  (4) Flood control
  (5) Mineral development
  (6) Agro-industries
  (7) Highways/Railways
  (8) Land use

(d) Quality of life values
  (1) Socio-economics
  (2) Resettlement
  (3) Public health
  (4) Nutrition
  (5) Recreation and aesthetics
  (6) Archeological and historical

Some factor-wise study of the impacts of Loktak Multipurpose Project are listed below.

(a) Physical Resources

1. *Water Quality*: With the construction of the Ithai Barrage, nutrient hooding in the Loktak Lake, from both internal sources, has far exceeded the assimilative capacity of the macrophytes which has considerably reduced the quality of Loktak Lake.
2. *Fisheries*: Disappearance of many indigenous species of fishes that would migrate from Chindwin river to the Imphal river.
3. *Wild life*: The project has caused rapid decline in waterfowl population thinning of phoomdis, deteriorating the habitat of the *Sangai*.
4. *Land use*: The project has cost 50,000-80,000 hectares of cultivable land and habitation.

The Assam Pollution Control Board (APCB), Guwahati have studied the Brahmaputra river system (Indian part) and the Barak (a stretch of 12 km. flowing by the side of Silchar town). The study reveals that apart from containing very little amount of inorganic/organic pollutants, the rivers shows signs of pollution and also noticed that high degree of bacteriological pollutants are there.

1. All throughout the year and in almost the entire course of Brahmaputra (from Dibrugarh to Togighapa, about 450 km.) the water quality has been contaminated by total coliforms and focal coliforms.
2. It may be mentioned here that waste of Togighapa Paper Mill was directly drained to the river Brahmaputra. The

Nagal Paper Mill, Togiroad Paper Mill, Kamrup Paper Mill, Indian Carbon, Bokajan Cement Factory, Dimapur Sugar Mill etc. are discharging their wastes in the tributaries of the Brahmaputra or the Brahmaputra itself thereby polluting the greatest water resources of Assam as well as of the North East.

3. The study on Barak also reveals that this river stretch is highly polluted inorganically, organically and bacteriologically due to the assimilation of raw sewage and waste water and other pollutants like garbage and commercials solid waste. Conquest upon the dissolve of effluents and toxic chemicals of HPC, Panchgram in the Barak river, water turns blackish tinge (from Panchgram to the downstream) during dry season. The poor people are bearing heavy toll by drinking unsafe water. (1, 2 and 3 *APCB Environmental Bulletin*, Vol. 5. July-September, 1995). As a result of direct discharge of solid waste, raw sewage of both domestic and commercial nature, the water of river, flowing through the heart of Imphal, is highly polluted and is unsuitable for all purposes.

The present situation is at the cost of minimal industrialization whereas with the LEP we can expect some sort of industrialization as we are yearning for it and a lot more urbanization. But commensurate development of urban drainage system, sewage and solid waste disposal system is doubtful. In such a case, a grim picture of environmental pollution awaits the region from the shadows of India's LEP.

Post Script

Categorically dealing on environmental impacts of LEP is only speculative in nature and is done on purely comparative basis taking account of central and local administrators' treatment of this subject. Nevertheless it lies as our prerogative to protect and preserve our environment in the face of India's economic liberalization programme and subsequent incorporation of the North East alongwith the rest of the country with the free trade zone of South East Asia.

Unfortunately as we observed in the preceding pages, economic resurgence with the least concern for environment remains top priority in India's planning mechanism. And India's LEP, of which the North East provides the much needed gateway is guided by such insensitive attitude towards environment and ecology. Coupled with the insensitivity of the Government and the manipulative orientation of the MNCs and international investors poised to take advantage of India's LEP, any meaningful formulation and implementation of National Environmental Policy remains a far cry. This attitude of insensitivity is well manifested in their thrust for Tipaimukh High Dam in the face of strong and vehement opposition raised by the local people for the last two decades.

As shown by the Tucurui graph, GHG emissions from reservoirs, the climate of the region is on the verge of a drastic change as and when the numerous high dams schemed in the region are materialized. Currently, we are battling against the lobbyists and protagonists of the State. However, with the operationalization of India's LEP, there is a very reasonable apprehension that the MNCs with their multi-billion capital would join in the push for big dams in the name of power generation, economic development and employment avenues.

The point here is we can't remain as naive as before in the face of the relentless pro-dam, pro-LEP onslaught. Not only the political destiny, our environmental and ecological destiny should be determined by the collective decision of our conscious and rational minds. In this connection, we may recall and analyze the pros and cons of Ithai Barrage and the Loktak Multi-Purpose Project. It has been proven beyond doubt that, it is just a grand investment policy, basically conceived with the objective to earn huge profit at the cost of irreparable loss to the local populace and the environment of Manipur. While the project is unable to provide even six hours of power per day, the NHPC is exporting power to other states even as the local populace are made to suffer loss of tens of thousands of hectares of agricultural land and drastic alteration in the riverine and lake eco-system. It has seriously threatened the only floating National Park in the world and thereby jeopardizing the lives of the rare *Sangai* which is already on the brink of extinction. It is high time that we learnt the lessons from the Loktak Multi-Purpose project.

It is evident now that nothing has been done to avail the benefit of LEP to the region. What we observe so far is the development of highways to facilitate trade and commerce through the thoroughfare provided by the region. We are being kept just as a by stander in the overall grand design of India's LEP. In a nutshell, the environment sacrifice we are force to make is not worth the cosmetic modernization assured by the protagonists of LEP.

REFERENCES

Dahlberg, Kenneth A. 1973. 'Ecological Effects of Current Development Process in Less Developed Countries' in Vann, Anthony and Paul Rogers (eds.). *Human Ecology and World Development.* New York: Plennum Publishing Corporation.

Dinwiddy, Bruce 1973. 'Current and Future Trend in Development Assistance' in Vann, Anthony and Paul Rogers (ed.). *Human Ecology and World Development.* New York: Plennum Publishing Corporation.

Imhof, Aviva, Susanne Wong and Peter Bosshard 2002. 'Key WCD Findings' in *Citizens' Guide to the World Commission on Dams, International Rivers Network.* Berkely, CA, USA.

Kothari 2004. 'National Environmental Policy—An Appraisal' in Kumar Madhuresh(ed.) *Globalization, State Policies Sustainability of Rights.* Mahanirban, Calcutta Research Group.

Kumar H.D. 2003. *Environmental Science-Economic, Social and Political Dimensions.* New Delhi: Daya Publishing House.

Pandey, M.C. 1995. 'Population and Population on Forest Produces in North Eastern Region' in Ray B. Dutta (eds.). *Population, Poverty and Environment in North East India.* New Delhi: Concept Publishing House.

Saldanha, Leo. F. 2002. 'Public Involvement in Environmental Decision Making' presented at a workshop on *Judicial Enforcement of Environmental Law in Karnataka.* Organized by Judicial Academy, Environment Support Group and Environmental Law Institute, August 3-4.

Section 3
Manipur: Clouds of Uncertainties—Redefining Frontiers through LEP

6

Redefining Frontier through LEP: A Colonial Articulation of Manipur

SANJEEV THINGNAM

The essay seeks to understand the process and possibilities of the linkages of the North Eastern region of India with Southeast Asia from the British colonial perception and how it gets reflected in the present policy dimensions. It is an attempt to highlight the interaction between the North Eastern states of India particularly with Manipur and South East Asia, which follows complicated trajectories precisely because of the conceptualization of the North Eastern states as a frontier region.

The significance of the states of North-Eastern region in granting specificity not only to the internal policy of India but also for its foreign relations can best be highlighted by foregrounding a historical paradox. Geographically speaking, the North Eastern region provides a unique access for India towards Southeast Asia and Indo-China. The region shares an international border of over 1500 km. with Bangladesh, Bhutan, Burma, China and Nepal. In contrast, the area linking the region with mainland India is roughly 20 km. only. It could therefore be used as a vantage point for entry into Southeast Asia. However, this possibility was never translated into actual practice. The essay's thesis contends that the root cause behind this was the conceptualization of the region as a frontier by the British policy makers. The major impediment in integrating the region with Southeast Asia was thwarted due to difference of opinion within the rank and file of the colonial administrators.

Traditionally speaking, the politics, culture and social development of this region was strongly influenced by historical processes emanating from Southeast Asia. The formation of the Ahom kingdom and the Meitei kingdom are testimonies of this historical process. Subsequently, the politics of this region was determined by the relationship between the Burman, the Meitei and the Ahom kingdoms. All these drastically changed with the transformation of the North Eastern region into a geo-strategic zone in the eastern theatre of the British Empire. There is enough literature on the process and consequences of this transformation in the writings of colonial administrators. The legacy of geo-strategic concerns persisted and got carried over even under 'independent' India's administration. Since the North Eastern region was conceptualized as a frontier region, liberation of India did not have a liberating impact on the relationship between the North Eastern region and Southeast Asia. Instead, the policy thrust was on border rationalization with Burma and China to make the region militarily secure from India's position. This had a paradoxical result. A region that has one of the most disproportionate ratios between national boundary and international boundary was completely cut-off from contact with the outside world. Colonial legislations such as the 'Inner Line Permit', 'Protected Area Permit' and 'Restricted Area Permit' continue to be imposed. Of late, in the globalize scenario, there are efforts to revive contact with East and Southeast Asia with the North Eastern region of India as the focal point through the much celebrated Look East Policy (LEP). It is crucial to note that the policy is to be implemented through a region, which has hitherto been perceived as a frontier region. Precisely, because of the historical complexities the expected contact would not be free of implications.

Conceptualization of the region's status as a frontier zone during the colonial period made a deep impact in post British Indian policy framework. While India is trying to integrate herself with the global economy, there are many regions and sub-regions within the country, which have not yet been integrated with the national economy. To a certain extent, globalization of the economy depends on inter-regional economic integration within India, a country of continental dimension. This internal integration is vital for actual utilization of all potential opportunities arising out of efficient division of labour. This is also important for the socio-political stability. It is important to evaluate the challenges and new opportunities presented to the North East by the liberalization process (Sachdeva 2000).

With the changing national and international economic scenario, it is pertinent to discuss the past and present economic-environment issues of the region. The economic integration of the North East frontier zone especially Manipur, known as the Gateway to Southeast Asia, with the countries of the Southeast and East Asia was actually conceptualised during the colonial period. We often tend to forget the fact that through the centuries there has been a natural exchange of people's, goods and services between the North East and the countries of South and Southeast Asia.

Several centuries ago, the Ahoms of Assam had migrated from the Shan State of Myanmar, where the language spoken is almost identical to that spoken in Laos and Thailand. The Chins from Myanmar have migrated over the past centuries to Manipur and Mizoram and the Meiteis of Manipur have ties for over 2000 years with the Burmans of Myanmar. There have been similar migratory movements to the North East from the Yunan Province of China. Therefore, for the peoples of the North East the exchanges of goods across borders artificially drawn up by the British merely reflect a continuation of their historical links with countries like Myanmar, Laos, Thailand and China (Pathasarthy http://www.in.rediff.com).

Indian policy makers and development experts have been arguing that the main stumbling block for economic development in the North East is the disadvantageous geographical situation (Sachdeva 2000). It is important to note that this isolated, landlocked region shares less than 2 per cent of its borders with the rest of India, and the rest with Bhutan, Bangladesh, Myanmar and the Tibetan region of China. This artificially created international border led to the obliteration of the region's traditional trade, commerce and other linkages, which existed in the pre Partition days. It is a matter of grave concern that using of the region's 2 per cent perimeter as a major linkage point with the rest of India and at the same time checking the inflow of goods and people from across the remaining 98 per cent has been a gigantic task (Sachdeva 2000: 145). This point has been highlighted in studies undertaken by Tata Consultancy Services and North East Council (1990). Lately, with the increasing globalization of the world economy there has been talk of converting this locational disadvantage into an advantage. This is particularly so when all the seven states are in close proximity to the dynamic Southeast and East Asian economies. Although there has been very little attempt to write the history of commerce and the external trade of the early North East, it is evident that certain lines of communication existed which facilitated the movement of people, culture and merchandise between the North East on the one hand and other parts of the subcontinent or south China on the other (Mukherjee 1992, Verghese 1996). A brief outline of the early political encounter with the British colonial empire will be helpful in explaining the process of conceptualization of the region in terms of a frontier zone curtailing possibilities of linkages with Southeast Asian countries and Far East. Simultaneously, it also reveals the efforts made by some of the colonial administrators to foreground the necessity and utility of connectivity and linkages to subserve colonial interests. Relegation of these efforts by those at the helm of colonial affairs was not without the logic of the frontier concept.

Early Political Intercourse with British

The condition of Manipur and its surrounding hills was not free from internal tussle and power struggles. It was marked by constant raids of the Manipuris into Burma, and of Burmese into Manipur along with fratricidal warfare and struggle for the throne (Mackenzie 1884: 149). The invasion of Manipur by Alompora (ALAUNG-PAYA KING OF AVA) was disastrous in its consequence to the Manipuri people, as they then for the first time sought external aid, and appeared a few years afterwards as supplicants for British protection (Dun 1975: 39).

Apart from internal conflicts among the princes for the throne, they invited the British authority to intervene. Subsequently, a treaty of alliance, offensive and defensive was negotiated on the 14th September 1762 with Huree Doss Gossien (Hari Das Gossain), on behalf of his master Jaee Sing (Jai Singh), by Mr. Verelst. In the treaty the aid of a contingent of British troops was promised that whenever the Raja might find it expedient to attempt the recovery of such portion of his territory as had been wrested from him by the Burmese he would make such grants of land to the English sufficient for the establishment of a factory and fort, and a distance of country round such factory and fort, of 8,000 cubits with rent (Pemberton 1835: 21). It would not be incorrect to assume that the signing of the treaty has direct or indirect links with Anglo-French colonial rivalry in India and Europe as well. During that time the British were engaged with France in the Seven Years War (1756-63) and it had serious repercussions on their competition for colonial expansion particularly in India. During the war Aluang-paya king of Ava (1752-1760) was instigated by the French to destroy the English settlement at Negrais, an Island at the mouth of the Irrawady in 1754 on the allegation that the British supplied arms to the Mons, one of the war-like tribes in Upper Burma. Consequently, about ten Englishmen and one hundred Indians were killed. The British authorities in India were looking for retribution of the atrocities at Negrais as they felt badly humiliated. These are some of the crucial factors behind the signing of the treaty (Dena 1991: 2-3).

The motivating force of the British officials was based on political and commercial considerations. To establish direct trading relationship with Chinese merchants and the British merchants, the expulsion of Burmese from the soil of Manipur became necessary. It would subsequently enable the Chinese merchants to bring their goods down as far as Manipur, in quantities suitable for the market. Secondly, the East India Company through an alliance with Manipur would be able to demand reparation from the Burmese for the humiliation at Negrais (Dena 1991: 3). Under the treaty, it was also agreed that there should not be any disturbance or hindrance on the free movement of English traders and English subjects passing into and through Manipur. Things that might interrupt in their free trade activities were to be avoided. It was regarded that the English enemies were to be considered as enemies of Manipur and *vice-versa*. Jai Singh and Verelst further agreed that neither of them should enter into any accommodation with the Burmese king without the advice from the other. Most importantly it was also agreed that the English troops and the Manipuri forces should jointly move against Burma in case of any harm done to them. Manipur was allowed to take full possession of Burma and Jai Singh was to make good to the English all such losses incurred by the latter (Ali 1923: 1). Apparently, the circumstances led the Manipuri king seek external aid, which could only be provided by the colonial empire. It coincided with the larger interest of the British, who were looking for an ally in the region to control the North Eastern Frontier (see The Treaty of 1762).

The Question of the Manipur Agency

In February 1861 the Civil Finance Commission proposed the

abolition of the Manipur Agency. But later on, Major McCulloch was informed that the Government had no such kind of intention (Mackenzie1884: 155). There were several political and economic reasons for not abolishing the post of Manipur Agency. Colonial accounts indicate a long history of failure to exercise control over the region:

> The past history of the country shows that no chief has been able to manage the people. They have, one and all, proved cruel, oppressive, and weak. The country has been the scene of civil wars, murders, devastations and misery while under the nominal control of the chief, while, as a rule, peace, order, and comparative prosperity reigned while a British was present. In addition to these arguments in favour of the appointment of an Agent is the circumstance that indigenous tea has been found in large quantities all through the country: the knowledge of this will ere long make it the resort of Englishmen in great number. It will be difficult, therefore if not impossible; to prevent constant collision between and the natives, unless a British Officer is on the spot. (Foreign Dept., 1864)

It explicitly stated that the Agency ought not to be abolished and every one in Munnipore (present Manipur) wanted it to continue.

A Political Agent could also do much good in terms of fostering trade and commerce. In 1851, the Government of India resolved to recognised the present Rajah, Kirtee Chunder Sing (Chandra Kirti Singh), and further 'authorized the political agent to make a public avowal of the determination of the British Government to uphold the present Rajah and to resist and punish any parties attempting here after to dispossess him' (vide government letter, NO. 843, of the October 3, 1851). The Hon'ble Court of Directors in their dispatch No. 14, dated the May 5, 1852, expressed considerable doubts as to the propriety of this steps, but remarked that it was a necessary consequence of the pledge thus given that the Government of India should attempt to guide the Rajah by its advice, and if needful; should protect his subject against oppressions. In turn they expected—as the price of protection afforded to him—that the Rajah would submit to the maintenance of a sufficient check over the general conduct of his administration so as to prevent it from being oppressive to the people. This dispatch certainly appears to give the Political Agent some control over the administration, and this power has after all been exercised beneficially, as, for example, by Colonel McCulloch, who put down the slave trade with Burmah, and substantiated for it a legitimate trade in buffaloes and ponies.

The construction of a road between Manipur and Cachar and the presence of a political Agent considerably extended the trade between Manipur and British provinces, and there sprang up a very important trade in tea-seed. But as Manipur and the countries round it were at best but 'half-civilized state', this increase in their intercourse with Cachar and the European tea planters was fraught with certain dangers, and appeared to McCulloch to make the presence of a representative of the British Government in Manipur even more desirable. Incidents like the murder of Monteiro and his followers made it necessary for some officers to be permanently posted in the country so as to investigate such matters on the spot, and, perhaps, to prevent their recurrence. The king personally in one of his talks with McCulloch had stated that he had little or no control over many of the hill tribes, and yet, if any agent of a tea planter was murdered in the hills, he would probably be blamed for it, and without the presence of a political agent he would find difficult to clear himself. The great object in having a Political Agent at Manipur was that as he concluded 'everything may be kept quite on our frontier' (Beverige1864: 102).

Political and Commercial Considerations

It was part of the policy of the British Government to protect traders of all dispositions who visited the Manipur valley to trade in it, or who passed through it to Burma for that purpose. All who passed through Manipur needed to get passes from McCulloch, and when they returned he saw the cattle's they brought, and after having proper inspection, collected taxes, paid it to the Rajah, got the proper Mohurs, and sent them on. This was done to prevent delay and oppression, which might take place if the business were left to the Raja's people alone. According to the treaty, heavy duties were not to be exacted on commodities. McCulloch himself endeavoured to encourage trade by every means within his power. He made efforts to evolve a traffic system (Mackenzie 1884: 157).

Dr. John M'cosh, M.D., F.R.G.S, late Bengal Medical service, an enterprising enthusiast who had studied this region extensively as part of his duty to collect information about the resources of this province and other various practical routes into Tibet, Burma, and China came up with certain crucial ideas. He was ordered by the Governor-General to publish this report under the title 'Topography of Assam'. He expressed his reservations about the lack of interest by the Government in this frontier as 'it is curious to see the Indian and the Home Government and the people of this country generally so morbidly sensitive about the North Western Frontier of India, whilst the North Eastern is utterly neglected, and that the political and commercial interests of the Empire are in that quarter left to their fate. Yet our warlike neighbours the Burmese invaded Assam in that Quarter, and under the leader Bundoola alarmed the authorities in Calcutta, and there they may some day do so again. To this day we know very little of these mountain passes, and I believe I am correct in stating that no European Officer has ever crossed over anyone of them' (Foreign. Dept.: 373-77). A pamphlet was presented by him on trade route scheme between India and China before the British Association at Bradford and he stated his views on the importance of the North-East Frontier *vis-à-vis* trade and commerce. The first and greater portion of the pamphlet is taken up with note on, and reminiscences of Assam, after which he proceeds to advocate:

> A line of road to commerce at the terminus of the North Eastern Railway of Bengal, and pass through Munnipore and upper Burmah to Bhamo, and thence on through Momein and Talifoo to the Yang-tsi-Kiang.

He continues:

> I hope the day is not far distant when the North-Eastern Railway of Bengal shall be carried onwards over the hills of Munnipore, across the broad kingdom of Burmah to Bhamo, and thence on through Momein and Talifoo to the very centre of the celestial Empire, when the tiger, the

leopard and the bear, the bison, the elephant and the rhinoceros shall be driven from their strongholds, and garden of tea and coffee, oranges and lemons shall take the place of the now impenetrable Jungle; when even fever shall be driven from its hot bed, and regions now fatal to European life shall be made healthy and enjoyable; when the brave hill tribes shall drop their bows and arrows, and take up the spade and pickaxe; when the slothful Burmese shall bestow as much care on the cultivation of his fields as in the tattooing of his person; when they shall cease to think themselves celestials and hold out the hand of good fellowship to the outside barbarian; when the prodigious commerce of the Indus, the ganges, and the Brahmapootra, the Ningthee, the Irrawady, and the Yang-tsi-Kiang shall be hoisted upon trucks, and rolled from east to west and from west to east in one grand tide, ever ebbing, ever flowing, ever lasting, and when London and Liverpool, Manchester and Bradford, Glasgow and Paisley, Dundee and Aberdeen, shall dip their pitchers into the scared stream and deal out its bounty to the people of the land (Foreign. Dept.: 163-168)

Various economic and political interests were involved in forwarding this scheme:

1. *Need of importing Chinese labour migrant*: After the discovery of tea in Assam and other adjoining areas, which were growing wildly upon the amphitheatre of hills by Mr. Bruce, Assistant to the Commissioner of Assam, then stationed at Suddia, later on Governor-General, Lord Auckland subsequently took deep interest in the demand for Assam tea. The European Capitalists entered largely into trading speculation, and many officers invested their saving in it, with sanguine hope of success, the share rose to a fabulous premium amounts. But the efficient labourers are inadequate that reduced the plantation to ruin (Foreign Dept.: 373-77).

   The Assamese were perceived to be indolent to labour, and

too feeble and inefficient as workmen, even if they were willing. The surrounding hill tribes, though powerful men, were too savage and independent to work for other people, and preferred expanding their energies on their own fields. Considering thousands of Chinese cultivators, living not two hundred miles distant, willing to immigrate to Assam, yet prevented from coming to Assam due to absence of passable roads security of life and property, it was thereby proposed to open a practical road between China and Assam and restore prosperity to these plantations by importation of Chinese labourers.

2. *Increasing French influence in Indo-China*: Dr. M'cosh being a pioneer upon this road, he pointed out in his 'Topography of Assam' the great importance of such an overland route. However, without assigning any reason the Government ignored the matter. The expedition led by Major Slander from Bhamo to Momein, could not accomplish the desired objectives in his mission but the French expedition starting from Saigon in Cochin China, pushed their way right to Umerapoora, and thence across to the Yang-tsi-Kiang. On the other hand the British imperialist expansion proved successful in China after putting down the Panthay rebellion. With the establishment of a British embassy at the Burmese court and stationing of a Political Agent at Bhamo, the King of Burma was now persuaded to adopt free trade policy. Soon, the British steamers carried out regular navigation from Irrawaddy as far north as Bhamo.

The hills tribes in west Burma came under British protection and most importantly with the establishment of a British resident in Manipur, a good road from the North East frontier to the Burmese Capital was developed. The territory between the Irrawaddy and the Yang-tsi-Kiang was well known to Chinese authorities. From times immemorial all intercourse between the courts of Ava and Pekin was maintained through this route, practical even for elephants. Moreover, the French expedition led to the publication of a full account of their journey, and from it every desired particular could be known. Thus the line of road proposed would commence at the terminus of the North Eastern Railway of Bengal, and passed through Manipur and upper Burmah to Bhamo, and thence on through Momien and Talifoo to the Yang-tsi-Kiang which was connected by cannals with most of the great cities of China, including Nakin and Pekin. Bringing the attention of the Government, Dr. M'cosh contended that the Indian Government was passive while on the other side the French Government in Cochin China, availing themselves of their being the first in the field, were straining every nerve to intercept Chinese trade and divert it down the great river of Cambodia to their capital, Saigon. British Merchants at Rangoon, though somewhat behind, were doing their best to have a fair share of trade and commerce. They have established regular steam communication with Bhamo, and have sailing boats and canoes in their service far above it, up the Penang River. But Dr. M'cosh had something more important than fostering of plantation in Assam. He visualized carrying North Eastern Railway of Bengal onwards over the hills of Manipur, across the broad kingdom of Burma to Bhamo, and thence on through Momein and Talifoo to the very centre of the celestial empire (Foreign Dept.: 373-77). He forwarded his pamphlet to higher officials for further perusal and in response they gave their remarks. Some interesting insights are revealed in some of the responses. The Chief Commissioner, British Burma, who considered the visionary schemes of M'cosh for the civilization of China thought that everything possible was being done to encourage trade with China, and deprecated attempts being made to direct public attention to almost impossible routes through Assam. Captain Strover the political agent at Mandalay opined that Dr. M'cosh like many other enterprising enthusiasts had written a long paper on a subject he did not fully understand. He believed that a big portion of the country between Manipur and Bhamo was low and during the Monsoon completely inundated, the proposal would cause a very considerable outlay in the construction of a railroad.

Captain McCulloch, the political agent of Manipur spoke positively on the question of railway linkage between British India and China. He noted that desirable in the first place to give great impetus to trade, the completion of a good road between Assam and the Manipur valley; secondly, the completion of the road from Chuttuck to the Manipur valley, and the bridging of the hill streams and thirdly, the continuation of the road in the direction of Bhamo, which on looking at the map would be found to be almost due east from the stations of Sylhet and Cachar in the British province. Mr. Eden, another British official, strongly endorsed the need for a railroad from Rangoon to Mandalay. Since the opinions of the British officials varied, the scheme proposed by Dr. M'cosh could not be translated into reality. Many of the officials emphasized on the political difficulties, high expenses and difficult topographical factors. An official commenting on the Scheme gave his view that facilities existed for the construction of this railroad from an engineering point of view, on moderately high ground whole way, and the trains from Bhamo besides conveying the produce ofYunan to the nearest shipping port (as compared with Calcutta) from Europe, via the Suez canal, viz. Rangoon, would pass through a country rich in every description of produce, metals and minerals, and drain the great and various resources of upper Burmah with far greater effects than any line from Bhamo to Manipur could possibly do. The trade route scheme was solely motivated by commercial interests of enterprising Europeans who rigorously argued for the pacification and subjugation of the 'wild tribes' of the region. In fact, even M'Cosh himself explicitly mentioned that he was not interested in the welfare of those people (Foreign Dept.: 163-68).

Text and Context

In the present economic and strategic policy issues, there are many schemes inherited from the colonial framework. With the baggage of this inherited colonial legacy looming large over policies in the post British period, implications concerning issues and challenges in the region as a whole and particularly in the state of Manipur as well can be analytically delineated keeping in mind the history of the region. India's 'Look East' policy—an economic and strategic orientation to Southeast Asia—was first enunciated in 1991 but its conceptualization as a politico-military space had been realized during the colonial period. Yet, the restructuring of free market programme was initiated at the end of the Cold War. After losing Soviet economic and political support on which it had relied, the Indian government sought for a new markets and economic partners abroad. India also began to look for alternate energy sources after US-led Gulf War on Iraq in 1990-91 destabilized the Middle East (Kumara: <www.wsws.org>).

It is necessary to examine the complimentarities, coincidences or contradictions in economic, strategic and security policy between India and the ASEAN region and to identify the driving force behind India's policy of 'Look East', and the role of major powers, notably the U.S. and China, in determining the nature and extent of interaction between India and ASEAN. ASEAN mattered verbally only in the past articulation of Indian foreign policy. Today, it is a throbbing commercial reality behind India's diplomacy. Intensification of the economic linkages with ASEAN has led India into a second phase of LEP. Phase one was characterised by trade and investment linkages. Phase two according to former India External Affairs Minister Yashwant Sinha is marked by arrangements for FTAs and establishment of institutional economic linkages between countries of the region and India. However, there are other features that define phase two of India's LEP. It has moved away from an exclusive focus on economic issues and shifting to a broader agenda that involves security cooperation, including joint operations to protect sea lanes and pooling resources in the war against terrorism. India's engagement in such multi-directional defence diplomacy in Asia can be seen from the angle of how globalization and its effect on the nation-state system and security, which encompasses national interest and induces inter-dependence and emerging multi-polarity, shape up future inter-regional interactions (Grare and Matto 2001).

Three other unique features can be identified in the phase two of India's LEP. First is the pursuit of physical connectivity to Southeast Asia. As a result of marginal trade with Southeast Asia during the Cold War, the consciousness that the region was part of India's extended neighbourhood melted away. And there was no reason to think of transport links with Southeast Asia. Establishing air and land links to East and Southeast Asia has become integral to phase two of the policy. As part of its road diplomacy, India is now actively building transport corridors to the region. These include the trilateral highway project involving Myanmar and Thailand and the proposed rail link between New Delhi and Hanoi. Secondly, the phase two has opened the door for the first time since 'independence' to break out of the political confines of the subcontinent that has severely limited India's grand strategic options. LEP has allowed India to break the artificial political barriers between the subcontinent and Southeast Asia. A summit of a new economic grouping called BIMSTEC will bring five nations of the

Subcontinent (Bangladesh, Bhutan, India, Nepal and Sri Lanka) together with two countries from Southeast Asia, Myanmar and Thailand, with a view to promote regional cooperation. With this, India will be in a position to finally trump the veto that Pakistan has exercised over economic cooperation in the subcontinent through the South Asian Association for Regional Cooperation (SAARC) (Raja Mohan. www.hinduounnet.com).

North Eastern Frontier as a Growth Zone

The idea of redefining and transforming the economic fortune of the eastern frontier of South Asia is no pipe dream but draws inspiration from the integrating influence of geography, which has invested this region with a wealth of natural resources. To recapture the historic glory through a realization of the frontier region's collective potential, the eastern region not only provides the land link for the dynamic East and Southeast Asia but also offers a market for goods, a source of labour and potentials for complementary development within the framework of a flying geese model of global economic restructuring (Rehman 1999).

There are four board proposed themes to prepare a new economic policy framework for the North East region (Sachdeva 2000):

(a) Economic integration of the North Eastern region
  (i) Among themselves,
  (ii) With the National Economy,
  (iii) With the countries of Southeast and East Asia;
(b) Identifying those thrust areas where the economies of the region have a potential to develop and attract domestic and foreign investment;
(c) Institutions required for the creation of a market economy in the region; and
(d) Human resources development.

Feasibility and Speculation

It is a proven fact that the North Eastern states of India are integrally linked largely to the Indian economy through the areas of

Bangladesh. The North East was the largest tea producing region in India till 1947. The process of reintegrating the North East with South Asia must be viewed in the broader context of the reintegration of a shared transport infrastructure, which not only runs through Bangladesh but also links up with Nepal and Bhutan to the north and Myanmar and China to the east. The North Eastern states were once seen as India's eastern gateway to the Yangtze and Mekong valleys in China and the Salween and Irrawady Valleys in Myanmar. As far back as 1945 Jawaharlal Nehru had visualized the North East as the centre of a major highway and rail line linking South Asia with China and thereby connecting East Asia with Europe (Rehman 1999: 108-09).

During the Tang Dynasty there were road linkages between South West China and the North East. A southern route from Yunnan passed through Ruili in China across the Irrawady to Bhamo on the Burmese side of the border to the Shan state of Burma and across the Chin Hills and Chindwin River into Manipur. This route is today being developed by China as part of its infrastructure programme under the GMS agenda to link up China. It is roughly aligned along the prospective development of the Asian Highway, which comes across the border from Thailand and moves up north to connect with Moreh in Manipur (India) and Tamu in Myanmar. The Asian Highway is being developed, Myanmar has identified the Mandalay route as its route of choice to link up with India and a serviceable road link between Tamu and Moreh is being developed by RITES, a public sector agency under the Indian government. These infrastructural developments in the North East and Myanmar will take the road further south in Myanmar down to Kalemyo on the Chindwin, which is being bridged as past of the Asian Highway network. The trade protocol has been concluded between India and Myanmar, where the region of Champai in Mizoram along with Moreh in Manipur, have been identified as exchange point for trade (Rehman: 1999: 112-13).

Other possible alignments linking Bangladesh and North East with Myanmar and Southwest China also need to be taken into account. Myanmar could be linked by rail along three possible routes:

(a) A southern line extending from Chittagong to Akyab and

then over the Aeng Pass across the Arakan Yoma to Prome Province in Myanmar and link up with the Mandalay line.

(b) A central line from Lumding in Assam, through the Naga Hills into Manipur, into the Kubaw Valley in Myanmar to connect with the northern most point of the Myanmar rail system at Myitkinia. The Myitkinia railhead could link up with the rail line being built by the Chinese, linking Kunming with Ruili on the Yunnan-Myanmar border.

(c) A northern route from Margharita through the Hukwang valley in Mayanmar to link up with the railhead at Myitkania (Rehman 1999: 116).

Efforts are also on to have a railway link established between the North East and Myanmar. A feasibility study has been undertaken. Airlines of major Asian nations have also agreed to fly through Guwahati on an unlimited basis, raising hopes for boosting trade in the region. When all these plans get fully effective, trade and commerce between India and the other Asian nations would increase and the North Eastern region would get the maximum benefit (Nitin 2005).

New Challenges Confronting North East

The immediate policy initiative requires identification of the existing problems. It urges the private sector to take part in the development process. These are some of the new challenges faced by the policy makers and the people who will be at the receiving end. Whether they will have a balanced multi-level planning system for regional development is a matter of debate. It is on the agenda that the power and funds to states and then to local bodies will be decentralised. In the prevailing circumstances, however, the logical conclusion of economic liberalization is decentralization at the political level and greater autonomy to investors. Under the new economic policy regime, apprehensions regarding the success of the North Eastern states to manage their own affairs remain at large in the backdrop of all the policies being crafted and designed in the political power corridors of New Delhi (Sachdeva 2000).

After having resurveyed the road and other facilities again, there is a major disjuncture between policy and implementation.

It is clear that none of the decision makers in Delhi seems to have taken into account the hurdles such as the peoples' concerns, poor infrastructural facilities, including the state of the road network and disturbed conditions on the border areas. Problems arising from the failure to integrate the region politically remain central in debates on substantial and meaningful development in the North East. Marked by deep rooted crises, the Central Government is more often perceived as another invader and never as a helping hand. Considered as another sub-colonization, the overweening presence (and corruption) of Hindi speaking civil servants as well as the pressure of the Indian army, with its overweening influence in every state in the region, the factors that explain (but do not justify) the current crises in the region are not invisible (Egreteau 2006). Now, with the changing global politico-economic scenario another class of policy makers somewhere down the line might have felt the need to follow the path of economic development rather than committing on military solution to restore the stability in the North East. The economic opening up of the landlocked North East to its neighbouring regions might be seen as a potent means of solving the insurgency problem. With the inclusion of the North East in the LEP India is trying to reach out to ASEAN through Myanmar and the North East. In April 1995 the first project was launched that could be considered viable with the opening of the Tamu (Myanmar)-Moreh (Manipur) cross-border post. Earlier, even though the town of Moreh was linked by National Highway NH 39 to Imphal (capital of Manipur) and to the rest of the North East, the bilateral trade with Myanmar/Burma was merely a local exchange of goods. On the Burmese side, there was an obvious lack of transport infrastructure. However, during the visit of J.N. Dixit, the then Indian Foreign Secretary, to Yangon (March 1993) India managed to discuss with the Burmese government the means of financing the construction of 160 km. long road on Burmese territory from Tamu to Kalewa and then to Kalemyo in the Kabaw Valley of the Sagaing division. Nevertheless, the rest of the road connecting Kalemyo to Mandalay is still in a pathetic condition. It is very difficult to reach Mandalay from Kalemyo in the span of a single day. India has now declared that it is not interested in financing or building the road further leaving it to the Burmese government to draw up plans and undertake the rest of the construction by itself, which it has not done so far, despite its commitment to the Trans-Asian Highway project meant to connect Bangkok with India.

Thus, this project was the first to attempt at opening up Manipur and the neighbouring hilly areas to the east. In the backdrop of these stark realities, it is pertinent to note that the North East is not as landlocked as it is claimed to be. Transnational insurgencies, large-scale smuggling, common cross-border affinities have intertwined many communities, business and political interest. The underground economy of the North East is far more globalized than its apparent landlocked position would suggest. The smuggled goods from Burma, Thailand and China are easily available in Imphal, Tinsukia and Guwahati. The North East is far more connected to the 'outside world' than the general perception in mainland India. But it is and will remain as troubled as it appears from the outside. In addition, with the lack of trust and suffering from negligence by the political elite, criminalization and increasing disparities, there is every chance that the region will unfortunately remain unstable unless New Delhi makes an all out effort to solve the problem internally. If the 'External factor' has a considerable weight, the internal dynamics (degeneration of the insurgency coupled with the inefficiency of the Central Government) might doom the North East (Egreteau 2006: 147). As M'cosh's proposed trade route schemes failed due to various impediments and varied opinion raised by the many colonial officials, the LEP launched by the Government of India would not be free from implications and challenges. Manipur fall within the gambit of larger India's geo-strategic interest and conceptualising frontier into a global economic space with certain military dimension. Conspicuously, there will be severe repercussion on political, social and economic life of the frontier peoples.

REFERENCES

Ali, Abdul 1923. 'Note on the Early History of Manipur'. Paper read at the Fifth Meeting of the Indian Historical Records Commission, held at Calcutta. January.

Beverige, HESQ 1864. 'On Special Duty in Munnipore'. to Aitchison C.U., ESQ, Under-Secretary to Government of India, FDP, No. 4, dated Sylhet, January 26.

Dena, Lal (ed.) 1991. 'History of Modern Manipur'. 1826-1949.

Dun, E.W. 1975. (Reprinted). *Gazetteer of Manipur*. Calcutta: Government Publications.

Egreteau, Renaud 2006. 'Instability at the Gate: India's Troubled Northeast and its External Connections'. Publication of the French Institutes in India, Centre De Science Humaines

Foreign Department, 1864. *Political*. 'A'/No. 102-113, April.

Foreign Department, 1864. *Political*. 'A', No. 373-377.

Foreign Department, 1864. *Political*. 'A', No. 163-168.

Grare, Frederic and Amitabh Mattoo(ed) 2001. *India and ASEAN: The Politics of India's Look East Policy*. New Delhi: Manohar Publishers.

Gokhale, Nitin 2005. 'Focus North East—Look East Policy? The Far-Sighted Road to Nowhere: The NH-39'. August 18. <www.tehelka.com>

Kumara, Sarath. 'Burma Visit Highlight India's 'Look East' Strategy'. <www.wsws.org>

Mackenzie, Alexander 1884. *History of the Relations of the Government with the Hill Tribes of the North-East Frontier of Bengal*. Calcutta: Home Department.

Mohan, Raja C. 'Look East Policy Phase II' <www.hinduonnet.com>

Mukherjee, B.N. 1992. *External Trade of Early North-Eastern India*. New Delhi: Har-Anand Publications.

Parthasarthy, G. 'The Road to Mandalay'. <www.in.rediff.com>

Pemberton, R.B. 1835. *The Eastern Frontier of India*. Delhi: Mittal Publications.

Rehman, Sobhan 1999. *Transforming Eastern South Asia: Building Growth Zones For Economic Cooperation*. Dacca: The University Press.

Sachdeva, Gulshan 2000. *Economy of the North East: Policy, Present Conditions and Future Possibilities*. New Delhi: Konark Publishers.

Verghese, B.G. 1996. *India's Northeast Resurgent: Ethnicity, Insurgency, Governance, Development*. New Delhi: Konark Publishers.

7

Look East Policy and Manipur: Uncertain Trajectories, Ambiguities–A Synoptic View

SENATE KHURAIJAM

We could, on the basis of national realities exchange knowledge, integrate markets, interconnect, but at the same time we must understand that there are problems that do not have national solution: radio-active clouds, world oil prices, diseases, warming of the planet or the hole in the Ozone layer. —Hugo Chavez

Chavez's words obliquely reflect the policy debates at the global level. It is against such a critical backdrop that debates around developments in the North East 'a late comer to development' can be assessed meaningfully (Shukla Commission 1997). Manipur, one of the constituent states, carries the baggage of worries as far as development policies like the Look East Policy (LEP) is concerned. The baggage of worries characterised by ambivalence include questions revolving round the hidden agenda of LEP, its implications for almost half a million jobless youth, transformation of Manipur into a market place like Singapore, militarisation disguised as trade and so on and so forth. What does it mean for the State government and its ability to determine the economic future of the population? Such anxieties are to be found in many public spheres, in the academic debates of Scholars Will the narratives of 'frontier', 'ethnicity', 'identity', take a back seat with the onslaught of the global economy lurking beyond the frontiers and elsewhere? Or is it

Fukuyama's 'end of history' argued in his analysis of a world where the struggle for recognition, the willingness to risk one's life for a purely abstract goal, the worldwide ideological struggle that called forth courage, imagination and idealism, will be replaced by economic, environmental and endless solving of technical problem, environmental concerns, and the satisfaction of sophisticated consumer demands (Fukuyama 1989: 16). The essay attempts to probe into some of the questions related to development policies like the LEP by employing the concepts of globalization and regionalism as tropes to articulate the contradictions of an open market economy after India hitched on to the free-market band-wagon in the early nineties of the last situation.

India's Asianism: North East – A Handyman, Manipur – A Cypher

It is a tendency reflected in the Government of India's effort to undertake 'regionalist thinking' in both economic production and symbolic reproduction under global capitalism. The change of the command in the capitalist world economy reflects the 'Victory' of a 'New' regime over an 'old' regime. Whether a fresh change of command and a new stage of capitalist development are imminent remains unclear (Giovanni 1994). Gamble and Payne conceive regionalism as a state-led project designed to reorganize a particular regional space along defined economic and political lines. The two apparently competing tendencies in the contemporary world political economy—regionalism as a statist project and globalization as a set of social process—appear still to be in balance; indeed there seems no reason to assume that one must eventually triumph over the other. Conceiving regionalism as a discursive construct serves better to explain the construction of regionalist project within late capitalism. A widespread view within the capitalist framework of development contending that regionalism constitute a temporary mediation between the logic of capital and the work of nation-states in the world economy, and that this mediation suggests a means by which nationalist/capitalist ideologues reposition themselves in the transnational economic arena. In the present historical juncture, regionalism intercedes between the eroding of national autonomy and the deterritorialising of capitalism to reterriotorialise transnational capital. With the growing influence of global trade in every sphere of the world, regionalism in the realm of international trade has far wider significance than regionalism in any other domain of civil society. As the contemporary world is rapidly surging towards greater trade liberalization, globalization and ruled-based multilateral trading system, the emergence of an evergrowing number of Regional Trade Agreements (RTAs) between countries have opened a wide debate on their role and significance in the present globalized multilateral trading environment. In the recent years, particularly since the 1990s, there has been a dramatic increase in the number of (RTAs) from 1947 to the present day, over 200 RTAs have been notified either through World Trade Organization (WTO) or the erstwhile General Agreement on Tariffs and Trade (GATT) (Abraham 2002).

India's interest in economic imperatives *vis-à-vis* increasing sensitivity to the rising Asian economic activities became clearly visible in the 1990s. The Asianist sensitivity became visible in India in the 1990s to economic imperatives. During the Deve Gowda government, the man who most explicitly represented business interests was Finance Minister, P. Chidambaram. He declared in 1997 that India could become an economic giant like Japan and that India 'will now Asianise itself' (Jaffrelot 2003). Today, Asia itself is neither a misrepresentation of the orientalist nor the collective representation of the anti-imperialist. Asia has now become a market, and 'Asianness' has become a commodity circulating globally through late capitalism (Leo Ching 2000).

With India following the dictates of capital and moving from an agrarian economy to a more service-oriented and consumerist economy, the optimism and energy is reconfigured in the mass images of Asianism. Hence, India's Look East Policy is a logical corollary. Trade between India and countries of the Association of South East Asian Nations (ASEAN) is expanding significantly. India has signed Free Trade Area (FTA) agreements with Thailand and Singapore in place including the Mekong Ganga Cooperation (MGC) and Bangladesh, India, Myanmar, Sri Lanka and Thailand-Economic Cooperation (BIMST-EC). Rajive Sikri, Secretary (East) of the Ministry of External Affairs, speaking at a Forum organised by Centre of North East India, South and Southeast Asia studies (CENISEAS) contended that the 'LEP envisages the North East region not as the periphery of India, but a centre of a thriving and integrated economic space linking two dynamic regions with a network of highways, railways, pipelines, transmission lines crisscrossing the region'. In spite of these grand overtures from the Union Government, there is increasing skepticism in the region. Analysts in the region have expressed genuine doubts over the issue of substantial and meaningful development in the North East. As far as the role of the North East *vis-à-vis* LEP is concerned, it will just play the part of a facilitator in terms of being a transit point in the sheer absence of any productive base. There are serious hurdles to the LEP developing its North East India thrust. Indeed there is a growing sense that there may be more rhetoric than substance to the talk of the region becoming India's gateway to South East Asia (Baruah 2005).

Historically, the North East had extensive links with the neighbouring region of Tibet, Bhutan, Burma and Indo-China. It formed the southern trail of the Silk route. The region had substantial economic and social intercourse with the neighbouring countries. There is evidence that trade and migration into territories today comprising Tibet, Myanmar, Yunan Province of China, Nepal, Bhutan and Sikkim were important to the economy of the region (Baruah 2004). However, partition of East Bengal and independence ended whatever remained of this intercourse.

The structure of the economy in the region resembles the economy of the least developed parts of the globe, with primary sector accounting for 55-60 per cent of the income, and under developed secondary and tertiary sectors. The secondary sector constitutes only a meagre 11-16 per cent of the total income, making it India's industrially most backward region (GoI 2004). India's policies on trade and industry and its strategy of an inward looking economy deprived the North Eastern states of their natural market. All products consumed in the North East come from distant manufacturing regions in India. A World Bank study estimated that costs of logistics and damages added 60 per cent to the cost of a bag of cement and 14 per cent to general cargo, moved from Calcutta to the North East (Khana 2005).

Characterised by a market economy where there is virtual absence of indigenous products in the face of an overarching presence of goods produced elsewhere consumerist Manipur is going into the risky business world. It means 'linking up' with the tracks of the world. The expression is ambiguous, suggesting a sense of mixed feelings—a perceived time—lag in development paradigm and self-asserting itself as an entity in the global dynamics. It cannot be reduced by a simple assumption that because of transaction taking place in national territory and in a national institutional setting it should *ipso facto* be intelligible in terms of the national. National institutions can become home to some of the operational rules of the global economic system. They become part of the spatiality of the global economic system (Sassen 2000). LEP as a project of neo-liberal reforms holds uncertain future for an under-developed Manipur. Neo-liberal reforms are vigorously contested in a process mediated by domestic states and elites; it remains crucial to understand the constellations of domestic forces engaged in these struggles in order to comprehend the nature of economic change. It raises questions about assumed relationship between markets, governance, democracy and civil society and about the way different political and economic institutions are forged and transformed. It is a highly contentious political agenda for which there is often only a limited domestic constituency. Its progress is often driven by the like-minded technocrats in local states whose power is little more than the leverage they gained as a mediator between domestic governments, international investors and financiers, and donor government (Robinson and Hewison 2005). Neo-liberalism does not stem from a politically neutral, dispassionate and intellectually complacent analysis. On the contrary, it represents an attempt to reinvent orthodoxy in the domain of economic ideas and ideology by global policy community that is profoundly influenced by the US, the key international financial institutions over which it exerts authority and financial sector interests associated with 'Wall Street' (Beeson and Woods 2003). As Chomsky argues, the end of the Cold War unleashed the hegemonic impulse of the US, while the onset of the long economic boom in 1990s under Clinton administration lent a degree of legitimacy to a global project of 'exporting' neo-liberal ideas to the rest of the world. It espouses a conservative political agenda in which the political leadership should attenuate the activism of civil society (which Manipur has too many) and allow technocrats the discretion, freedom and scope to pursue the market-oriented economic agenda (Beeson and Islam 2005).

Elites with professed claims of pragmatism and sections of the urban-middle class are full of optimism that LEP is a harbinger of development and a road way to an 'Asianist' mode of 'modernism'. It only accentuates the old debate of 'modernization' without 'industrialization'. The ballooning euphoria is not going to lift higher because of the ugly realities on the ground. The political 'class of the state has been propitiating the godly figures at the centre in order to gain benefits; it is not making them angry by following their diktat. Since the revenue of the state is not generated from the people through taxes and other means but rather through the 'gift of grants' from the Central authority, the accountability of those who are in power in the state towards its people weighs less than the source of income. Because the state is the major source of employment without any other source, its importance in the running of society is heightened as a structure of monopolized power (Yenkhom 2005). Manipur is still industrially very backward even in comparison with states in the backward North East region. Its per capita income is far below the all India average. There are not enough industries to keep pace with the rapid growth of population and to deal with the growing problems of unemployment, poverty, lack of housing, healthcare and associated facilities. Moreover, there is problem of comparative neglect of industrialization in the state planning (Parasain 2000). There is virtual absence of industries worth mentioning except traditional cottage ones such as Khadi and Village Industries, handlooms and handicrafts. The contribution of the manufacturing sector to the total state domestic product is found to be 8.4 per cent to 7.4 per cent of the total working force population engaged in the sector (GoM 2003). The Five Year Plans of Manipur did very little for development of medium and large industries. Industrialization is undoubtedly desirable. On the state-wise distribution of domestic industrial investment proposals' front the share of North East (after adoption of North East Industrial Policy, 1997) is only 1.86 per cent of the total during the last 15 years of neo-liberal economic reforms (Maisnam and Khuraijam 2006). Manipur's share is best left to be imagined. As a result Manipur remains a consumer state in spite of its rich potential to become a producer state. The problem with the policy making projects are that they are conceived from the top and either ignore the ground realities altogether or are based on patron-client relations between some presumed 'leaders' of the state and the centre. LEP therefore looms large over the policy and political horizon with immense uncertainties.

The Military Might: The Moreh–Monger (Indo-Myanmar Trade)

Economic engagements with the neighbouring countries are based on the strategic and military posture of the successive Governments in New Delhi, rather than a development paradigm. To disinterested regimes consolidating power in the remote centre of Delhi and with grand designs of independent industrialization, the North East is best left to army and police to manage, while the only development objective seemed to be to build infrastructure to militarily secure its frontiers (Khana 2005). The accretion in military strength, both manpower centric as well as military hard ware acquisition based on real or imaginary threat assessments has contributed immensely to consolidation of the military's role in Indian politics. The government's militaristic approach predates economic reforms. What economic reforms have done, however, is that FDI, foreign trade and foreign investors as new 'stake holders' in India's political economy have lent the policy of suppression greater urgency. It is more crucial because this coincided with the consolidation of the army's role in internal affairs (Navlakha 2005). Significantly, the Government of India enacted the Armed Forces Special Powers Act in 1958 when there was hardly any insurgency in the region. As a result, when the North Eastern Council was established in the early 1970s, it was placed under the Home Ministry. Politicization of economic issues has reached its height recently with the requirement of certificates from the Home Ministry for the provincial government to get funds sanctioned by the Ministry of Finance (Yumnam 2005).

Indo-Myanmar security issues are presently discussed at the level of Home Secretaries, at the Joint Secretary level and at the level of local army commanders, who met frequently. Its engagement with Myanmar is rooted in its perception of the North East as the gateway to ASEAN nation. Highlighting his dualist sense of economics and insecurity, Rajeev Agrawal joint Secretary (North East) in the Indian Home Ministry in a TV interview said:

> We find that over a period of time they (Myanmarese) are much more responsive towards our concerns. In the last national level meeting, it was agreed that there would be coordinated action against Indian insurgents in Myanmar

> by their forces and also simultaneously Indian security forces will take action inside our border.... Two areas need to be targeted—Gun running and narcotics.... It will benefit the North East quite a lot if the trade routes are improved, a large of Indian business man can go there and send things. It can boost to production facilities in the North East.

Manipur has almost half a million (4,48435) job seekers registered in the Employment Exchange. Statistics over the last one decade shows increase in the number of Employment Exchanges (11 to 17) and decrease in the number of vacancies. The problem of (un)employment is continuing to be a matter of serious concern to the state's economy (GOM, 2003). It only testifies the dismal performance of the policy makers and its sheer lack of sense in putting forward a vision. The 'intelligentsia' as well as the state actors cannot simply rest on the philistine hope that LEP would give employment opportunity to the people of Manipur. The allegorization of the *Nongpok Thong Hangba* (Opening of the Eastern door) is deemed to be challenged by the (in)security factor and the vanity of an 'Asianist' dream, severely compounded by the sorry state of affairs in the state.

The Indo-Myanmar border town, Moreh has been a significant place for the traders and small time businessmen of Manipur. They are usually self-financed who have to resort to *Moreh-lallonba* (Moreh trader) for a living. Government vehicles with flag and beacon light do frequent the township, including bureaucrat, police and army officers (mostly with family), school and college students for 'educational tours' and 'shopping.' The local traders are there since the 1960s and are more used to illegal cross border trading. It was on 12th April, 1995, the Indo-Myanmar cross border trade was formally opened by the then Union Minister of Commerce. P. Chidambaram and his Myanmar counterpart, Minister for trade Lt. Gen. Tun kyi. Full swing trade has not taken off owing to discrepancies of cross border knowledge for trade among the traders, insufficient infrastructural facilities, and non-formalization of currency exchange rate. Myanmar military government decides the currency rates (Singh 2000).

Major trade thrives on the borders of Myanmar and Thailand on its eastern border and Myanmar and China on its Northern border. It accounts for approximate one billion US dollar because of complete deregulation of the area and permitting for trans-border exchange of commodities without any customs or banking restrictions. Aggressive economic expansion of China to Southeast Asia countries like Myanmar is perceived as a threat in terms of flooding Indian market with cheap Chinese goods. China is the biggest economy in Asia after Japan in constant dollars and largest in purchasing power parity, and the largest recipient of FDI (Rajan 2003). India made goods fail to catch the fancy of the consumers as China has been making significant inroads into India's backyard through crossborder economic and strategic penetration (Malik 2006). The Moreh markets in Imphal (International market) are usually flooded with cheap China made goods. Household items, electronic items, synthetic blanket, cosmetics, toiletries, plastic products, cigarettes and medicines are some of the goods. The moot question whether India can compete with China is left to be answered. In this mad 'gold rush', Manipur will remain fretting as mere consumer. One of the objectives of the Indo-Myanmar Border-Trade Agreement is 'to exchange the locally produced commodities by the people living along both sides of the border' (Thomas 2000). Manipur does not produce a single item of goods, which are permitted as per the agreement. Goods produced in the Indian mainland passes through the NH-39. There is half truth in Rajeev Agrawal's interview. Indian businessman can go there and send things is true, it can boost production facilities in the North East is symptomatically ambiguous.

Conclusion

Following its mantra of a free market reforms, it is observed that Look East Policy is an 'Asianist' dream of the Indian state in the volatile global economy. The State of Manipur must undertake the task of engaging itself a reality-check. Global economy transcends the authority of the national state even as it locates itself into national territories and institution (Sassen 2000). The decision making body within the gamut of LEP should be accountable to anyone especially to the people of Manipur. Accountability is the corner stone of democracy (Sarkar 2000). There is no way to give all the people of India a human condition of living both in terms of civil and political freedom and of a reasonable material support for exercising that freedom. Market cannot simply allow settling most of the choices involved (Bagchi 2004). Manipur should be genuinely worried over availability of choices. It is not only about the anxiety of preparedness. It is about the capacity to take risk and manage it. The anxiety generated points to Manipur being left behind stranded on the shore watching the fading image of the ship sinking below the horizon.

REFERENCES

Abraham, Joseph 2002. 'Regionalism in International Trade; Role of WTO'. *Yojana*. Vol. 46, June.

Bagchi, Amiya Kumar 2004. *The Development State in History and in the Twentieth Century*. New Delhi: Regency Publication.

Baruah, Sanjib 2005. 'Gateway to the East, A Symposium on North East India and Look East Policy'. *Seminar No. 550*, Guwahati.

———— 2004. 'Between South and Southeast Asia; North East India and Look East Policy'. *Ceniseas Paper 4*. Guwahati.

Ching, Leo 2000. 'Asianism in the Age of Late Capital'. *Public Culture*, Vol. 12. Winter Gamble, Andrew and Payne, Anthony 1996. *Regionalism and World order.* New York: St. Martin Press.

Giovanni, Arrighi 1994. *The Long Twentieth Century: Money, Power and Origins of Our Time.* New York: Verso.

Fukuyama, Francis 1992. *The End of History and the Last Man.* Penguin Publication.

Government of India. 1997. *Transforming the Northeast: Tackling Backlog in Basic Minimum Services and Infrastructural Needs,* Planning Commission.

———— 2004. *Economic Survey,* New Delhi.

Government of Manipur 2003. *Economic Survey of Manipur.*

The Imphal Free Press. 2006. June 3.

Islam, Iyanatul and Mark Beeson. 2005. 'Neo-liberalism and East Asia: Resisting Washington Consensus'. *The Journal of Development Studies.* Vol. 41, No. 2, February.

Jaffrelot, Chritophe. 2003. 'India's Look East Policy; Asianist Strategy in Perspective'. *India Review.* Vol. 2, No. 2, April.

Khana, Sushil. 2005. *Economic Opportunities or Continuing Stagnation.* <www.india-seminar.com>

Maisnam, Chinglen and Senate Khuraijam. 2006. 'Political Economy of the Neo-liberal Economy Policy and the North East', *International Young Scholars' Seminar*. New Delhi.

Malik, Mohan. 2006. 'China's Strategy of Containing India'. *The Imphal Free Press*. April 23.

Navlakha, Gautam. 2005. 'National Security; To Control Something that is out of Control'. *EPW.* Vol. XL, No. 31, August.

Parasain, G.P. 2000. *Indo-Myanmar Border Trade and its Impact on Development. The per Capita Income of Manipur is Rs. 10,658 is compared to Industrialization and Infrastructural Development of Manipur, Border Trade, North-East India and Neighbouring Countries.* New Delhi: Akansha Publication.

Rajan, Ramkrishen. 2003. *'Emergence of China as an Economic Power; What does it imply for South East Asia?' EPW*, Vol. XXXVIII, No. 26, July.

Robinson, Richard and Hewison Kevin. 2005. 'East Asia and Trails of Neo-liberalism'. *The Journal for Development Studies*. Vol. 41, No. 2, February.

Sarkar, Subhalakshmi. 2000. *Fiscal Aspects: Myth and Reality, Critical Essays on Economic Liberalization*. New Delhi: SFI Publication.

Sarma, Atul. 2005. *North East as Gateway to South East Asia: Big Dream and Home Truths*. Presidential Address, Seventh Annual Conference, NEEA, Itanagar.

Sassan, Saskia. 2000. 'Spatialities and Temporalities of the Global: Elements for a Theorization'. *Public Culture*, Vol. 12, Winter.

Singh, Iboton. 2005. 'Political Economy of Manipur; Transformation within the Mixed Economy Paradigm'. *Eastern Quarterly*, Vol. 3 Issue III, December.

Singh, Rajmani. 2000. *Indo-Myanmar Cross Border Trade: An Overview, Border Trade, North-East India and Neighbouring Countries*. New Delhi: Akansha Publication.

Thomas, C. Jashua. 2000. *Indo-Myanmar Border Trade; An Assessment of the Moreh-Trade Sector, Border Trade, North East India and Neighbouring Countries.* New Delhi: Akansha Publication.

Woods, N. 2003. *US Hegemony and International Organizations*. London: Oxford University Press.

Yenkhom, Jilla. 2005. 'The "Priestly" State: Flyover Development; Politico-Aesthetics, Protest in Manipur'. *Eastern Quarterly*, Vol. 3, Issue II, September.

Yumnam, Amar. 2005. 'Development Intervention in the North East: A Critique'. *Eastern Quarterly.* Vol. 3, Issue III, December.

8

India's Look East Policy and Manipur's Economy: A Critical Scrutiny

HANJABAM ISWORCHANDRA SHARMA

Contemporary Manipur has been experiencing the bitter taste of social and political crises, and to add to the taste, all is not well on the economic front too. Its economy has been invariably labelled neo-colonial, captive, dependent and tertiarised. From essential to luxury items, the State is dependent on imports from outside and its exports remain negligible. It symbolizes an economy which is open from outside but essentially closed from inside (Chongtham 2005: 6). The State is still lagging far behind the country in almost every aspect of development. A cursory glance at some of the key indicators/indices of development speaks volumes of Manipur's pathetic picture *vis-à-vis* development. The per capita income of Manipur in INR 10,658 as compared to India's INR 16,487, a per capita income gap of 41.74 per cent. The incidence of poverty in Manipur is 28.54 per cent in 1999-2000 compared to India's 26.10 per cent. The road density of Manipur is 48.19. kms per 100 sq. km. against all India figures of 100.99 km. per 100 sq. km. (Sangubam 2003: 26). Agriculture is at subsistence level in spite of the introduction of High Yielding Variety (HYV) in the post-Green Revolution period. Large and medium scale industries (LMSI) are virtually non-existent. The essay takes a brief look at the present economic scenario of Manipur, especially the bread and butter sector and its prospects and problems in the wake of India's Look East Policy (LEP), which rigorously thrusts free trade with the Southeast Asian countries.

Manipur's Economy: A Rudderless Economy

Manipur's economy can be characterized as a tertiarised one, an economy that is dependent more on exchange rather than production. The state economy witnessed a scene of structural retrogression with falling primary sector, slow growth of secondary sector and a speedy growth of tertiary sector. The primary sector contributed 32.09 per cent of NSDP in 2002-03 which declined from 37.87 per cent in 1993-94. It employed 49.69 per cent of total workforce in 2001 reflecting a sharp decline from 69.27 per cent in 1991. Agriculture contributed the lion's share with 27.20 per cent in the primary sector. Forestry and logging contributed 1.96 per cent of Net State Domestic Product (NSDP). The forest area in Manipur covers 78 per cent of the total land area and its contribution of mere 1.96 per cent clearly reflects a depleted forest resource in Manipur. Fishery shared 2.93 per cent of NSDP in 2002-03 that is higher as compared to the national share of 1.1 per cent of GDP at current prices in the same period. It reflects a potential for this sector in Manipur. The 0 per cent contribution of mining and quarrying clearly depicts situation of poor mineral resources in the state. Secondary sector registered a slow growth from 15.73 per cent of NSDP in 1993-94 to 16.84 per cent is 2002-03. However, the secondary growth is construction led rather than manufacturing led. Constriction contributed 12.25 per cent of NSDP in 2002-03 whereas manufacturing's contribution was 6.73 per cent in the same year indicating a weak industrial base. Manufacturing is further divided into registered and un-registered. The share of registered group is 0.14 per cent of NSDP in 2002-03 as compared to 6.73 per cent of unregistered group, a clear sign of substantial contribution of informal sector or household industry. The secondary sector, like the primary sector, also registered a fall in the share of workforce from 9.69 per cent in 1991 to 6.54 per cent in 2001, a jobless growth in the secondary sector. The tertiary sector accounts for 51.07 per cent of the total NSDP in 2002-03. But this must not carry us away as important sectors like banking and insurance, transport and communication contribute only 6.40 per cent. The larger share of tertiary sector has come from public administration and other services (health, education, sanitation etc). The lower share of power, transport and communication and banking in the NSDP is a symptom of weak infrastructure of the State. The tertiary sector registered a growth in the share of workforce from 20.34 per cent in 1991 to 43.77 per cent in 2001. However, the structure of the economy has moved along the usual line of falling share of agriculture and rising share of other sectors. The secondary sector growth has been distorted with very little impact on the productive base of the economy and large size of tertiary sector is indicative of an economy largely based on exchange rather than production (Chongtham 2005: III). Industrialization is still a distant dream as traces of sick small scale and industrial units with utterly insignificant capital input and product output are the only visible signs of industrial activities in the State.

Historically, Manipur economy has been an agrarian-based economy and the importance of agriculture has not withered away even as its share in the economy in terms of income and employment has declined in the recent times. Majority of the population in Manipur depend on agriculture and allied activities for their livelihood. Agriculture in the State is confined to only 10.48 per cent of the total geographical area. The percentage of agricultural land in the valley districts and the hill districts is 47 and 53 per cent respectively. Agriculture is so important in the State that estimate of the state domestic product fluctuates sharply from year to year according to the success or failure of crops (Sangubam 2003: 34). Rice, wheat, maize, oil seeds and sugarcane are some of the important crops grown in Manipur. Among these crops, cultivation of paddy is the largest both in the plain and hills, and covers 82 per cent of the total cultivated land area. Out of the total food grain production of 482.72 metric tonnes in 2001-02, rice accounts for 439 metric tonnes (about 83.12%). So, rice is the only main crop grown in Manipur and its production is not satisfactory; they are mainly grown for self-consumption. Introduction of HYV seeds in post Green Revolution phase has significant impact on agricultural production, but the State is far from self-sufficient in food grains. The food grain production in the State always falls short of the requirement of the State and is met through import from mainland India and even from Myanmar also. The food grain shortage was a massive 30 per cent in 2002-03. The plan target of total food grain production in 2005 was 571.5 metric tonnes but it managed to produce only 426.85 metric tonnes. The agricultural productivity in the hills is even worse than the valley owing to institutional, geographical and technological factors.

The practice of jhum and non-availability of High Yielding Variety (HYV) seeds suitable for the hills have failed to catch up with the productivity level of the valley. Land people ratio in the hills is substantially higher than the valley. Yet agriculture in the hills continues to be of low productivity because of the prevailing land ownership system (Elangbam 2005: 162). The deteriorating pattern of land holding in valley owing to the demographic pressure has created a major hurdle in the development of agriculture. Marginal holding are below two hectares. Medium and large holders have virtually disappeared. It leads to capital alienation, low investment in land and commercial hiring of animal and power at high cost (Chongtham 2006: 2). Underutilization of irrigation potential of the State is creating a bottleneck for agricultural development. Irrigation goes down well in paper but in reality it is a different scene altogether. Medium and major irrigation works have created potential amounting to 59,000 hectare whereas the actual utilization is 15,000 to 20,000 hectares or 25 per cent to 35 per cent of the potential. Unfortunately, the problem of irrigation is more of a problem of administration and implementation failure (Yumnam 1999). Underutilization of available irrigation facility along with the lack of proper irrigation leading to under-cultivation of land hamper the practice of multiple and intercropping in Manipur, which can boost agriculture productivity.

Another aspect of the problem in the agrarian sector is that of credit. Almost majority of the cultivating household are in debt. Farmers seldom take loan from the bank for agricultural purpose; they rather resort to local moneylenders and relatives. Investment in land farm is negligible and 90 per cent of borrowing is meant for consumption. Debt reduction, agrarian resurgence and dynamism are necessarily weak (Chongtham 2006: 2). To sum up, land holding pattern, jhum cultivation in the hills; underutilization of irrigation facility and the lack of institutional credit have dragged agriculture into rough weather. And to add fuel to the fire the state government does not have a state agricultural policy document. Historical experience in the world has shown agriculture as the main instrument for development. Similarly in Manipur, agriculture must be the epicenter for development.

Deindustrialisation rather than industrialization has been the industrial scenario in Manipur. The state is nowhere on the industrial map of India. The state remains as an industrially backward state with all the district under the category of "No industry district" by all India standards. Manipur's dream for industrialization came after attaining statehood. It coincided with the 4th Plan, with the establishment of Manipur Spinning Mill Cooperation and Khandsari Sugar Mill in 1973. Prior to the 1972 planning policy for industrial growth, industrialization was managed through specific instructions from the Central Government. The State Industrial Policy of 1982 was the first attempt to collate the perception of state government in matter relating to the industrialization of Manipur. It laid primary emphasis on development of the small scale sector but also gave due attention towards development of large and medium scale industries. The Industrial Policy of 1996 which was framed keeping in view of the Indo-Myanmar Border Trade have also not managed to increase the tempo of industrialization in Manipur as reflected by the sluggish growth and falling role of workforce in the industrial sector in the half decade that follow. It is also clearly reflected in ailing public sector undertakings. The following is the list of some public sector undertakings in Manipur struggling to reach break even (Sangubam 2005:55):

(1) Manipur Industrial Development Corporation
(2) Manipur State Road Transport Corporation
(3) Manipur Spinning Mill Corporation
(4) Manipur Handloom and Handicraft Development Corporation
(5) Manipur Cycle Corporation
(6) Manipur Electric Development Corporation Ltd.
(7) Manipur Tribal Development Corporation Ltd.
(8) Manipur Cement Ltd.
(9) Manipur Agro-Industries Corporation Ltd.
(10) Manipur Chipping Plant.

The persistence of industrial backwardness in Manipur has been blamed on infrastructural bottleneck, viz. lack of proper transport and communication, power shortage, paucity of funds, lack of entrepreneurship and technical skill and more importantly neglect in the Five Year Plans. With the advent of the ideology of privatization and the virtual withdrawal of industrial entrepreneurial support system, Manipur is yet far away from real industrial development (Chongtham 2005:157). The absence of central public sector undertaking in Manipur may be of border effect. Producers avoid locating industries near the border since trade barriers limit the market for goods and the area that supplies input. It is more rational to locate in areas closer to the core of the domestic market. The border effect thus leads producers to locate industries away from international borders (Baruah 2004:16). As the large and medium scale industries are in moribund and fail to give the standing example of efficiency and productivity, industry in Manipur has become synonymous with small scale industries (SSI). SSI too is not in laudable position. The share of Manipuri's SSI to India's total has decline from 0.49 per cent in 1990-91 to 0.28 per cent in 2000-01 and more serious of all is that 48.92 per cent of the total SSI unit were sick in 2000 (Prasain and Singh 2005). In this technological era handloom and handicraft industries still hold importance in the economic and social life of Manipur. Handloom industries employ more than 3 lakh people. But they are facing tough competition from products imported from mainland India and Myanmar. Whether it is LMSI or SSI or handloom industry immediate and proper medication is the need of the hour. Inception and gaining momentum of the LEP has prompted the state to draft its most ambitious industrial policy in 2003, giving thrust to different possible areas. Apprehensions of whether the new industrial policy will meet the same faith of the Industrial Policy, 1996 remain a question which can only be decided by the full operation of LEP.

Modern day economic problems associated with unemployment, regional disparity, power shortage, low productivity, lack of transport and communication infrastructure, corruption, black marketing, poor public health, education and other social services have been endemic in the state. The structure of Manipur's economy in the post-independence period shows incongruities and distortions symptomatic of an economy which has not been properly planned with specific objective and target (Chongtham 2005: III). These acute economic problems aggravate and exacerbate the serious political and social issues in the state.

Indo-Myanmar Trade: A Dress Rehearsal for LEP

Trade between Manipur and Myanmar is not of recent origin. It can be traced to the growth and development of the Manipuri civilization way back in the ancient period. Ever since the growth of the Manipuri kingdom and the Ava (Burmese) kingdom, relationship between the neighbours has witnessed several ups and downs. With the advent of British rule in the subcontinent, nature of the relation between Manipur and Myanmar became a matter of deep concern for the British who always felt threatened by French colonial expansion and influence in Indo-China. In the post British period, legal recognition in trading ties came in 1995 with the formal launching of Indo-Myanmar Border Trade on April 12, 1995. The launching of Indo-Myanmar Border Trade came in the wake of India's economic liberalization and its policy for strengthening economic ties with the neighboring countries. Historical and friendly neighbourhood policy pursued by the then Indian political leadership was also a driving force behind the launching of the Indo-Myanmar Border Trade (Yumnam 1999: 2). It had initially raised high expectations in impoverished Manipur. People in Manipur by and large believed New Delhi's tall claims that Indo-Myanmar Border Trade would eventually boost the industrial sector and generate income and employment in the State. It is pertinent to note that the Manipur Industrial Policy of 1996 was formulated taking into consideration the Indo-Myanmar Border Trade. Manipur saw the legalized border trade as an opportunity for enhancing the general standard of living of its population (Yumnam 2005). However, existing realities tell a different tale. The Indo-Myanmar Border Trade has completed a decade, a decade of meretricious trade.

The Indo-Myanmar trade agreement envisaged that border trade will take place initially through the land custom post at Moreh in Manipur and Champai in Mizoram corresponding to Tamu and Rhi in Myanmar. There are three approved land custom posts in the Indo-Myanmar border, viz. Moreh (Manipur), Champai (Mizoram) and Nampong (Arunachal Pradesh) for trading activities with Myanmar. However, only one customs post at Moreh is operational for conducting border trade. The trading system was opened under the barter mechanism. The traders are permitted to go inside 40 km. on either side of the international border. There are 22 items, which have been identified and disclosed as exchangeable items under the Indo-Myanmar Agreement. Main items of export include wheat, flour, bicycle and its parts, bleaching powder, tea, stainless steel etc. and main items of import include betel nuts, rajma, turmeric, kuth roots, gram, resin, reed brooms etc. (http://www.aseanindia.net/.). A conspicuous feature of the trading items is that none of the Indian export items are produced in Manipur. It largely undermines the development of substantial productive base in the State. In the face of the existing incongruities, a decade of border trade shows declining trend in the official volume of trade. According to official data, goods worth INR 31,70,51,137 were exported when the import volume was INR 15,17,64,137 during 1996-97 but in 2004-05, it dwindled to just INR 5,64,45,050 in export and INR 5,00,81,749 in import (*The Sangai Express*. August 2006). But trade in official items is going on smoothly without interruption. Products ranging from cloths, electronic goods, edible items, detergent and other consumer items imported from Myanmar have flooded the local markets. Though the official volume of trade has declining sharply, there is a growth in the non-official volume of trade with rupee as the medium of exchange. Daily volume of imports to India under this arrangement is approximately to the tune of INR 5 lakh. The commodities include consumer items ranging from clothing to electronic goods. Most of the goods originate from countries like Taiwan, China, Thailand, South Korea and other Southeast Asian countries (Yumnam 1999: 5). The burgeoning imports from Myanmar along with the products from mainland India have significantly crippled the fledging small scale productive units in Manipur. Instead of strengthening the industrial base of Manipur, Indo-Myanmar trade has increased the degree of tertiarization in Manipur. Pervasive presence of products from mainland Indian industries as a sequel to the merger and more recently, products from South East Asian countries in the post-border trade phase have contributed immensely to the thwarting of industrialization initiatives in the State (Elangbam 2005: 165-66).

The logic of trade as an engine of growth has not clicked in Manipur. It has been observed that the small size of market fails to absorb sufficient volumes of output that leads to low induce surplus volume of output thereby leading to incentive in investment. If it was the case in Manipur, the Indo-Myanmar trade might have boosted the productive base. The tottering industrial sector in

Manipur is not the result of their product unable to sell on account of the small market size. It is rather the result of their product being of low quality amidst infrastructural limitations, lack of entrepreneurship and technical skill. Moreover, the pattern of export in Indo-Myanmar trade has also created less incentive for industry in Manipur as most of the export items originate from other states. Most of the proposed projects for Indo-Myanmar trade still remain in paper. The state government's proposal to the North East Council for assistance in setting up an EPZ has not received favourable response. Total cost of EPZ is estimated at INR 100 crores (www.mastec.nic.in). On the other hand, infrastructural facility for the smooth functioning of Indo-Myanmar Border Trade seems to have been showered on the side of the border. In a highly publicized event in 2001, the then Indian External Affairs Minister, Jaswant Singh inaugurated the 160 km. Tamu-Kalemu-Kalemyo road in Myanmar. The INR 90 crore road built by India's Border Road Organization was India's gift to Myanmar. In his inaugural speech, Singh said that the natural movement of goods, people and services for the North East is not through Calcutta as he foregrounded the importance of opening up the natural outlet of the North East (*Assam Tribune*, 2001, cited in Baruah 2004: 22). India has also offered 10 million line of credit to Myanmar as a gesture of goodwill and to promote bilateral trade and economic cooperation (*The Hindu*, November 8, 1997).

The existing road between Imphal and Moreh is too narrow. It causes hindrance for the movement from Imphal to Moreh. Even as the trade route directly passes through Chandel District, people are yet to get any kind of advantage or benefit from the Indo-Myanmar trade. Most of the people in the district are still dependent on traditional jhum cultivation or charcoal trade for their livelihood (*The Sangai Express,* August 1, 2006). Myanmar has an upper hand in the Indo-Myanmar trade. The Myanmar authorities have constructed a modern market at Namphalong as compared to the shady and muddy one at Moreh on the Indian side. In other words, the Myanmar side is evolving with the market logic while the Indian side is trailing behind (Yumnam 1999: 6). The Indo-Myanmar border trade has become a haven for drug trafficking and black marketing, with reports of Indian security forces joining the bandwagon. The Indo-Myanmar border which was for some years used as a route for heroin smuggling from Myanmar to the outside world has been transformed to a route of Ephedrine Hydrochloride smuggling. Ephedrine is used in making Amphetamine tablets, a drug being used as a substitute of heroin by many drug addicts. According to local sources, some merchants in the Indo-Myanmar border trade who have turned into this narcotic trade estimate that at least 22 kg. of Ephedrine is being smuggled from India into Burma everyday (MIZZIMA News Group, February 12, 1999). One of the most significant items exchanged through the Manipur-Myanmar border is narcotics. Most surprisingly, it has been reported that many defence personnel including BSF of India in the Manipur-Myanmar border were involved in the informal trade in narcotics (Baruh 2000: 57). There is an element of truth and logic when people doubt the involvement of the security personnel in contraband trade. The contraband trade is estimated to be of about INR 250 crores annually (Yumnam 1999: 6). Indo-Myanmar trade has failed to live up to the expectation of the people and needs a post-mortem. The Indo-Myanmar trade which can be regarded as a dress rehearsal for the much awaited LEP, i.e India's free trade with South East Asian countries through Manipur, has turn out to be a failure. This has raised doubts about LEP whether LEP will give the same result as that of Indo-Myanmar Trade. The failure of Indo-Myanmar Border Trade has serious implications on the implementation and operation of LEP.

LEP: Boon or Doom

Initiated by the late P.V. Narasimha Rao in 1991, 'Look East Policy' has gained momentum recently. India's eastward campaign is driven by the vision of an Asian Economic Community (*India Today*, July 4, 2005). A new dimension was added by the first Indo-ASEAN car rally which coincided with the third Indo-ASEAN Summit held in Vientiane, Laos. The rally flagged off by Indian Prime Minister Manmohan Singh at Guwahati in November 22, 2004 (passing through Manipur on November 24, 2004) streamlined India's strengthening bonds with the ASEAN countries. It was a great event as it promoted reestablishment and opening of a land route from India to the ASEAN countries that would promote connectivity enhancing side-by-side, opportunities for trade, investment, tourism and people to people link between India and ASEAN (Kumar 2005). The LEP has created euphoria especially among the people of Manipur.

The inward looking policy of India had developed a strong sense of negligence and isolation amongst the people of Manipur. General perception holds LEP as an instrument of bringing closer ties with mainland India by breaking the physical barriers. Through this policy the people of Manipur expect some benefits from the developing economies of Southeast Asian nations in terms of tourism, inflow of foreign investment, essential commodities at low prices. Mainstream Indian media projects the LEP as the panacea for all socio-economic problems in Manipur. However, the ultimate apprehension is whether it will be a boon or doom for the State's fragile economy.

From India's point of view, the policy is a single-shot multi-target approach. Through the introduction of railways and inclusion of Manipur in the Trans Asian Highway map, the Indian government is trying to show that it is concerned with the development of the region and therefore, Manipur will remain no longer be neglected. There is no clarity about how India is going to utilize Manipur in the LEP. From the international experiences, Manipur fits into LEP in three ways—(a) Land bridge (b) Trade post, and (c) Export hub. In the first case, if Manipur can serve as a land bridge between India and Southeast Asian countries, the state will be reduced to the role of a passive spectator. In the second case Manipur can be utilized as a trade post for India and Southeast Asia in which the goods to be traded are piled up in Manipur. But the possibility of Manipur being a trade post is very low as India's trade with Southeast Asian nations is still largely a maritime one along with the virtual absence of adequate infrastructure in Manipur. The third option has Manipur being utilized as an export hub; this is precisely what people in general expect in the State. This option entails setting up of EPZs and SEZs for the processing of exportable goods. However, in the face of infrastructural inadequacies, the option of being an export hub is very thin. Assam is a strong contender for this option among the Northeastern states as a result of its resources, infrastructure and experience in international trade as a major exporter of tea. It is logical to expect that Assam will be in a position to derive maximum benefits from the new trade regime because of her strategic location and relatively better infrastructural facilities compared to other states in the region (Baruah 2000).

Manipur's chance of deriving benefits from LEP is extremely limited even if the State is transformed into an export hub. Setting up of SEZs and EPZs will be accompanied by export and import banks. However, the export sector will not be able to produce the carry-over effect. In other words, it will not be possible for the export sector's positive effect to generate the desirable activities in other sectors due to prevailing economic conditions in the State—low industrial base, low road density, power shortage, ill equipped transport and communication, isolated markets and lack of entrepreneurship and technical skill. Even with a strong stimulus from export, transmission of growth from the export base to the rest of the economy will still be contingent upon other conditions in the economy (Meier 1973). Power shortage is acute in Manipur. In spite of claims by the government of 97.70 per cent of the villages in the State being electrified, reality is otherwise. There has been a pervasive shortfall in the supply of power with the inability of the government to meet the demand even as a large number of hydroelectric projects are envisaged in the New Industrial Policy, 2003. Notable projects awaiting implementation are Tipaimukh Hydro Electric (HE) (Multipurpose) Project, Loktak Downstream HE Project and the Irang HE Project. The experiences of Loktak HE Project have been a sore point with the people as all the promises made by the project turned false. With large scale displacement of human and animal population, submergence of immense tracts of arable land and land under cultivation have made the people acutely conscious of the harmful effects of such mega power projects in Manipur. Consequently, it has dragged the Tipaimukh Project into troubled water. Power problems are not of recent origin. But sudden emphasis on power projects on the eve of LEP has raised doubts in the minds of the people at large. Whether power generated through these projects are meant for domestic and industrial use or for the Trans Asian Highway is a serious question.

Transport and communication can be a deciding factor in spreading the positive effect from the export sector. Introduction of mobile telecom services in the State is not the end of the story. International experience tells us that telecommunication and electricity facilities subsequently follow the route of road transport. After the operation of India's trade with Southeast Asia through Manipur the national highway will definitely undergo certain change. But the concern is over inter-district connectivity and hill-valley connectivity. As mentioned earlier, road density in Manipur is very low compared to the all India average. Leaving aside the horrible condition of the roads, density is 1000 km. per 1000 sq. km. in the valley. Road density in the hills is even worse. In the hill districts road density ranges from 90 km to 220 km. Existing road systems also suffer from other deficiencies like poor geometry, narrow and weak bridge, insufficient cross drainage etc. At present even sub-divisional headquarters and other administrative centres are not adequately connected. There are a number of villages, which have no roads or are connected. A miniscule number of villages are connected by only fair weather roads (Sangubam 2003: 27). These are some of the major issues which will impede the positive effect from the export sector. Other issues include general ignorance about international trade as it will be the first major experience with international trade.

The State is not self sufficient in most of the essential items and LEP means the inevitability of international trade. It will be interesting to see how the State copes with the policy. Possibility of deriving benefits from the policy is bleak. In view of the implementation of the policy, the state government has announced a plethora of projects in the New Industrial Policy 2003 including projects on export. However, various projects in the past along with the Indo-Myanmar Border Trade raise question marks over the viability and feasibility of these projects. Two important areas *vis-à-vis* are agro-based industries and tourism. These are the areas where the State can have maximum benefit with minimum cost. Agro-based industries must be paid high priority among the existing industries in view of the availability and quality of the raw material. More importantly, agro-based industries unlike other industries such as chemical, pharmaceutical, engineering and consumer goods industries require less technical inputs and heavy infrastructural investment. Manipur has immense potential to attract tourists owing to its natural scenic beauty, glorious cultural heritage, mosaic of tribal and non-tribal cultures, bio-diversity, pleasant climate and pollution free environment. The government both at the centre and the state need to evolve a completely different orientation from the prevailing one in order to make tourism an industry. It is high time to initiate the measures to harness the potential.

India is already an active participant in the ASEAN +4 (China, Japan, Korea and India) and BIMST-EC. It has signed FTAs with Thailand in 2003 and the Comprehensive Economic Cooperation Agreement (CECA) with Singapore in 2005. Operationalization of

India's trade with Southeast Asia through Manipur is not far away. Time is running out for Manipur. A Strong and vibrant economy in the State for effective and meaningful participation in LEP in a short period of time will be a mammoth task. In the face of existing realities and the pace of development or rather underdevelopment that characterizes Manipur's economy it will be eventually be a tale of despair. The powerful market forces of globalization will crush the State. Manipur has been a market for mainland India and LEP will further reduce it to a market for the developing economies of Southeast Asia. Haphazard urbanization, consumerism, drug and human trafficking, ecological and environmental degeneration are the likely outcomes of LEP in Manipur. There is every possibility of our indigenous populace and culture being negatively impacted by LEP. India's hunger for strategic influence in Southeast Asia may end up with Manipur being reduced to the sacrificial lamb at the altar.

Table 8.1: Distribution ofWorkForce in Manipur by Occupational Sector Per Cent

Census year	*Primary sector*	*Secondary sector*	*Tertiary sector*
1961	66.26	23.05	10.69
1971	71.27	14.53	14.20
1981	68.59	9.68	21.73
1991	69.97	9.69	20.34
2001	49.69	6.54	43.77

Source: Census Report 2001.

Table 8.2: Percentage Distribution of Net State Domestic Product of Manipur by Industry of Origin at Current Prices

S. No.	*Industry of Origin*	*1993–94*	*1994-95*	*1995-96*	*1996-97*	*1997-98*	*1998-99*	*1999-2000*	*2000-01*	*2001-02*	*2002-03*
1.	Agriculture Livestock	31.19	30.06	31.13	32.06	31.18	29.6	27.78	29.81	26.92	27.2
2.	Forestry and Logging	3.54	3.31	2.54	2.12	4.55	4.56	2.08	2.22	1.98	1.96
3.	Fishing	14	3.38	3.12	2.67	2.55	2.53	2.49	3.03	2.84	2.93
4.	Mining and Quarrying	0	0	0	0	0	0	0	0	0	0
	Sub-Total: Primary (1 - 4)	**48.73**	**36.75**	**36.79**	**36.85**	**38.28**	**36.69**	**32.35**	**35.06**	**31.74**	**32.09**
5.	Manufacturing	7.39	7.38	7.30	6.96	6.51	6.74	6.90	6.12	6.70	6.73
	5.1 Registered	0.19	0.23	0.28	0.36	0.16	0.11	0.05	0.07	0.09	0.14
	5.2 Un-registered	7.20	7.15	7.02	6.60	6.35	6.63	6.85	6.05	6.61	6.59
6.	Construction	7.31	8.12	9.87	11.13	10.88	9.66	11.24	7.63	10.27	12.25
7.	Electricity, gas and water supply	1.03	0.08	-0.94	-1.49	-1.59	0.35	0.97	0.9	0.09	2.14
	Sub-Total Secondary (5-7)	**15.73**	**15.58**	**16.23**	**16.60**	**15.80**	**16.75**	**19.11**	**14.65**	**17.06**	**21.12**
8.	Transport, Storage and Communication	3.43	3.56	3.29	3.22	3.13	3.27	3.08	3.63	3.75	4.24
9.	Trade, Hotels and Restaurants	12.18	12.54	11.76	11.07	11.37	13.04	10.29	10.70	12.84	13.15
10.	Banking and Insurance	1.67	1.31	1.39	1.59	1.42	1.38	1.29	1.41	1.86	2.16
11.	Real estate, ownership of dwelling, business services	3.35	3.56	3.30	2.90	2.91	3.18	2.64	2.94	2.86	2.99
12.	Public administration	13.64	14.57	14.91	15.17	14.61	13.86	16.96	16.44	16.57	15.07
13.	Other Services	11.90	12.18	12.34	12.60	12.48	11.77	14.29	15.17	13.32	13.46
	Sub-Total: Tertiary (8-13)	**46.40**	**47.72**	**46.98**	**46.55**	**45.92**	**46.50**	**48.55**	**50.29**	**51.20**	**51.07**
	Total Net State Domestic Product	**100**	**100**	**100**	**100**	**100**	**100**	**100**	**100**	**100**	**100**

Source: Statistical Abstracet of Manipur, 2006.

REFERENCES

Baruah, Sanjib. 2004. *Between South and South East Asia: North East India and the Look East Policy. CENISEAS*. Guwahati.

Baruah, Srinath. 2000. 'Certain Observation on Informal Border Trade with Neighbouring Countries and Economic Prospect of the North East Region' in Gurudas Das (ed.) *Border Trade North East India and Neighbouring Countries.* New Delhi: Akansha Publication House.

Bilateral Trade: 'Indo Myanmar Bilateral Trade' <www.aseanindia.out/asean/country/profile/myanmar.trade.policy.htm>

Chongtham, Prioranjan. 2005. *Agrarian Structure and Production Relation in Manipur,* Unpublished Ph.D. Thesis, Imphal: Manipur University.

————. 2006. 'Agricultural Development in Manipur'. *Working Paper Vision 2020*. February 16-17. Imphal: Manipur University.

Singh, Iboton. 2005. 'Manipur's Economy: Historical Roots and Structural Evolution'. *Eastern Quarterly*. Vol. 3, Issue III. October-December, New Delhi.

Elangbam, Bijoykumar. 2005. 'Development Discourse in Manipur: Hills *Vs* Valley', *Eastern Quarterly*. Vol. 3, Issue III. October-December, New Delhi.

Statistical Abstract of Manipur. 2001. Government of Manipur. Directorate of Economics and Statistics. Imphal.

————. 2004. Government of Manipur. Directorate of Economics and Statistics. Imphal.

————. 2005. Government of Manipur. Directorate of Economics and Statistics. Imphal.

Memorandum to 12th Finance Commission. 2004. Finance Department. May, Government of Manipur.

Draft Annual Plan. 2006-07. Government of Manipur.

India Today. 2005. 'Manipur: Gateway to the South East Asia'. July 4.

'Indo Myanmar Border Trade Promotion' <http://mastec.nic.in/indomyanmar.html>

Kumar, Akshay. 2005. 'UPA'S Economic Diplomacy'. *Employment News*. June 11-7. New Delhi.

Manipur Industrial Policy. 1996. 'North East India Databank' <http://nerdatabank.nic.in/mnid>

Meir, Gerald. 1973. *Leading Issues in Economic Development*. Oxford: Oxford University Press.

MIZZIMA News Group. 1999. February 12. <http://www.mizzina.com/mizzina-workers/research/1999/inden3.html>

Prasain, G.P. and Kh. Tomba Singh. 2005. 'Sickness in Small Scale Industries in Manipur', *NURJ*, Vol. 3. September. pp. 109-18.

Sangubam, Brajamani. 2003. *Economic Growth in Manipur and Empirical Analysis*, Imphal.

Taxmann. 2005. *The Economic Survey 2004-05*. New Delhi: Taxmann Publication.

The Hindu. November 8. 1997. <http://www.mizima.com/mizima-workers/research/1999/index3html>

The Sangai Express. 2006. August. Imphal.

Yumnam, Amar. 1999. 'Indo-Myanmar Trade through Moreh: Time to Show Time to Reap'. Seminar on Transborder Trade in North East India. July 28. Guwahati: OKD Institute of Social Change and Development.

———. 1999. 'Socio-Economic Profile of Manipur'. *Economy of Manipur Series* No. 7, September. Department of Economics. Imphal: Manipur University.

———. 2005. 'Indo-Myanmar Trade through Moreh: Status and Assessment', in Gurudas Das (ed.). *Indo-Myanmar Border Trade: Status, Problems and Potential*. New Delhi: Akansha Publishing House.

9

Understanding Underdevelopment: A Contextual Reading of India's Look East Policy and Manipur

THINGNAM KISHAN SINGH

I

Nothing exists outside history. Taking cue from the dialectics of the historicizing operation that subsequently converges into a common focal point even after following two distinct paths—the path of the object and the path of the subject. An attempt to comprehend the existing politico-economic landscape of Manipur can assume theoretical standpoints where the historical origins itself appear primary or the more intangible historicity of the concepts and categories by which efforts to understand those thing appear fundamental. Manipur's political economy both as the object of study as well as the subject of study necessarily finds itself entangled in the discursive rims of historical co-ordinates that are becoming ever more readily persisting pre-capitalist economic features. Corollary to this development stands the process of the underdevelopment of its capitalist potential. The essay tangentially attempts to argue the conjunctive and complementary role expected to be played by India's Look East Policy in furthering the process of underdevelopment of Manipur's economy.

Scrutinizing the changes that took place in Manipur's economic structure during the British colonial period, it can be seen that these changes were contingent not only upon the impersonal forces of the world capitalist market, but also upon the policies pursued by the colonial power itself. The state in its colonial framework hardly reflected the aspirations of the Manipur people—even in the vaguest manner—as it was not a representative organ of the people, but rather of a foreign colonial power in spite of its collaboration with the monarchy in its efforts to appropriate the wealth of the land. As seen elsewhere in other colonies, the state thereby functioned as a dictatorial power devoid of the people's welfare. It can be argued that the state acted on behalf of the metropolitan bourgeoisie in so far as the interests of the expatriate businessman who had dealings with each individual colony. Instances can be seen in the persistent attempts made by the colonial power to develop and boost trade and commerce between Manipur and British India. Further policies pursued to serve the interests of the bourgeoisie witnessed the subsequent growth of a trading class in Manipur comprising mainly of Marwaris from British India.

The exact character of the takeover of Manipur as a British dependency in the late 19th and early 20th century was a result of the role which it had begun to play in the geo-strategy matrix vis-à-vis French expansionism in Indo-China and the sub-continental economic system during the period of British imperialism. It is pertinent to note that Ahom had already contributed substantially to colonial economic interests through its oil, tea and timber. Crucial to this integration within the imperialist economic system is our understanding of the proliferation and growth of peripheral capitalism, which is distinguished by its reliance on the import-export sector, to the detriment of the development of the internal economy. Manipur's transition from self-sufficiency in pre-capitalist modes of production-evident in the pre-colonial period as an importer of consumer commodities in exchange for the export of raw materials that constituted mainly of forest and agricultural produce. At each stage, Manipur and its people were increasingly drawn into the import-export economy and Manipur's existence became more and more dependent on its ties with the British colonial economy sprawling over the entire length and breath of the vast Indian sub-continent.

Peripheral capitalism, in a colonial economy, is characterized by a high degree of integration into the world capitalist market, but a low degree of development of the capitalist mode of production internally. The economy is not 'auto centric', the internal market is underdeveloped while external dependence is aggravated (Amin 1974). Production inside the peripheral social formation is for profit, but this profit is obtained through international trade, not through the creation of surplus value consequent upon the exploitation of labour-power in capital production. Producers are not alienated from their means of production; they can continue to own their own tools, as in the case of Manipur, their land. Capitalist social relations develop in a haphazard manner; these are incompletely formed, although new social classes begin to emerge as producers get increasingly polarized and differentiate into rich and poor, and as groups of brokers and traders emerge to compliment the activities of the metropolitan bourgeoisie. A crucial factor of pre-colonial self-sufficiency through household and cottage based production (Ali 1988: 93) found rapid erosion in the post 1891 period as British political agents rigorously propelled trade and commerce with heavy imports from British India into Manipur (Mackenzie 1884).

II

The post-British phase failed to witness any significant or substantial change in terms of economic development as Manipur's economy still remain appended to the larger framework of India's planning and development which ironically remained metropolitan centric. Along with other states of the North East, Manipur represented the classic case of a frontier, which needed to be defended militarily rather than being allowed to pursue the path of development (Konthoujam 2006: 47). Centralized Indian planning through its Five Year Plans concentrated development and economic advancement in certain metropolitan zones and left the North East outside its development frame. As a part of 'independent' India since 1949, Manipur's tryst with development was conspicuously shadowed by the overarching logic of underdevelopment. Categorized as a part C state with administration in the hands of the Central Government in New Delhi, the persisting legacy of a peripheral economy operated full swing in the face of increasing 'security' concerns *vis-à-vis* its status as a border territory. The political economy of India's development on the capitalist path of development found a corollary in the underdevelopment of Manipur and the North East region (Ahmad and Biswas 2005). British colonial legacy of associating the North East as a militarily secured frontier zone was perpetuated on grounds of 'national security'. With the 'security' phobia exercising a pervasively pernicious grip in the mainstream Indian mindset, the policy makers and political leadership in mainland India remained oblivious of the need for development in Manipur and North East. Evidence can be lucidly drawn from the meagre amount of outlays for the initial Five Year Plans when Manipur was a centrally administered Union territory. A comparative study of the first four Five Year Plan of Manipur with the overall plan outlays of India during this period reveals the insidious logic of underdevelopment and peripheralization of Manipur's economy. Fixed at INR 154.89 lakh (1956-61), INR 625.11 lakhs (1961-66) and 0.06 per cent (1951-56) of the all India figure, a further twist in the story was the inability of Manipur under central administration to spend even these meagre outlays. It is pertinent to note that Manipur as Union territory under the Central Government's administration actually experienced shortfall in expenditure during these initial plan periods. Such deliberate acts of marginalization provide ample evidence of the persistence of the logic of underdevelopment in Manipur.

India's capitalist logic of development—evident in its indicative planning and mixed economy with deficit financing of the private sector by the state naturally concentrated and confined development in certain pockets. It has been widely argued that the Indian state failed to discard the legacy of colonial development—the capitalist mode of production—in 'decolonized' India as a result of the interplay of the alliance between Western metropolitan capital and the indigenous capitalist class had already made significant inroads in the colonial economy during British rule. After British departure, the state becomes instrumental in propelling capitalist development by evolving complex strategies for achieving growth of capitalism in India (Bhambri 1988: 6). Mobilization of large resources for investment and the resultant high capital-output ratio reveals the logic of capitalist contradictions. Capital driven development was concentrated in certain specific locations in mainland India while the North East as a region continued to real under the pernicious grip of underdevelopment. Manipur and the North East remained firmly entrenched in the Indian imagination as the peripheral frontier aloof from the development sphere of the Indian state (Konthoujam 2006: 47).

Primarily an agrarian economy with a primitive agricultural infrastructure, Manipur's status as a surplus producer of rice during British colonial period has witnessed rapid decline in the post British phase. It has turned into an importer of rice (Chongtham 2005: 158). Agriculture continues to play a dominant role in the state's economy in spite of the increasing food grain imports indicating the serious nature of its economic crisis. Even as agriculture continues to employ economy the maximum workforce, and contributes substantially to the Net State Domestic Product (NSDP) increasing food grain imports from outside undermine its importance. On the other hand, declining contribution of agriculture to the NSDP does not represent a concomitant increase in the secondary sector, as industrialization is still a distant dream. Tertiarization of Manipur's underdeveloped economy has taken place rapidly with massive increase in government jobs. This is in marked contrast with the all India trend where growth in the tertiary sector came from trade, hospitality industries including hotels, catering services and tourism, banking and insurance, real estate and consumer related services. A cursory glance at the per capita income, one of the traditional indices of development reveals the precarious condition of the state's economy. Against the all India figures, Manipur continues to lag far behind with insignificant annual growth rates.

A disturbing feature in Manipur is the virtual absence of industrial and economic infrastructure even after five decades of Indian economic planning. Sheer absence of infrastructural development serves as the logical framework of the state's existence as peripheral economy. Infrastructure in Manipur is dismal at a figure of 75.37 as against the all India average of 100. The 11th Finance Commission Report shows Manipur at the bottom of social and economic infrastructure with other states of the region and Jammu and Kashmir. A comparison with states like Kerala, Karnataka and Maharastra reveals the sorry state of affairs in Manipur. One look at the power sector—a basic requirement for all development activities—in Manipur indicates the utter incapability to meet even demands for domestic consumption. Even as the state has not witnessed the birth of a single large-scale industrial unit, power supply for domestic consumption and small-scale units has always been marked by acute shortfalls. The Electric Power Survey of Indian reports that the demands of power in Manipur always remain unmet. As per the Annual Administrative Report 2001-02 the annual demand for power in the state was 156 MW in 2001-02 while the demand met was just 93 revealing a shortfall of 63 MW. Manipur still relies heavily on power imports from neighbouring states to meet the domestic demand. In 1998-99 it had to purchase 1,74,076 MW Hydel power from Loktak Hydro Electric Project, a National Hydel Power Corporation project (NHPC) based in Manipur and largely responsible for large scale environmental and ecological disaster and massive human displacement, 1,03,874 MW from Kopili Hydro Electric Project (KHEP), 31,326 MW from Agartala Gas Turbine Power Project (AGTPP), 1,08,785 MW from Assam Gas Base Power Project (AGBPP) and 28,534 MW from Meghalaya State Electricity Board (M-ESEB). With this dismal performance, development activities in the state naturally get crippled. Such dismal scenes where demands for domestic power consumption cannot be fulfilled logically entail the failure of the even the marginal small-scale units in the state. These units have largely been the result of persistent entrepreneurial drives in the state. Present condition of these small-scale units speaks volumes for the nature of industrial backwardness as the average employment per unit of manufacturing enterprises is around five only during the period 1987-88 to 2002-03. Direct production declined between 1987-88 and 1991-92 from INR 1.62 lakh to INR 1.37 lakh in 2002-03 there was marginal increase with the figure standing at INR 1.71 lakh. Classified as the only visible category of industrialization in the state, there are just 108 manufacturing units as recorded in 2002-03. The pace of development in this sector is hardly worth being seriously considered as a viable economic force.

Steeped in traditional mode of production, Manipur's economy is still marked by the dominance of cottage based or household industry that basically caters to the immediate needs of the people. Competition with cheap consumer goods manufactured outside remains a distant dream, as the mode of production in the state is still primitive. Handloom and handicrafts feature as the mainstay of production in Manipur. A traditional cottage industry base on household labour where members of the family are collectively involved in the production process, handloom is dubbed the largest cottage industry in the state. Handloom weavers are categorized as self-employed artisans who carry on this profession in their own homes. In spite of Manipur possessing 2.7 lakh looms comprising of fly shuttle, throw shuttle and lion looms with a weave population of more than 2.8 lakhs, the primitive and non-mechanised nature of production make it unworthy of competition with the massive influx of cheap machine made products from mainland Indian Industries. Nothing substantial has come out of the slipshod measures adopted in line with the recommendations made by the High Power Committee (HPC) during the Ninth Five Year Plan period. Provisions for welfare measures and better working condition to handloom weavers in form of various packages have failed to transform the sector as theses measures are largely of a haphazard nature the never really moves towards structural transformations. Equally pernicious is the large scale appropriation of unique and traditional Manipuri designs used by indigenous weavers over the centuries—*Ningthou Phee*, *Lanthan Khulak, Khame-Chatpa, Ahamilnmi, Moirangphee, Lashingphee, Leiroom, Heijamayek, Tindongbi, Leirong* and *Akoibi* designs among others. Rooted in the historical development of the Manipuri civilization, each of these designs carries symbolic connotations of its culture and experience. Widespread appropriation and abuse of these designs through machine made clothing from mainland Indian Industries present a potent threat to the indigenous weavers who are in no position to compete with the massive influx of factory products. Another area of concern in the handloom sector is that of dyeing of fast colour on various kinds of cloths using indigenous plants, leaves, flowers and barks. Manipuri art of dying has remained an important hallmark in the history of the land and its people. With massive dumping of cheap cloth from mainland India mills and factories, the indigenous art of dying is rapidly moving into the margins. At present, Manipur can hardly speak of its indigenous art of dying without taking notice of the dwindling number of people who are actually involved in this work.

A similar picture can be seen in the handicraft sector too. Once the pride of Manipur and the envy of the neighbouring kingdoms of Ahom, Tripura and Ava (Burma), praised and admired by the British colonizers, Manipuri handicrafts in the post British era represents a woeful saga of incessant and acute deprivation. In spite of abundant resources—material and human—handicraft is increasingly finding it difficult to sustain the level of production. Experts have identified over fifteen species of bamboo in Manipur alone out of one hundred and thirty species bamboo found in India.

Five varieties of cane are also found in the state. As per the Directorate of Commerce and Industries, Manipur, important items in the bamboo and cane product range include the following:

1. Baskets like items for packaging, measuring, storing, carrying goods, washing and fishing etc.
2. Mat like items for ceiling, partition, fencing etc.
3. Fishing traps/tools
4. Furniture like table, chairs, sofa set, stools etc.
5. Walking stick
6. Umbrella handles
7. Trays
8. Decorative pieces like table lamps, wall hangings, ashtrays, flower pots, vast, etc.
9. Caps/Hats.
10. Ply board (Bamboo laminated)
11. Tooth pick/Incense sticks
12. Musical instruments like flutes
13. Suit case
14. House construction Material.

With an estimate of 1.50 lakh people engage as artisans in the handicraft sector, Manipur's potential has never been unleashed or harnessed effectively. Locally known as *kouna*, a weed of the phragmities genus artisans in the state have used it with tremendous dexterity to product some of the most sought after mats and mattress of different sizes. Abundance of this reed is the basis for its increasing level of production. It has become an important item in the handicraft sector with heavy demand from foreign countries like the United Kingdom, Netherlands, Germany, France, United Arab Emirates and Switzerland, Latin American countries are also showing keen interest in *Kouna* products. Recently, the State Government (Directorate of Commerce and Industries, Manipur) has made plans to set up ten units for *Kouna* production after identifying suitable areas:

I. Imphal West District

1. Konjeng Leikai

2. Mayang Imphal Bengun

II. Imphal East District

1. Kongba Nandeibam Leikai
2. Khongman

III. Bishnupur District

1. Moirang
2. Keinou
3. Phubala

IV. Thoubal District

1. Khangabok
2. Shikong
3. Chairen (East)

It remains to be seen whether the potential of this handicraft item can be fully exploited to boost the state's sagging economy. Modernization of handicraft sector has been a predominant demand in the state. The nature of the existing economy and production in the state is far removed from signs of modern industries.

III

In the backdrop of this prevailing scenario of acute underdevelopment and absence of infrastructural base necessary for production, the logic of the Look East Policy and its impact on Manipur needs detailed studies. A dramatic shift can be seen in terms of the prevailing global economic trends. Political environment, geo-strategic need and internal security concerns. Formulated during the tenure of Narasimha Rao's Prime Ministership, the policy is responsible for a series of political and military interface between India and Vietnam, Cambodia, Indonesia, Thailand and Myanmar besides the increasing trade and economic ties with ASEAN. Ventures like the BIMSTEC (Bangladesh, India, Myanmar, Sri Lanka, Thailand Economic Corporation) and Mekong Ganga Project signal a move towards increasing economic cooperation. The BIMSTEC has recently been expanded to include Bhutan and Nepal. Free trade between the countries of the Bay of Bangal grouping and Southeast ASEAN countries figure prominently in India's Look East Policy. Facilitation of these projects entails the sponsorship of the World Bank as plans for the 1360 kilometre Trans Asian Highway to link India, Myanmar and Thailand in the first phase and with Indo-China in the second phase is on the card. In due course of time, the Trans Asian Highway will become part of a much larger Trans Eurasian Highway linking South Asia, Southeast Asia, China and Europe.

Serious rethinking is needed as far as the implications of the Look East Policy in underdeveloped Manipur are concerned. Traditional household or cottage based industries and marginal small-scale units mark the nature of production in the state. Virtual absence of substantial economic and industrial infrastructure makes the fragile economy susceptible to hazardous pressures from outside. Both the governments at the Centre and the State have not done anything in terms of formulating a concrete policy to initiate substantial production in Manipur, which aims at self-reliance and self-sustenance. It has been seen elsewhere that respective state governments in India do everything they can to protect their own industries and producing units. The battle between the West Bengal Government and Anand Cooperative Ltd. of Gujarat over dairy products and sale in West Bengal is a glaring example. Manipur has not witnessed any policy that aim to promote and protect its production units. The state is virtually a big market for products coming from mainland India.

A contextual critique of the Look East Policy underscores the serious threat it poses to Manipur's underdeveloped economy. As discussed elsewhere, globalization propelled moves have proved detrimental to the growth and development of the North East region as a whole (Maiti 2002: 50) (Ahmad and Biswas 2004). Reading of these issues *vis-à-vis* the peripheral economy status of Manipur and the North East logically underscores the presence of interests detrimental to the growth and development of the region (Maiti 2002: 50). In the virtual absence of industrial infrastructure and any significant large-scale industries in the state, it will not be in its interest to open up to the outside world merely in terms of physical connectivity. Such an opening basically implies the opening up of the region as potential market of consumer goods produced elsewhere. In spite of the fact that virtual absence of significant industrial and production units in the region makes it dependent in terms of consumer goods from outside, the traditional life-style of a largely rural set up makes it possible for the household industries to service. Cottage industries handloom and handicrafts constitute the mainstay of the economy of the state and region both in terms of its export value and internal market value. Opening up of the state and the region without a complimentary transformation of its industrial base would naturally entail the destruction of these small scale units (Ganguly 2002: 58). At this juncture, it is pertinent to not that there has been no significant move on the part of the policy makers in New Delhi to develop economic and industrial infrastructure in the region. Mere opening up in terms of providing accessibility to the region therefore entails the risk of destroying the fragile household industries in the region. It will only tend to serve the interest of the global capitalist market where trans-national corporations visualize even the most underdeveloped regions as potential markets for the consumer goods produced elsewhere. Accessibility and connectivity can problematic in the absence of industrialization. Ecological and environmental problems are logical corollaries of such haphazard urbanization.

The logic of trade as an engine of growth and development needs careful rethinking *vis-à-vis* Manipur's underdevelopment and its existence as a peripheral economy. Whether the state can become a really substantial partner in the development prospect envisaged by the LEP still remains to be answered. Analyses have raised concerns about the trade potentials of the region. As Indian exports to Southeast Asia comprise items not produced in the North East region, the logic of physical connectivity is seen solely in terms of providing a transit point (Oinam 2005). It has been argued that until and unless items produced in the North East find a central place in the export process, LEP merely entails a transit point in the region. A crucial reminder at this juncture is the virtual absence of industrial or production units in the region that can constitute the bulk of Indian exports to Southeast Asia. Underdevelopment and the legacy of a peripheral economy make it stark that the region will only continue to play a peripheral role in the world economy. It will take a lot of factor into consideration to envisage Manipur and the North East in evolving a framework that radically seeks to remove it subjugated heritage and reorient itself on the path to integrated socio-political and economic development. Manipur as a peripheral economy can only witness the massive erosion of its marginal productive base. Look East Policy eventually seeks to further the cause of globalization at the expense of the underdeveloped world.

REFERENCES

Ali, Md. Ashraf. 1988. *Economic History of Manipur*. Unpublished thesis submitted to Manipur University. Imphal.

Amin, Samir. 1974. *Accumulation on a World Scale*. New York: Monthly Review Press.

Ahmad, Raiful and Prasenjit Biswas. 2004. *Political Economy of the Underdevelopment of North East India.* Akansha Publishing House. New Delhi.

Bhambri, C.P. 1988. *Politics in India 1947-1987*. New Delhi: Vikas.

Chongtham, Priyoranjan. 2005. 'Manipur's Economy: Historical Roots and Structural Evolution'. *Eastern Quarterly*. Vol. 3, Issue III, October-December. New Delhi.

Ganguly, J.B. 2002. 'Globalization and North East India: Opportunities and Challenges for the Twenty First Century', in Bimal J. Deb. *Development Priorities in North East India.* New Delhi: Concept.

Konthoujam, Indrakumar. 2006. 'Imaging the North East: Towards a Contextual Understanding'. *Alternative Frames.* Vol. I, Issue II, January-March. Imphal.

Mackenzie, Alexander. 1884. *History of the Relations of the Government with the Hill Tribes of the North-East Frontier of Bengal.* Calcutta: Home Department.

Maiti, Ashok Kumar. 2002. 'Globalization vis-à-vis Regional Development in North East India', in Bimal J. Deb. *Development Priorities in North-East India*. New Delhi: Concept.

Oinam, Bhagat. 2005. 'Manipur', in Murayama (eds.). *South-Regional Relations in the Eastern South Asia: With Special Focus on India's North Eastern Region*. Wakaba: IDE-JETRO.

Thingnam, Sanjeev. 2006. 'Redefining Frontier through Look East Policy: A Colonial Articulation of Manipur'. *Alternative Frames.* Vol. I, Issue III. April-June.

Section 4
Myanmar Factor and the Global Dynamics

10

Indo-Myanmar Relations in the Greater Perspective of India's Look East Policy: Implications on Manipur

LANGPOKLAKPAM SURAJ SINGH

The recently concluded 12th Home Secretary Level Talks between India and Myanmar, from 13 to 14 September, 2006, in New Delhi, on wide ranging issues such as cross border insurgency, narcotics and small arms proliferation, border trade, HIV/AIDS etc., brought once again to the fore the long term implication of the bilateral relations between the two on Manipur and the entire North East. The paper attempts to trace the growth of Indo-Myanmar relations and its implications on Manipur. At present Indo—Myanmar relations happen to be at one of the most decisive and crucial stages. India, the emerging Asian power, and Myanmar, the biggest country in Southeast Asia mainland with its abundant natural resources, are clubbed together in one of the most geo-strategically and economically significant regions of the world. The two are in the tri-junction of South, East and Southeast Asia.

Geopolitical shifts in South and Southeast Asia and the increasing wave of globalization after the end of the cold war brought about the need for a new orientation in India's Foreign policy. This need for a more pragmatic and dynamic foreign policy culminate in India's Look East Policy (LEP). The rapid multi-polarization in the new sphere of geo-politics compelled the country to move nearer to the regional and sub-regional power centres for security and economic interests. India's relation with Myanmar is of utmost importance in the context of our new orientation and area specific approach to the LEP. Policy makers in South Block perceive Myanmar as a bridgehead to Southeast Asia. On Myanmar's part also the growing relationship is increasingly regarded beneficial in the sense that it can counterbalance China by using India as a bargaining chip, and thereby enhance its position in the international arena. In this scenario Manipur occupies a crucial space in the emerging configurations. New Delhi's concern for Manipur and the North East is conditioned by more of security issues than economic ones in spite of its conspicuously different projections. An indepth analysis is needed to ascertain to the validity of New Delhi's claims of benefit in the North East through this policy.

A brief glance at the historical and social aspects involved between the North East and Myanmar will help in elucidating the nature of the issues involved:

(i) There was socio-cultural interaction between the North East and Myanmar, which was, at the same time, chracterised by competing politico-military activities between the King of Ava (old Burma) and the Meetei Kings of Manipur and the Ahom Kings of Assam;
(ii) During the British colonial period it was a part of the British Indian Empire till 1935;
(iii) During the freedom struggles in the subcontinent, Indian and Myanmar leaders, particularly Jawaharlal Nehru and Aung San were in close touch;
(iv) For many of the original natives along either side of the 1,643 km. long India-Myanmar border the political boundary line has little or no meaning. The trans-border tribes were allowed free movement on either side because of their close cultural affinities and economic ties;
(v) Another important manifestation of the expansion of Indian culture to Myanmar is the presence of a large number of mainland Indian communities. It includes Tamils, Punjabis and Bengalis;
(vi) The embodiment of Buddhist culture as result of deep culture and intellectual interactions during the Buddhist period.

Indo-Myanmar Relations: A Background

Post British history of India's relations with Myanmar is full of ups and downs till the early 90s though there were no problematic issues of immense complicacy between them.

The First Phase: 1948-62

India had friendly relations with Myanmar from the time of the country's independence in 1948 till the General Ne Win led coup of 1962. India and Myanmar signed a Treaty of Friendship in 1951. Prime Minister Nehru and his counterpart U Nu worked with close understanding between each other. India helped the country with military and economic assistance when it was grapping under endemic insurgency and civil war. It was a time when the whole of Myanmar, except for Yangon (then Rangoon), was under the control of insurgents, both communist and ethnic. The Government of Myanmar was aptly referred to as 'the Rangoon Government' (Lintner 1994: 78). Prime Minister U Nu appreciated India's gesture. As a result Nehru and U Nu came very close to each other. U Nu cooperated with Nehru in spearheading the Non-Aligned Movement. And it was during this period that, as a token of friendship, Nehru completely transferred the ownership right of the whole area of the teak rich and immensely fertile Kabaw Valley to Myanmar without anything in return, which still infuriated the local people of Manipur.

The Second Phase: 1962-88

The period under Gen. Ne Win and his Revolutionary Council was an era of complete political isolation of Myanmar. It was also a time when India, on her part, sidelined her national interests while apparently putting up a show of sticking to ideological and moralistic values of liberal democracy. Prime Minister Indira Gandhi had meetings with Gen. Ne Win during her tenure. The Land Boundary Agreement and the Maritime Boundary Agreement are signed in 1967 and 1986 respectively are testimonies (MEA 2004). Prime Minister Rajiv Gandhi made an official visit to the country in 1987. However, the fact also remained that the relationship was mostly formal.

The Present Phase: Since 1988

India's Myanmar policy since 1988 could be divided into three sections. First, it was strongly critical of the junta regime; secondly, a gradual move towards neutrality; and finally, increasing inclination towards the regime (Langpoklakpam 2006: 218). India supported the democracy movement in Myanmar. Dissidents were given asylum. Many national leaders and organizations extended patronage to the dissidents and democracy activists. Besides, Myanmarese dissidents in India were allowed to organise public demonstrations and protest movements for their cause. India also made repeated appeals to the ruling State Law and Order Restoration Council (SLORC) for the release of Aung San Suu Kyi. A programme called 'Voice of Burmese People' was subsequently started from September 1989 in the All India Radio's Myanmarese service to express solidarity with democratic forces (Steinberg 1990: 598). Besides, there was widespread belief that in the aftermath of the '88 Uprising' the Embassy of India in Yangon was involved in the process of providing the Myanmarese students safe passage to India and assurance for political asylum thereof. At this juncture India assumed that a democratic regime in Myanmar would be more sympathetic to its national security interests (Langpoklakpam 2006: 212). The early 1990s saw a gradual policy shift in the attitude of the Government of India towards the SLORC regime. India's overarching security concerns *vis-à-vis* the volatile and conflict ridden North East eventually led to a dramatic reversal of its apparently pro-democratic pantomime. Within the government there was strong protest from many of the military, intelligence and foreign ministry officials against the policy of supporting the democracy movement and sidelining the junta regime in the greater national interest (Konsam 2004). The need for rethinking on India's part was motivated by its desire to moderate the Chinese sphere of influence over Myanmar, the growing economic clout of ASEAN and national security interests in the North East compelled India to rethink its attitude towards the SLORC regime. When the Narasimha Rao Government embarked on its LEP, immediately after the economic reforms of 1991, Myanmar could no longer be sidelined. Improved India-Myanmar relations formed the first and critical step in India Southeast Asia ties while improving security in the North East region and paving the way for future economic development in the region (Bahroo 2005).

India's first initiative in the newly reoriented Myanmar Policy was the formal reception given to the Myanmarese delegation led by the Director General of the Foreign Office in August 1992, and the reciprocal visit by an Indian delegation led by the then Foreign Secretary J.N. Dixit in March 1993 (MEA 1992-93 and MEA 1993-94). This was followed by an MOU signed in January 1994, at the secretary level, to concretise border trade. The Chief of Army Staff, General B.C. Joshi, visited Yangon from 9-13 May, 1994 to discuss matters related with insurgency and other strategic issues with his Myanmarese counterpart (MEA 1994-95: 5). And on 12 April, 1995 Trade Minister of Myanmar, Lt. General Tun Kyi and Commerce Minister of India, P. Chidambaram inaugurated the much-hyped Moreh-Tamu Border Trade jointly. This was considered a landmark in India-Myanmar relations.

In between, the conferring of Jawaharlal Nehru Award for International Understanding to Aung San Suu Kyi created some problems in the improving relations. In 1997 Myanmar was taken in the fold of ASEAN. India's desire for increased economic engagement with ASEAN to reap dividends in the form of trade agreements made Myanmar an imperative factor in its ongoing 'Look East Policy'. Its strong and active initiatives in sub-regional groups like Bay of Bengal Initiative for Multi Sectoral Technical and Economic Cooperation (BIMSTEC), established in 1996, and Mekong Ganga Cooperation (MGC), established in November, 2000, for a Free Trade Area and development of regional infrastructures, necessitated New Delhi to work in tandem with Yangon—as Myanmar is a member of both these groupings.

Several high level visits have also taken place from both sides. A significant one was the visit of India's Minister of External Affairs, Jaswant Singh, to Myanmar in February 2001—the first visit by an Indian Minister after the 1988 Uprising. He inaugurated the 165 km long Tamu-Kalewa-Kalemyo Road (named Indo-Myanmar Friendship Road), entirely funded and constructed by India as a symbol of friendship. This road will also form an important segment of the much-talked Transnational Highway. In November 2003, yet another significant visit from India was that of the Vice-President, Bhairon Singh Sekhawat. Myanmar, on her part, reciprocated the Indian gesture with the visit of the Chairman of State Peace and Development Council (SPDC), Senior General Than Shwe, in October 2004 to New Delhi. Eight agreements in the area of commercial and strategic concerns were signed between the two. And in the last few years the most remarkable landmark in cementing the Indo-Myanmar ties is that of the official visit of President APJ Abdul Kalam to Yangon in March this year. Wide-ranging discussions and agreements were carried out in various areas of common concerns. Thus in the last few years strong and increasing closer ties between the two countries can be seen, completely contrary to its earlier stance of supporting those struggling for restoration of democracy in the country. In the meeting of the ASEAN Regional Forum (ARF) in July this year in Kuala Lumpur, India's State Minister of Defence declared that India would not isolate Myanmar in an attempt to encourage democracy in the country. The changing shifts in India's economic and strategic needs and its desire for a strong foothold in Southeast Asia through its all inclusive 'Look East Policy' necessitated a close relationship with Myanmar.

China: A Deciding Factor

China has always been a key factor in the newly emerging India-Myanmar relations. In the context of larger China-Myanmar relations, Myanmar's increasing dependency on China in economic terms as well as for military armaments has been a matter of concern for India (Singh 2000). Increasing ties between Myanmar and China is perceived as detrimental for India's interests in the long run. From New Delhi's outlook, China's penetration in Myanmar when juxtaposed with its ties with Bangladesh is taken as serious encroachment into Indian sphere of influence (Malik 1994: 141).

Myanmar's relation with China was never cordial before 1989 because of Beijing's strong involvements against anti-Yangon activities. It was in the aftermath of 1988 Uprising, with the increasing international isolation and with no country to turn in for meeting its military requirements, Myanmar gradually move closer to China. Eventually, China changed from being an enemy to a benefactor. Thus, the long years of Myanmar bashing and indifference by India created a big vacuum, which was gradually filled up by China, much to the chagrin of New Delhi. Since 1989 New Delhi is keeping a close eye on Chinese capital, aid, military equipment flowing into Myanmar (Selth 2002: 53). Myanmar's improving relations with China is marked by (i) frequent exchange of official visits from both sides; (ii) significant increase in bilateral volume of trade; (iii) Myanmar's heavy dependence on China for arms supply; (iv) China's increasing participation in the development process of Myanmar; and (v) expansion of China's economic activities in India's North east through Myanmar (Langpoklakpam 2006: 208-9). In the backdrop of these developments, Myanmar's relations with China and its overall implications on India's national interests can be analysed mainly from two angles: strategic considerations and economic compulsions.

(i) Strategic Considerations

Myanmar considers China as its main partner and source of its strategic needs while China perceives Myanmar as an important instrument in its strategic designs in the region. As a result of the arms embargo by Western countries since the early 1990s, China became the only major country supplying defence material to Myanmar and also helping it in the construction of military installations. In 1989-90 alone, the SLORC regime procured as much as US$ 1.2 billion worth of weapons from China (Seekins 1997: 529-30). Considered the largest arms deal in the history of Myanmar, it consisted of advanced military hardware. It was followed by procurement worth US$ 400 million which concluded in November 1994 (Chi Shad Liang 1997: 84-85). These developments are viewed with awe by New Delhi.

There are reports of involvement of Chinese military expert in upgrading and developing of Myanmar's naval bases in its islands and coastal areas. It is believed that all these installations in Sittew, Mergue, Great Coco Island, Ramree Island, Hainggy Island (in the estuary of Irrawaddy River), Zadekyi Kyum Island are all equipped with high frequency Direction Finding (DF) and Signal Intelligence (SIGNIT) facilities (Bert 2004: 273). The SIGNIT facility in Great Coco Island, which is located just 50 km. North of India's Andaman Islands, is capable of monitoring activities at the Indian Naval Base and Tri-Service garrison at Port Blair in the Andamans (Ball 1998: 221-22). Nature of Chinese expertise involved in the sites has been matter of concern in India (Ball: 222). All these new installations with Chinese involvement have introduced a whole new dimension to India's threat perceptions from a powerful neighbour (Malik 1997:

56). Myanmar can no longer be left purely under the sphere of Chinese influence.

(ii) Economic Compulsions

Beginning of economic cooperation between Myanmar and China in the immediate aftermath of the '1988 Uprising' proved to be a boon for both, though the degree in case of the later is higher. For China it is double benefit: first, Myanmar provides a large market for its cheap finished consumer goods; and secondly, it gets access to the abundant natural resources of Myanmar including oil and natural gas. Volume of trade between the two countries increased markedly including border trade (started in 1988). At present the whole of upper Myanmar consisting of the Northern and Central region has purely become a Chinese economic zone. Moreover, in order to maximise its influence on the commercial sphere of Myanmar, China extended soft loans, technical expertise and help in infrastructural development projects. In the fiscal year 2003, the total volume of trade between the two was valued at US$ 1152.6 million and accounted for 18.90 per cent of Myanmar's total foreign trade (Far East and Australasia 2005: 733) recording an increase from US$ 418 million in 1999 (FEER Asia 2000 Year Book). According to India security analyst, the Chinese see Myanmar as a route of Southwest China to the ocean and the world beyond for trade and economic relations (Singh 2000).

India needs enormous energy and looks forward to Myanmar's vast reserve. India is appalled at the increasing Chinese presence in Myanmar's growing energy sectors, around the coastline of Rakhine State, in the Bay of Bengal. Chinese companies have picked up offshore blocks A-4, D, M and M-10 and are likely to get C-1, C-2 and M-2 (*The Hindu*, January 17, 2005). In January 2006 Petro China (a Hong Kong based Chinese company) signed a MOU with Myanmar to supply 6.5 trillion cubic feet (t c f) of gas for 30 years from block A field (*The Times of India*, March 28, 2006). This is the same field in which two Indian Public Sector companies, Oil and Natural Gas Corporation (ONGC) Videsh Limited and Gas Authority of India Limited (GAIL), own 20 per cent and 10 per cent stakes respectively. Much to India's discomfort, China has already taken up necessary measures for laying down a 2,380 km. pipeline from Kyanukpyu (in the Bay of Bengal) to Yunan province of China. China also agreed to give US$ 84 million in the form of soft loans (*The Times of India*, June 16, 2006). The fact remains that increasing relations between India and Myanmar, and India and ASEAN can be seen to be motivated in part by New Delhi's desire Chinese influence.

Economic Cooperation: Era of New Venture

Economic cooperation between India and Myanmar has become imperative as India embarks on its LEP. Economic engagement with ASEAN as a regional grouping is also a priority for India. As the only Southeast Asian country sharing a land border with India, Myanmar is also important in the context of India's growing involvement in sub-regional groupings such as Bay of Bengal Initiative for Multi Sectoral Technical and Economic Cooperation (BIMSTEC) and Mekong-Ganga Cooperation (MGC) which are directed towards free trade, common development of infrastructure and integration of national economy in the global economy.

India's relations with Myanmar underwent a major change in 1994 with the signing of a MOU on trade and economic cooperation, particularly in terms of border trade (MEA 1993-94: 5). With 22 items of trade the opening of the Moreh-Tamu trade post in April 1995 was an attempt to kickstart border trade between the two countries. Steps have also been taken up to materialize the Zokhawthar border post in Mizoram State adjoining Rhi in Myanmar in January 2004. The amount of bilateral trade between India and Myanmar, as per the 2003-04 estimates, is around US$ 470 million while the share of border trade amounts to a meagre INR 18.25 cores in the year 2003-04 (Khathing 2004). Necessary initiatives are also being taken up between the two countries to materialize projects like the Kaleidan River Multi-Model Transport project; India-Myanmar-Thailand Trilateral Highway linking, India's Moreh to Mae Sot of Northern Thailand through Bagan in Myanmar; development of Tamanthi Hydro Electric Power Project; India-Myanmar Gas pipeline and so on. India plans to take part in the construction of a deep-water port at Dawei (Bert 2004: 274). All these symbolize increasing trade and business relations between the two.

India is also engaged in the maintenance of the 165 km. long Tamu-Kalewa-Kalemyo Road which was gifted to Myanmar in 2001. The road, which is the first project of infrastructural cooperation between the countries, is of immense strategic significance as it gives India connectivity to the commercial markets in Southeast Asia. India and Myanmar signed yet another MOU on July 27, 2004 for development of Myanmar's railways which has a 4,525 route km. line. Under this agreement India is to provide US$ 56.358 million to Myanmar (*The Hindu,* July 28, 2006). Rail India Technical and Economic Services Ltd. (RITES) will carry it out. These are the signs of growing economic cooperation between the two countries.

India's GAIL and ONGC Videsh Ltd. are currently engaged in gas extraction work in Rakhine State in the Bay of Bengal. The two public sector companies also own equities of 10 per cent and 20 per cent respectively in the AI field (*The Times of India*, March 28, 2006). With increasing competition from China in this sector India is planning to lay a 1,400 km. gas pipeline from Myanmar's Sittwe area to Gaya in Bihar State of India through the North East, particularly Mizoram and Assam—thus skirting Bangladesh. The pipeline will cost US$ 3 billion (*The Hindu,* June 16, 2006). If all goes as it is Myanmar could supply 10-15 per cent of India's gas consumption by 2025 (Varadarajan 2005).

Economic cooperation and trade relations between India and Myanmar have increased with the visit of SPDC Chairman Sr. General Than Shwe to India in October 2004 and the reciprocal visit by India's President A.P.J. Abdul Kalam in March 2006. In both the visits many agreements in the areas of trade, infrastructure, energy, human resource development, education and technology came into effect with far reaching impact in the development to both.

Insurgency: India's Obssession

'Independent' India's beleaguered history reflects a persisting obsession with 'security' *vis-à-vis* the North East. Legacy of anti-colonial struggles since British period has placed the North East as a strategically insecure region. Post British political configurations and realities have been marked by widespread insurgency contesting mainstream Indian hegemony and domination. Persistence of insurgency has been a cause of real concern for both India and Myanmar, though the degree varies. Need for closer coordination between the respective security agencies of either side is strongly felt (Bhaumik 2005: 41). Therefore, containment of insurgency in

North East India highly calls for mutual cooperation between the two countries.

The issue of India's insurgency linked security concern in the North East forms an important part of any bilateral talk between the two countries. Initiatives were taken up by India for getting help from the Yangon regime in the containment of insurgency. Myanmar reciprocated India's request at various instances. In May 1995, the then India's Chief of Army Staff Gen. B.C. Joshi visited Yangon to discuss insurgency and other security related issues with his counterpart. Consequently a joint counter-insurgency operation known as 'Operation Golden Bird' was launched in the same year in the India-Myanmar border. This was followed by an attack of Myanmarese army on insurgent camp located inside Myanmar (Bhaumik 2005: 41). Misunderstanding erupted between the two because of India's accusation of the Yangon regime of giving shelter to two Pakistani Nuclear scientists. However over the years improvements in term of military to military understanding could be seen. It will not be wrong to say that the increasing relations between the two are putting lots of pressure on the India insurgents (Konsam 2005: 295).

It has been reported that there was a military crackdown of on ULFA insurgents by Myanmarese army somewhere in the Sagaing division (*The Times of India*, June 11, 2006). Sr. Gen. Than Shwe, in his visit in 2004, also assured India that it would not allow Myanmar's soil to be used by Indian insurgents. And on April 20, 2006 the military officials of the two countries agreed to extend coordination and strengthen joint intelligence mechanisms during a meeting in Dimapur in India (*Mizzima News*, April 21, 2006). In the recently concluded Home Secretary level talk also there was proposal from Indian side for a joint Bhutan like operation for flushing out the Northeast insurgents from Myanmar. Consequently, operations by the Myanmarese army have once more started against the insurgents from the first week of October. In the years to come there will be lots of pressure on the North East insurgents.

Narco-Trade: A Parallel Economy in the Border

Large-scale narco-trade operating illegally in the border areas of India and Myanmar is also of serious concern for the two, which necessitated a greater cooperation in this area. Narco-trade has become a two-way traffic in this region. Heroin and synthetic drugs come from Myanmar to India while chemical like acetic anhydride and ephedrine, essential for converting raw opium into heroin, are transported from India (Lintner 1994: 29).

India's 1,643 km. long porous and topographically hostile border with Myanmar proves to be immensely difficult for the authorities to monitor. With complacency and corruption amongst the Indian agencies responsible for border control and law enforcement, it provides easy entry of large amounts of narcotic substances into India. Despite the reduction in opium production in recent years, Myanmar still remains the second largest producer of opium in the world and a large supplier of heroin according to the United Nations Office on Drugs and Crime. Consequently, narco-trade flourishes in the North East. Supply of drugs, which originates from Eastern and Northern Myanmar enters the border states of Manipur, Nagaland and Mizoram through different routes and then spread throughout the country and outside (Langpoklakpam 2006: 213). The problem is further aggravated with the emergence of new synthetic drugs. viz. methamphetamines and ecstasy in the narco-markets of Myanmar in the late 90s (Lintner 2000: 165-66). These new drugs started entering India in large quantities, as these are much cheaper and easier to transport than the traditional ones like heroin.

Flow of narcotic drugs in the North East India from Myanmar has increased manifold since 1992 because of the multiplication of refineries in Myanmarese areas quite close to the Indian border. Six new refineries were reported along the Chindwin River, closer to the Indian border (Lintner 2000: 176). Engaging Myanmar is the need of the hour. As such, the issue of narcotic trafficking remains an important area of discussion in all the bilateral talks between India and Myanmar since the beginning of formal engagement in 1993. Abundant drug and human trafficking along the border have become a menace. Ultimately it becomes a necessity for India to take the SPDC regime into confidence for a joint initiative against the spreading danger of narco-trade and its negative fallouts. Both the governments need a serious deliberation.

Democracy in Myanmar

Changes in Indian policies do not imply that it is not in favour of a political transition in Myanmar. However, a conspicuous silence regarding democracy in Myanmar can be noticed as far as India is concerned. This is very much clear from the press briefing of Foreign Secretary Shyam Saran who spoke of the continuing engagement on the eve of President Dr. A.P.J. Abdul Kalam's visit to Myanmar in March 2006 (Saran 2006). This amply reveals New Delhi's dubious stand on democracy in Myanmar. Pro-democracy people in Myanmar, on their part, consider Indian efforts to make an amicable and balanced approach to the issue of improving relations with SLORC on the one hand and supporting the movement for democracy on the other ambiguous and contradictory (Langpoklakpam 2006: 217).

Restoration of democracy in Myanmar is also becoming an important issue in India's growing relationship with the country. Daw Aung San Suu Kyi's receipt of Jawaharlal Nehru Award for International Understanding in 1995, acknowledging her struggle is still fresh in the minds of the Junta. Meanwhile India is eagerly watching the Seven-Point Road Map to Democracy taken up by the SPDC regime in 2003. It has also expressed the need for an all inclusive and broad based approach for early transition to democracy. Though India does not show strong enthusiasm for democracy in Myanmar like that of USA it is not passive like China. New Delhi is hoping for a role in the ongoing process in the near future taking into consideration its good rapport with Yangon. ASEAN countries also share this view. Since the failure of their constructive engagement policy in bringing any significant change in Myanmar these countries expect India to play a more constructive role. However, New Delhi is more interested in developing strategic and economic cooperation with the country while keeping the issue of democracy still alive for an opportune moment in future.

Implication on Manipur

In the backdrop of the prevailing situation, Manipur's position in the equations of India-Myanmar relations needs careful scrutiny. Its implications on Manipur have to be looked into with depth. Manipur being a prospective gateway to the mainland Southeast Asia becomes important in the context of its locational importance in the greater perspective of India's LEP.

Manipur, one of the states in the Northeastern region on India boarding Myanmar, has got relations with the later dating back to history. Manipur as an Asiatic Kingdom has closer ties with Myanmar (then called 'Awa' by the Manipuris) than with the rest of mainland India. There were ups and downs in the relationship. Instances of matrimonial alliances between the Manipuri Kings and the Myanmare Kings feature prominently in history. This connection was there even during the British occupation of Manipur. However, with Manipur's merger to the Indian Union in October 1949, and the subsequent limitation of political boundary, nature of relationship changed. Mobility of people was curbed as free movement was confined only to the hill natives who live on either side of the border. Relationship becomes confined only mostly to a limited informal border trade among the hill peoples and to a greater extent to illegal trade in contraband goods, Chinese consumer items, narcotics, small arms and precious stones. These goods flow without restrictions to this side of the border. So at the time of opening the Moreh-Tamu Border Trade there was nothing new, except that negotiations and deals of illegal activities become much easier. Besides, the place has become a focal point for strong power struggle among different forces, both state and non-state actors. New Delhi's interest in the state is based on security issues. It is in this background coupled with the general considerations of India's Myanmar policy in the wider spectrum of its LEP that we need to analyse Manipur's position.

On April 20, 2006 a 20-Member Myanmarese delegation led by Brig. Tin Maung Ohn met Indian-army officials at Rangapahar Cantonment at Dimapur in India's Northeast State of Nagaland. The meeting agreed to extend coordination and strengthen joint intelligence mechanism as regard to the curbing of insurgent movements (*Mizzima News*, April 24, 2006). Then there is the recently concluded 12th Home Secretary Level Talk between India and Myanmar where the main issue remained that of flushing out insurgents from areas of the latter. India needs the regime's cooperation to ensure that the large number of outfits operating in Northeast India is denied sanctuary in Myanmar's territory (Ramachandran 2004). On May 2 and July 20, 2006, a convoy of sealed Indian army vehicles entering Myanmar through Moreh has been observed. The popular assumption is that these may have contained small arms given by India as a token of friendship to Myanmar for use against the North East insurgents.

Senior Gen. Than Shwe in his visit to New Delhi assured that it would not allow Indian insurgents to operate from Myanmarse soil. In the last part of 2004, Home Ministry of India had submitted a list of insurgents and there camps in Myanmar for necessary cooperation from the country mentioned (*Burmanent News*, October 14, 2004). India's overriding security concerns and subsequent desire to contain insurgency in Manipur became the focal point of its engagement with Myanmar. Insurgency in Manipur assumes importance in India's relation with Myanmar.

Opening of the border trade between India and Myanmar has indirectly helped in exposing the porous nature of the boundary. Lack of proper monitoring mechanism on the part of the authority makes the scene chaotic. Moreh, the border town of Manipur adjoining Myanmar, has become a conflict zone. Tussle for power among different opposing forces for the control of Moreh is a vivid reality. Indian security forces are not behind in this tussle either, sometimes their interests going much beyond their duties related with maintenance of law and order.

Border Trade or Pandora's Box

The Moreh-Tamu Border Trade aimed at the opening of a gateway to Southeast Asia is another important link area in India-Myanmar relations. Moreh became an important centre for border trade with the entire people of Manipur expecting economic prosperity. Indian imports and exports through Moreh started with Rs. 5.39 crores and INR 00.46 crores respectively in 1995-98 reached a high point of INR 37.19 crores in terms of import and INR 25.17 crores in terms of export in 1997-98 (Khating). New Delhi thinks of combining trade with infrastructural development in the region in conjunction with the desire to connect India with the rest of Southeast Asian economies by land route. The main objective is the availability of a cheap mode of transport to Southeast Asia through Manipur. Joint development projects between the two are in the offing. India's initiative in building the Moreh-Kalewa-Kalemyo road linking Manipur with Mandalay, and its keen desire to construct other road links in Myanmar lend substance to its LEP Initiatives for a Trilateral Highway linking Moreh to Mae Sot in North East Thailand through Tamu and Bagan in Myanmar, and a Trans

Asian Railway linking Jiribam in Southwest Manipur to Moreh then to Tamu have been made. Manipur is poised to be India's gateway to the Southeast and subsequently Myanmar is perceived in terms of a land bridge to Southeast Asia and Southwest China. Manipur's location gives this unique advantage.

Contrary to Indian claims and expectations the border trade has failed to alleviate the condition of Manipur economy. It has proved to be a dampener to people's aspirations for trading opportunities. A decreasing trend in terms of legal trade (since 1998-99) can be seen. In 2003-04 the volume of export and import came down to INR 9.41 crores and INR 8.85 crores respectively (Khating 2004). On the other hand, informal trade with transactions in narco-trade increased manifold. Moreh's official trade is only a fraction of its large and flourishing informal trade. The main reason for this large-scale illegal traffic is that Myanmar does not impose any restriction on third country goods in transit (Verghese 2002: 189). Thus, the opening proves beneficial for informal trade but not for those who carry out trade legally in the meagre 22 items included in the trade agreement of 1994. Business is not beneficial for traders because of the existence of many hurdles in the process of trade transaction itself. Particularly a trader travelling from Moreh to Dimapur along the NH 39 has to cross nearly 53 check posts with many of these belonging to non-state actors. Moreover, due to the non-conducive situation in Moreh, business has shifted to Tamu's Namphalong market. Main reasons are lack of development efforts, slipshod border development measures, strong turf war and volatile conditions.

New Delhi is particularly worried about the massive influx of Chinese goods. Gradual domination of the entire border trade by Chinese goods is a major irritant. From the most sophisticated electronics goods to the simplest vegetable products like garlic, commodities are brought to Manipur through the Moreh-Tamu transit from China. Cheap Chinese manufactured goods are used in abundance in every household in Manipur because of its durability, quality and affordability as compared to expensive Indian products. Ultimately the fact remains the India-Myanmar Border Trade has failed to bring the minimum expected gains to the local people of the state. It has rather created a situation of turf war among the different forces, both state and non-state actors.

Menace of Drug-Trafficking and AIDS: The Crisis Within

With the recent ban on opium production, a sifted in the form of large-scale increase in the production of synthetic drug could be seen in Mayanmar. Whether it is heroin or amphetamine, the volume of drugs entering Manipur is increasing. This is because Manipur has become an important transit-route for Myanmarese narcotic products to mainland of India and other international markets. Patna is one such major drug distribution centre (Image Asia 1998: 62). Beside, the presence of large number of mobile drug manufacture units along the Chindwin River close to the Manipur border is another factor. Manipur has become a ready market as well as an easy transit-point for drugs coming from Myanmar.

Increasing influx of drugs in Manipur has its fallouts in the rise in the incidence of AIDS in state. Manipur is third among the states of India having highest number of HIV cases. Illegal supply of chemicals necessary for drug production from India has made trafficking in this part of India-Myanmar border a two-way traffic. And with it the dreadful disease in the form of AIDS has also transcended borders. As such the menace of drug trafficking and the dreadful spread of HIV/AIDS have become common concern for both the policy markers in New Delhi and Yangon. Despite efforts, the immediate effects are on the people of Manipur. Negative effects like HIV/AIDS, and drugs and arms related factional wars have become part of Manipur life. This remains a challenge for India in its Myanmar policy.

Assessment

When viewed from Manipur's perspective, Indian initiative seems to have more political and security concerns rather than the economic concerns related with the border trade. New Delhi's interest in the region has more to do with security concerns *vis-à-vis* the prevailing conflict than with genuine economic development and trade promotion. Economic analysts in the region think that the Central Government in the centre is not keen with the overall development of the state, inclusive of the India-Myanmar border trade, which is now in total disarray. No one seems to know who is incharge of the border trade. Policy makers in New Delhi have already forgotten the intertwined relationship between economic development and socio-political problems. In the heat of containing insurgency most of the significant bilateral development projects are left in the lurch. Millions of rupees are pumped by the Indian Government to maintain its security forces in Manipur and other states bordering Myanmar while necessary infrastructural developments related with the border trade are blatantly ignored.

Lack of necessary developmental efforts and the continuing backwardness of the region have made the fallouts of the border trade more distinct. Drug and human trafficking, small arms trade and smuggling have become the means of life culminating to drug related crimes, kidnapping, ransoms, factional wars and the rise of HIV/AIDS. Though the Indian Union Minister of State for Commerce and Industry, Jairam Ramesh, in his recent visit to Manipur from 28 to 30 September, announced a composite check post with all facilities needed under one roof to be located in Moreh (*The Sangai Express*, September 30, 2006), sincere concretization of the announcement remains to be seen meanwhile, if a concrete policy is not taken up, the negative multiplier effects will degrade the whole region or, in the extreme case, it will intensify dumping ground of cheap manufactured goods made outside Manipur. Moreh-Tamu trade needs to be mobilized for the benefit of the North East. This problem needs to be tackled at the earliest by creating substantial economic and industrial infrastructure in Manipur lest the negative effects catch up with the whole situation.

India, while moving forward with its broad LEP, needs to give a minute and systematic policy approach commensurate with the distinctive needs of the region and the state. Improving relations with its neighbour and opening borders lone in the absence of proper policy planning will neither solve the multi-faceted problems faced by New Delhi in Manipur nor bring socio-economic changes in the region. Consequently, India's Myanmar policy itself loses meaningless for Manipur and the North East. Initial hopes of the people of Manipur that there will be a major opening in the Eastern direction, the opening of the traditionally believed *Nongpok Thong* (Eastern Gate), which will bring prosperity, seems to be gradually disappearing. Contrary to their expectation nothing sort of significant progress came. Practically positive improvement in the direction could be possible only when the right type of planning is taken up with sincerity on the part of policymakers in New Delhi, taking into confidence the local authorities, and by going much beyond its narrow outlook of security maintenance.

Political pragmatism should be combined with development realities in taking up any policy implementation and planning on the part of New Delhi. Synchronization of India's Myanmar policy with the interest of those who are directly linked with the issue is a necessity. Only then India-Myanmar cooperation will become meaningful for the North East region, and Manipur can play a positive role in India's Myanmar policy in its greater perspective of LEP.

REFERENCES

Annual Report, 1992-93. Ministry of External Affairs. Government of India. New Delhi.

Annual Report, 1993-94. Ministry of External Affairs. Government of India. New Delhi.

Bahroo, Laxman, 2005. 'India's Foreign Policy Challenges: Today and Beyond'. *Security Research Review.* <www.bharat-rakshak.com/srr/volume12>

Ball, Desmond, 1998. *Burma's Military Secret: Signal Intelligence (SIGINT) from 1941 to Cyber Warfare*. Bangkok: White Lotus Press.

Bert, Wayne, 2004. 'Burma China and the U.S.A.' *Pacific Affairs*. Vol. 77, No. 2. Summer.

Bhaumic, Subir, 2005. 'Guns, Drugs and Rebels'. *Seminar*, No. 550. June.

Chi, Shad Liang, 1997. 'Burma's Relations with the People's Republic of China: From Delicate Friendship to Genuine Co-operation', in Peter Carely (ed.). *Burma: The Challenge of Charge in Divided Society.* London: Macmillan.

CIA, 2006. *The World Factbook*: *Burma*. <http://sportsforum.ws/book/geos/bm.htm>

Dixit, J.N. 1996. *My South Block Years: Memoirs of a Foreign Secretary*. New Delhi: UBSPD.

Far East and Australasia, 2005. 36th Edition. London: Europa Publications.

'*Far Eastern Economic Review*', 1999. Asia 2000. *Year Book*. Hong Kong.

Images Asia, 1998. 'All quit on The Western Front? The Situation in China State and Sagaing Division. Burma'. Chiangmai.

Kalam, A.P.J. Abdul, 2006. *Speech to Union of Myanmar Federation of Chamber of Commerce and Industry*. March 10.

Khathing, J.S.R. 2004 , 'Indo-Myanmar Border Trade'. Paper presented at *the National Seminar on Border trade Between India's North East and Myanmar. Problems and Prospects* on 8th and 9th November 2004 in Imphal.

Konsam, Ibo Singh, 2004. 'Indo-Myanmar Border Trade'. Presented at the

National Seminar on Border trade Between India's North Eastern and Myanmar: Problems and Prospects. November 8 and 9. Imphal.

——————, 2005. 'Insurgency in North East India and the Myanmar Connection', in Agnihotri, S.K. and Ray. B. Datta (eds.). *Perspective of Security and Development in North East India.* New Delhi: Concept Publishing Company.

Langpoklakpam, Suraj Singh, 2006. Movement for Democracy in Manipur. Akansha Publishing House. New Delhi.

Lintner, Bertil, 1994. *Burma in Revolt: Option and Insurgency since 1948.* White Lotus. Bangkok.

Malik, J. Mohan, 1994. 'Sino-Indian Rivalry in Myanmar: Implications for Regional Security'. Contemporary Southeast Asia. Vol. 16, No. 2, September.

——————, 1997. 'Myanmar's Role in Regional Security: Pawn or Pivot'? *Contemporary Southeast Asia.* Vol. 19, No. 1. June.

Ministry of External Affairs, 1995. Government of India Annual Report 1994-95. New Delhi.

Ministry of External Affairs, 2004. 'Government of India, Myanmar'. *Foreign Affairs.* May.

Mizzima News, 21 April, 2006. New Delhi. <www. Mizzima.com>.

Mizzima News, 24 April, 2006. New Delhi.

Pedersen, Morten B. Rudland, Emily and May, Ronald J. (eds.) 2000. *Burma Myanmar: Strong Regime Weak State.* Crawford House Publishing. Adelaide.

Ramchandran, Sudha, 2004. 'Delhi in Steps with the Generals' *Asia Time*, November 3.

Saran, Shyam, 2006. *Briefing in the eve of President of India's visit to Myanmar.* March 7.

Seekins, Donald M. 1997, 'Burma-China Relation: Playing with Fire'. *Asian Survey*. Vol. 37., No. 6. June pp. 525-39.

Selth, Andrew, 2002. 'Burma and Superpower Rivalries in the Asia Pacific'. *Naval War Collage Review*. Vol. 58, No. 2, Spring.

Singh, Jasjit, 2000. 'Our Eastern Neighbour'. Paper presented at the *Looking East: A Symposium on the Need to Refocus our Foreign Policy*. No. 487. March.

Steinberg, David I. 1990. 'International Rivalries in Burma: The Rise of Economic Compitition'. *Asian Survey*. Vol. 30. No. 6. June.

The Hindu, 2005. New Delhi, 17 January.

The Hindu, 2006. New Delhi, 16 June.

The Irrawaddy, 2005. Vol. 13. No. 10. October. Chiangmai.

The Sangai Express, 2006. Imphal. 30 September.

The Times of India, 2006. Guwahati, 16 June.

The Times of India, 2006. Guwahati. 28 March.

Varadarajan, Siddharth, 2005. 'India, China view for Energy Influence'. *The Hindu.* 17 January.

Verghese, B.G. 2002. *Reorienting India: The New Geo-Politics of Asia.* Delhi: Konark Publishers.

11

Trade, Security and Strategic Concerns: The Politics of India's Look East Policy

SANATOMBA KANGUJAM

The hype generated over India's Look East Policy (hereafter LEP) did not come as dramatic surprise to the people of Manipur since the opening of the 'Eastern Gate' as a belief was rooted in their consciousness. It finds expression in the ancient Manipuri sacred text called *Puya* that *Nongpok Thong* or the 'Eastern Gate' would eventually open after a long period of 'enforced closure'. Such beliefs instilled positive expectations amongst the people who hoped that something miraculous would happen to Manipur ushering an era of prosperity and reunion with the kindred tribes of the 'East'. Naturally the general belief went parallel with India's announcement of a policy of looking eastward which marked a major shift in its economic policy. Even as news of India's LEP spread rapidly, people in general were optimistic about the imminent economic advantages that could be derived from such an initiative. Ironically, the logic of the unfolding events falsifies such hopes despite India's grand design to project the LEP as a viable developmental alternative.

India's LEP: A Policy Sans Mandate

The Government of India (GoI) after decades of wilful negligence has all of a sudden changed its perception towards the North East. The most apparent reason behind this policy shift could be attributed to gradual realization of the region as a potential economic zone, apart from being a corridor to Southeast Asia. But the chief moving forces behind this new economic initiative are the various private sector corporations and business firms of metropolitan India. Economic trends triggered by the onset of globalization compelled the Indian state to formulate policies, which apparently follow current global trajectories. India's LEP is direct fallout of the structural adjustment programmes initiated in 1991 in response to the pressures of international finance capital. It is a tacit move to integrate the Indian economy with the world economy through regional co-operation. India's LEP is thus a manifestation of this process of globalization deliberately orchestrated on the pretext of facilitating economic development.

According to the Indian Chamber of Commerce (ICC), a lot of benefits could be derived from such regional economic co-operation (Arif 2006). It has been stated that the North East region together with Eastern India, Bangladesh, Bhutan, Nepal, Myanmar and Thailand constitute a formidable market of 400 million people that can increase the scope of larger investment in the region. It would also lead to the creation of efficient common infrastructure by setting up cross border infrastructure particularly in energy and transportation. There would also be increase in scope for attracting larger multilateral funding thereby increasing export from the region. Transport linkage would enable higher trade and cost competitiveness. This would also solve the problem of the North East being landlocked by providing access to ports of Bangladesh and Southeast Asia. Besides, the fiscal incentive available for investment in the North East will become more attractive for the USA and European investors. Such is the vision espoused by the ICC, whose sole objective is the maximization of profit, in its attempt to portray the LEP as a people-friendly and development-oriented project.

A critical analysis, however, reveals dubiousness in the Centre's motives since it seeks to open up the border without proper consultation with the peoples or civil societies of this region. It has been about one and a half decade since the LEP was first envisioned in the early Nineties. Yet the centre has done hardly anything to elicit the views of the peoples in this regard. A disturbing feature of the ongoing debate revolves around the exclusion of the North East peoples from any decision-making process *vis-à-vis* the LEP. It cannot be denied by any figment of imagination that the peoples of the region who are going to be the most affected as a result of the implementation of the LEP are left in the lurch. The politics of exclusion—an inherent aspect of globalization where schemes, plans, policies and decisions are made elsewhere far away in distant ivory towers hardly in touch with the stark realities on the ground—has made its onslaught without ever divulging the merits and demerits of the said project. The operationalization of this project has the potential of completely altering the original landscape—social, economic and cultural—of the North East. Therefore, the peoples of the North East have every right to be informed and consulted on this project, which will have direct bearing on every aspect of their lives.

The centre has not initiated any measure worth the name to spread awareness among the masses of the region about the probable consequences that could be associated with the LEP. This is not to deny the limited academic exercise undertaken at the higher level in the forms of seminars and a few other publications. But the fact remains that the scanty information available so far has not been disseminated to the masses. Here lies the crux of the issue rendering India's LEP as a policy lacking peoples' mandate. Literal absence of any genuine consultation and participation of the peoples of the North East in the formulation of this policy lends an elitist orientation to India's LEP. This is in fact a clear violation of the draft UN declaration of the rights of indigenous peoples which *inter alia* envisages certain provisions requiring the states to obtain 'free and informed consent' of the indigenous peoples prior to the approval of any project affecting their lands, territories and other resources particularly in connection with the development, utilization and exploitation of minerals, water and other resources (Chakma 2003: 82). The absence of free, prior and informed consent of the indigenous peoples of the North East in the formulation of India's LEP is tantamount to violation of the right to development endorsed globally. In the light of this gross injustice, it is increasingly difficult to subscribe to the statist version that the policy is designed for ushering development in the North East.

Engaging the Military Junta: Strategic U-turn

The enthusiasm recently exhibited by India towards Myanmar can be gauged from the unfolding security paradigm in the Eastern front. Earlier, India had staunchly supported the movement for democracy in Myanmar prompting many pro-democracy activists and student leaders to take refuge in India following the military takeover of Myanmar in 1988. India had maintained an isolationist policy *vis-à-vis* Myanmar while simultaneously extending all sorts of logistic support to the dissident groups fighting for restoration of democracy. India also joined the international community in criticising human rights violation by the military junta and endorsed all the United Nations resolutions demanding restoration of democracy in Myanmar. Informed sources revealed that Indian diplomatic mission in Bangkok had been accused of funding the NCGUB while establishing covert ties with the Democratic Alliance of Burma. The conferment of the Jawaharlal Nehru Award for International Understanding, the most prestigious international award conferred by India, to Aung San Suu Kyi, leader of the dissident National League for Democracy in 1995 marked the zenith of New Delhi's support for democracy movement in Myanmar. Such diplomatic postures adopted by India widened the gulf that existed between the two countries. It gave impressions of mutually irreconcilable differences between the two neighbours.

Of late, there has been a gradual shift in the Indian attitude towards the military rulers in Yangon. Observation made by certain analyst indicates that the twin factors of Chinese expansion and containment of insurgency in North East India made it imperative for India to reassess its policy towards Myanmar (Konsam 2005a: 288). In fact, the growing expansion of Chinese influence in Myanmar which eventually pose a strategic threat to India's national security coupled with series of armed resistance movements launched by various shades of insurgent groups taking shelter in Myanmar compelled India to review its foreign policy *vis-à-vis* Myanmar. Therefore, India's LEP, which finds its articulation partly in Indo-Myanmar Border Trade, is deeply intertwined with the existing as well as the emerging security development. The essay attempts to scrutinise India's security agenda behind an apparent economic facade of the much-publicised LEP and tangentially explores how far India has moved in that direction.

The political vacuum in Myanmar created by international isolation in the wake of the popular 1988 uprising provided China with an opportunity for economic and strategic penetration into Myanmar. Intensive research indicates China's desperate search for markets for its cheap finished consumer goods even as it became more interested in the contracts for extracting Myanmar's rich natural resources (Langpoklakpam 2005: 209). The reciprocal visits between Chinese and Myanmarese officials led to gradual opening of Myanmarese economy to China with the latter becoming the first country to establish formalised border trade with the former. Separate trade agreements were signed between the two countries in 1989 and 1993 that ultimately resulted in increased trade volume. China extended possible economic assistance to Myanmar in the form of soft loans, technical knowledge and expertise thereby rendering Myanmar a Chinese satellite. Through its economic power China intends to exercise political influence over Myanmar in its bid to enhance its strategic interests in the region especially the Indian Ocean region. In turn, China provided Myanmar with all the diplomatic protection from international pressures against the junta apart from supplying military equipments to Yangon.

China's help to the Myanmarese government with telecommunication network in Northern Myanmar and also the Chinese plan to construct a 1,350 km. railway tract through Laos, Myanmar and China (Kunming) going up to Thailand (Bangkok) is seen by India with suspicion (Oinam 2004: 99). The emerging security configuration in Southeast Asia has rendered Myanmar an important component of Chinese strategy to prevent its encirclement by the United States and its allies as well as to secure vital naval routes to oil supplies from the Middle East (Kangujam 2005: 34). The Chinese maritime expansion in the Bay of Bengal and Arabian Sea with the logistic support of Myanmar and Pakistan respectively has created a situation of perceived Chinese encirclement of India (Konthoujama 2005: 64). In fact, Chinese maritime expansion and inroads into the Indian Ocean through Myanmar is a cause of serious concern for India mainly in the light of Chinese assertion that the Indian Ocean is not India's Ocean. In the strategic perception of India, Chinese dominance in the Bay of Bengal is an obstacle to its aspiration for economic and strategic influence in Southeast Asia. India finds it hard to tolerate the installation of Chinese monitoring centre in the Coco Island, close to Andaman and Nicobar Islands, which is an overt strategic incursion into the Indian maritime zone. Besides, the Chinese presence all along the Myanmar's border is perceived as a direct threat to India's security. As such, the strategic concern caused by Myanmar-Pakistan-China nexus in an attempt to encircle India in the long run entails the need on the part of India to reverse its foreign policy in dealing with the military regime of Myanmar.

Another significant factor accounting for India's strategic shift towards Myanmar is the security threat to India's territorial integrity posed by numerous armed resistance groups of the North East with sanctuaries in Myanmar. Constant Myanmarese encouragement to the insurgent groups in India's North East was largely responsible for the Indian government to reverse its earlier isolationist stand (Langpoklakpam 2005: 213). It became imperative for India to elicit the support of the Myanmarese military regime in flushing out the insurgent groups, some of which are of Myanmarese origin or having connections with Myanmarese insurgents. India had to seek the military junta's co-operation due to growing realization of Myanmar's geo-strategic importance to counter insurgency. Consequently, as revealed by certain informed sources, a number of officials from the foreign office, defence and intelligence establishment had opposed Indian Government support extended to the pro-democracy movement and the 'limited support' extended to the Myanmarese rebels (Konsam 2005a: 288). The logic behind their argument was that if India did not improve relations with the junta, Myanmar would become a Chinese satellite. This argument got substantiated chiefly in view of the fact that the junta is there to stay as transition from military rule to democracy in Myanmar is a distant dream. As a matter of policy, based on real politick, India refrained from lodging a formal protest to the SLORC regime against its policy of dishonouring the electoral verdict of the Myanmarese people in 1990 thus paving way for normalising diplomatic relations with Yangon. In this context, India's security anxiety—getting Myanmar to act against North East Indian insurgent groups taking shelter in Myanmar—rather than a desire to give the LEP a continental orientation explains India's U-turn vis-à-vis Myanmar. It is pertinent to note that India had all along maintained a maritime outlook towards Southeast Asia (Baruah 2004: 28).

It was against this backdrop that U Ba Swe, Vice Foreign Minister of Myanmar paid a visit to India in 1992 on the invitation of the Indian government. His visit resulted in identification of concrete areas for bilateral co-operation including border trade, prevention of narcotics trafficking and contact between the civilian and military authorities in the border regions of the two countries to prevent illegal activities (MEA Annual Report 1992-93). Later, the Indian side intensified diplomatic offensives against Myanmar marking an era of 'Constructive Engagement', a policy that implies active co-operation with that country in the economic sphere without interference or intervention in its domestic political affairs. Such a policy adopted by India towards the military rulers in Yangon was much to the displeasure of the Myanmarese pro-democracy groups. Hence, India virtually deviated from its cherished principles of supporting democracy movement in Myanmar as it found its own interests increasingly paramount in the backdrop of various considerations like the emerging strategic equation in Southeast Asia. In spite of being the largest democracy in the world, India could hardly stand the trial of circumstances mainly when it comes to questions involving its interest. By aligning itself with the junta, India had laid a bad precedent for extending recognition and conferring legitimacy to the military regime of Myanmar. Serious fallout of such an alignment is the militarization of the Indo-Myanmar region in an unprecedented scale. Mention may be made of the joint counter-insurgency operation consisting of Indian and Myanmarese army known as 'Operation Golden Bird' launched in 1995 in the Indo-Myanmar borders resulting in busting of many North East Indian insurgent camps.

Behind the Veil of Border Trade: A Security Obsession

It was in the midst of such development that the idea of Indo-Myanmar border trade got revived after decades of hibernation when the then Foreign Secretary J.N. Dixit led a delegation to Myanmar in 1993; informal trade between the two countries is not a new phenomenon. Ironically, a sincere desire on the part of the Indian government to promote a smooth and efficient border trade was absent right from its very inception as India's policy towards Myanmar is guided overwhelmingly by its security obsession. It has always remained conspicuous that the logic of enhancing border trade as such was not the decisive determinant behind India's recent engagement with the military junta. The concept of border trade has been meticulously dragged into the picture only with a design to lend an economic character to the various diplomatic initiatives undertaken with regard to Myanmar.

Formalization of border trade between India and Myanmar was secured through the signing of Indo-Myanmar Border Trade

Agreement on January 21, 1994, which was operationalised on April 12, 1995 with Moreh in Manipur officially declared open for trade. However, an interesting revelation points to the fact that the main area of discussion between the Indian delegation and the Myanmarese authorities in all rounds of talks during 1994 had always focused on 'better border management' which in turn covered issues like insurgency, terrorism, narcotic trade and boundary issues (Langpoklakpam 2005: 215). Pertinent to recall in this context is the fact that another agreement in addition to the border trade agreement known as the 'Memorandum of Understanding on Co-operation between the Civilian Border Authorities' of the two countries to prevent illegal and insurgent activities was also executed on the same day. The reasons behind India's security concerns along the Indo-Myanmar border can however be explained by the existence of drug trafficking, small arms trade and insurgency. Border trade, therefore, in India's perception is an institutional device to monitor movement of insurgent groups in the border areas and Chinese incursion into Myanmar. It is worth noting that exchange of visits between the Indian and the Myanmarese authorities from 1992 to the present revolved round the issues pertaining to tackling of insurgency and its associated phenomenon of arms smuggling. In all the agreements reached between the two countries, high level of bilateral understanding is demonstrated for a well coordinated military campaign against armed nationalist groups in the border regions. Myanmar went to the extent of declaring that it would not allow its soil to be used by any group against India while the latter tried its best to appease the junta. One glaring example is the gifting of the 165 km. long Indian-built Tamu-Kalewa-Kalemyo road linking India's North East as a token of improving relationship. India stressed on construction of roads and development of the border areas with a strategic calculation for containment of insurgents operating in the region.

A significant aspect of Indo-Myanmar relations lies in convergence of strategic interests between them as the Naga insurgents campaigning for 'Nagalim' or Greater Nagaland, which includes certain portions of Myanmar, poses a security threat to the military rulers in Yangon. The junta is also apprehensive of the Naga insurgents lest they could be used by the Western powers especially the United States to topple the military regime and restore democracy in Myanmar. The junta badly needs Indian help to fight against Myanmarese ethnic separatist groups that control several provinces in its North Western parts. The fact that the geographical areas controlled by the ethnic minorities are highly inaccessible requires joint military operations.

The year 2004 witnessed a great improvement in the bilateral relationship between India and Myanmar when senior General Than Shwe, Chairman of the SPDC paid a state visit to India from October 25-29 holding talks with Dr. Manmohan Singh, Prime Minister of India on a wide range of issues. The two sides reiterated their firm determination to maintain peace, tranquility and stability along the entire length of their border as an essential prerequisite to successful implementation of cross-border projects and to bring about economic prosperity in the area (*Strategic Digest* 2004). Both sides have also come up with several other cross-border projects such as the Tamanthi Hydro-electric project, the Rhi-Tiddim and Rhi-Falam roads and the Kaladan Multi-modal Transport project. Such projects are apparently meant for uplifting the economic condition in the border areas and improving connectivity between the two countries. However, it has been widely argued that the implementation of such projects will certainly lead to human rights violation and environmental problems. Both sides have already reached an understanding on clearing the areas of hostile elements as a necessary pre-condition for smooth and meaningful execution of the projects. In this regard, large-scale deployment of army for maintenance of security in the areas is quite logical.

Following the understanding between India and Myanmar, a number of military operations have been launched by the Myanmarese army busting many camps of the rebel groups from the Indian side. The Burmese military also sealed its border to block the insurgents when the Indian military forces launched a major operation codenamed 'Operation All Clear' involving 6,000 troops to crack down the rebels in Manipur. It can be recalled that even in the late Nineties, Yangon literally gave consent to the Indian Army to track down the North East insurgents in Myanmarese territory and uproot them on foreign soil (*The Telegraph,* March 21, 2006). A top-secret operation, it denoted the extent of cooperation and understanding between the world's largest democracy and the despotic military junta.

In December 2005, Myanmarese troops overran two camps of the NSCN (Khaplang) in Saigang division bordering India even as the junta began concerted operation to flush out North East insurgents taking shelter in that country. It is worth stating that the NSCN (K) has as many as 50 camps including its general and council headquarters in Myanmar. Media reports indicate some other insurgent groups from Assam and Manipur also share some of these camps with the NSCN (K) (*The Telegraph*, December 16, 2005). It may also be recalled that the Myanmarese army had attacked the camps in the summer of 2004 although the scale of offensive was comparatively low.

The 21-member Myanmarese delegation that came to Nagaland on April 20, 2006 told Indian army officials that they had adopted a zero-tolerance approach to militant activity while identifying NSCN (K) as one of the unwanted elements in their territory. Yangon has been specifically targeting the NSCN (K) apparently because of the very fact that it dominates the so-called Eastern Nagaland, which incidentally happens to be within the territorial boundary of Myanmar. The Government of India has also allegedly extended co-operation to the junta in its counter-insurgency operation against the NSCN (K) with a motive to marginalise it into an insignificant entity. The territorial demand of the NSCN (K) consists of large areas falling on the Burmese side thereby posing a serious problem to India as it is well beyond her jurisdiction to address the issue. On the contrary, the NSCN (IM) seems to have scaled down its earlier demand from sovereignty to integration of Naga-inhabited areas of the North East under a single political unit within the framework of the Constitution of India. In other words, India wants Yangon to deal with the NSCN (K) militarily while New Delhi shall take care of the NSCN (IM) through peaceful dialogue. The strategic thinking of Indian political and military establishments is based on the notion that insurgency in the North East would come to an end once the Naga insurgency is done away with. However, such a notion holds little ground in the present context as the emerging dynamics of insurgency in the North East demonstrates that Naga insurgency has ceased to be 'mother of all insurgencies'.

The recent visit by President Kalam to Yangon in March 2006 is crucial in a sense that it was the first by an Indian President. Sources from the media indicate that Kalam's visit to Yangon was meant to oversee the implementation of several strategic projects undertaken by India (*The Telegraph*, March 8, 2006). One of such projects is the Kaladan Multi Modal Transport Project, an artery that will link Kolkata to South Mizoram, through the Arakan Coast of Myanmar. Construction of road through Arakan will help India check anti-India rebel groups operating from there. It may be recalled that the Indian government had cultivated the National Unity Party of Arakan in a larger strategy to counter rebel groups from the North East. India also maintained close ties with the KIO and CNF for the same purpose, i.e. to deny the use of their territory for anti-India activities. Visit of the Indian President also secured the signing of a framework agreement on the setting up of a ground station in Myanmar for receiving data from the Indian Remote Sensing satellite. The Indian space agency was reportedly involved in building the facility, which is now ready for use. Such a facility will certainly help in gathering information about the locations of the insurgent camps and monitor their movements. In this context, mention may be made of the request made by General Than Shwe to the Indian government for emergency military supplies including helicopters, helicopter gunships, heavy rockets, navigation equipments and most importantly the global positioning system devices for his beleaguered troops in countering anti-India rebels based in Myanmar. However, India had suggested that the equipment be deployed in joint operations with the Indian military given the lack of training on the part of Myanmar's security forces to use the equipments (Ramachandran 2005). Both the countries have been deliberating on a joint counter-insurgency operation inside Myanmar.

More check posts are coming up in the Indo-Myanmar Border to facilitate meetings between the armies of the two countries as part of India's LEP (*The Telegraph*, April 29, 2006). A check post which has already been set up near the border gate no. 1 at Moreh is said to house office of Central and State governments, including land customs, taxation, forest police and para-military forces, and medical as well as food-testing laboratories. Reports indicate that new posts would be opened at Lungwa in Nagaland's Mon district, Bihang in Churachandpur district of Manipur and at Sapi and Lokawather in Mizoram. Pertinent to note in this regard is the nod given by the Union Home Ministry to a scheme to raise the iron fencing equipped with concertina ring, along Mizoram's 404 km. border with Myanmar. The 8-ft high iron fencing along the Indo-Myanmar border has been erected to stem the rising trend of cross-border movements. Similarly, about 400 km. of Tripura's 856 km.

long borders with Bangladesh has already been fenced by the Central Government to prevent cross-border insurgency. The Union Home Ministry is also determined to complete fencing of 736 km. by the end of December 2007 even if it has to resort to force for ensuring smooth completion of the said project (*The Telegraph*, June 13, 2006). The fencing is primarily intended to curb recent trends of North East insurgent groups' crossing over to training camps in Myanmar (*The Telegraph,* April 17, 2006).

In spite of the fencing, several projects to improve connectivity in the country through construction of roads on either side of the international border have been undertaken by both the governments to check illegal movements. In March 2006, Dr. Manmohan Singh, the Prime Minister of India informed the Lok Sabha that Myanmar had agreed to a suggestion offered by India regarding facilities for joint interrogation and consular access to Indian insurgents apprehended in the neighbouring country. As the unfolding events demonstrate, the understanding between India and Myanmar is not confined to the higher echelons of the two governments but also gets reflected at the levels of sector commanders on either side of the borders. Media reports reveal that the Indian and Myanmarese armies would embark on a 'strategic co-ordination' between themselves immediately with an objective to tackle the insurgent outfits based in each other's territories in a 'meaningful way' (*The Telegraph,* June 3, 2006). As such, the Indo-Myanmar region is likely to witness a series of joint counter-insurgency operations in the near future.

The Shwe Gas Pipeline: Road to Militarization

Increasing American monopoly in the production and sale of petroleum during the post-Gulf War era precipitated a major crisis in India's energy policy. The United States had directly resisted the proposed 2,575 km. gas pipeline from Iran through Pakistan to India despite the understanding between the three countries to go ahead with the project. Pakistan's hostile nature also acted as a deterrent to such an initiative as the gas pipeline has to pass through disturbed and often dangerous physical and political quarters. Import of gas from other countries too has been stalled due to unstable political situation prevailing in those countries. India failed to get through in the international competition for energy as the economic powerhouses especially the United States tried to balance growing Asian demand with its own rising requirements. Such a situation compelled India to search for alternative energy sources that found its expression in India's LEP. India's concern for energy ultimately bore fruit when it secured the signing of an agreement in principle with Myanmar and Bangladesh to build a pipeline from Myanmarese offshore gas fields via Bangladesh to India, following a Tripartite Ministerial Meeting held in Yangon on January 12-13, 2005. Myanmar had earlier agreed to sell India gas from the Shwe gas field off the coast of Arakan State.

Daewoo International, a South Korean corporation signed a Production Sharing Contract (PSC) with the Myanmar Oil and Gas Enterprise (MOGE) in August 2000 for the right to carry out oil and gas exploration in the A-1 offshore block of Myanmar's Arakan Coast, extending over an area of 3885 square km. The exploration conducted by the Daewoo International resulted in the discovery that the whole A-1 block could hold more than 20 Trillion Cubic Feet (TCF) equivalent with 3,500 million barrels of oil. Total value of the natural gas is estimated at 19 to 26 million US dollars, which is expected to increase further. Current stakeholders of the Shwe Gas Project are Daewoo International and KOGAS of South Korea and the ONGC Videsh and GAIL of India. The Gas Authority of India Limited and ONGC Videsh Limited through an agreement in January 2002 hold 30 per cent stake in two exploration blocks—A-1 and A-3—offshore. South Korea's Daewoo International Corporation has 60 per cent and 70 per cent stakes in blocks A-1 and A-3 respectively while Korea Gas Corporation holds the remaining 10 per cent in the block A-1. It may be noted that ONGC Videsh Limited is the overseas arm of the Oil and Natural Gas Corporation and GAIL is India's largest gas transmission and marketing company.

The entire length of the pipeline is 897 km. of which Bangladesh side has to facilitate 289 km. of the pipeline. The proposed pipeline will affect 400 square km. in the state of Mizoram alone and a stretch of 5 km. on its side will be reserved and fenced off for security. However, negotiations between the Indian and Bangladesh governments have run into rough waters with Bangladesh applying conditions for carrying Myanmarese gas through its territory. The three conditions set by Bangladesh are provisions of transit facility through India to facilitate transmission of hydroelectricity from

Nepal and Bhutan to Bangladesh, assured and unhindered utilization of corridors for trading between Bangladesh and Nepal or Bhutan through Indian Territory and effective measures to reduce trade imbalance between India and Bangladesh (Khan 2005). India had earlier agreed to these conditions of Bangladesh and included them in the draft MoU signed between the three countries after initial hesitation. Later news reports dismissed the prospect of signing a bilateral treaty as part of the tri-national agreement although officially India denied holding such a position. The two countries could not make any progressive headway thereafter. Subsequently, the delay in reaching a consensus between India and Bangladesh sealed the fate of the proposed tri-nation pipeline after Myanmar backed away from the deal to supply India with the gas. Sidelining India, the military junta in Yangon signed a memorandum of understanding with China's Petro China on December 7, 2005 for the sale of 6.5 trillion cubic feet of gas from Burma's A-1 block in the next 30 years. Informed sources indicate that the MoU between Myanmar's Shwe Gas and Petro China includes preliminary plans for the construction of an overland pipeline through Myanmar to Kunming in China's Yunnan Province. Myanmar has extended its favour to China after repeatedly urging India to speed up alternative plan including setting up of pioneer projects near the gas field. The deal between Myanmar and China caused a severe blow to India as nine years of planning went up in smoke instantly. Thus, India lost the gas war to China as a price for years of neglect and faulty diplomacy in the East.

Nevertheless, the severe setback India suffered in its quest for energy security did not deter India from pursuing its goal more aggressively in recent months. Undaunted efforts made by India in this regard seems to have born fruit when Myanmar's Ambassador to India, U Kyi Thein assured his country had enough gas supplies to meet the demands of both China and India (Ramachandran 2006). This statement has allayed Indian apprehensions that the sale of gas to China would affect its availability to India. However, India has to win back the favour of the Myanmarese junta at a high price. India has reportedly agreed to buy gas on a 'take or pay' basis under which India would give Myanmar guaranteed earnings for its gas every year even in case of failure in accessing the gas. It became crucial for India to give immense concessions to Myanmar for various reasons. The threat to India's security that the Sino-

Myanmar military and economic cooperation posed was perhaps the main factor behind the Indian rethinking. India also sees Myanmar as its land bridge to Southeast Asia for boosting its 'LEP'. Most importantly, India realised that it needed the junta's co-operation to tackle insurgency in its North Eastern states (Ramachandran 2006).

Unable to strike a deal with the Bangladesh government over the gas pipeline, India has presented eight alternative routes including one via the North Eastern part of India that excluded Bangladesh. Bypassing Bangladesh will help India skirt the contentious issue of importing gas from Myanmar without having to offer any concession to the Bangladeshi government. In fact, the proposals put forward by Bangladesh were found to be quite unacceptable to India. The proposed pipeline shall pass through the Indian states of Mizoram, Assam, Bihar and West Bengal. To this end, the state run GAIL got a feasibility report of the project to import gas from Myanmar bypassing Bangladesh with the help of the SUZ Tractable of Brussels (Belgium) as technical consultants. In this case, India will have to install an additional 1000 km. of pipeline through the geographically tough North East region thereby increasing extra expenditure. However, it is calculated that the additional expenses of laying pipeline are well commensurate with the purpose since the gas from Myanmar is expected to flow over a period of 15 to 20 years or more.

Various efforts made by India to woo Myanmar resulted in the signing of a memorandum of understanding (MoU) on cooperation in petroleum sector in 2007 March when President A.P.J. Abdul Kalam visited Yangon. The MoU was reportedly signed by Joint Secretary in the Ministry of Petroleum and Natural Gas and the Director General of Energy Planning Department of the Ministry of Energy of Myanmar.

Apart from causing severe cultural and environmental destruction, the Shwe Natural Gas Project is expected to unleash large-scale militarization and human rights violations on both sides of the international border. Cases relating to human rights violations in the context of the construction of the Yadana and Yetagun pipelines during the Nineties have been well documented by the UN Commission on Human Rights and other international bodies like the Amnesty International. Previous experiences indicate increasing militarization of the affected areas with local villagers being compelled to leave their lands without proper compensation. The military appropriating agricultural lands and forcing the villagers to provide food for the troops were also recorded. The Myanmarese junta also resorted to forcible conscription of the local people as porters and labourers to construct military camps and to build roads along the pipeline corridor. Arakan and Chin States of Myanmar have witnessed increased militarization and extensive human rights violation in the last decade as a consequence of Yadana and Yetagun gas pipeline (www.shwe.org).

A greater magnitude of demographic dislocation is also expected once the construction of oil pipeline linking Arakan State's port of Akyab (Sittwe) with China's Kunming starts. The 1000 km. long conduit would be passing through areas north of the Mandalay-Lashio highway. Consequent upon this plan, some of the ceasefire groups were forced to surrender and the SSA (Shan State Army-North) was forced to move south of the road in 2005. Two of the ethnic armed opposition groups of Myanmar, which have entered into ceasefire with the junta—Shan State National Army and Palaung State Liberation Army—were pressurised to give up arms in April 2005. Besides, the SSA-North's Third Brigade was forced to relocate from its operational areas north of the highway in September by the Myanmarese Army. In this regard, one senior Shan ceasefire officer was quoted as saying that the KIA's 4th Brigade, the only group which remains currently north of the road had also come under strong pressure to move out of the area (Shan Herald Agency April 22, 2006).

Similarly, construction of the Shwe Gas Pipeline through Arakan and Chin States would necessitate establishment of permanent military camps. Military operations against Myanmarese ethnic armed opposition groups and Indian insurgent groups having bases in those areas would become highly inevitable for ensuring security to the gas pipelines. The Shwe Gas Pipeline will provide excuse to further militarise and exploit the frontier areas of Arakan and Chin States in the way the Yadana and Yetagun projects had provided a pretext for Myanmarese military regime to extend its reach into minority and opposition areas (*The Other Media*). If the earlier trend of human rights violation is an indication, the communities living in and around the pipeline corridor could experience certain consequences in the wake of extensive militarization, which is quite impending. The villagers can expect increased extortion of local food supplies, land confiscation for new military installation and pipelines, forced relocation of villagers, forced labour and increased sexual violence against local women. Such human rights violation tends to exacerbate internal displacement of civilians in Arakan and Chin States thereby causing massive influx of refugees into Bangladesh and India. Crucial fallout could be increased restriction on freedom of movement that shall affect the economic activities of the poor local populace. It will also undoubtedly undermine free activities of the rebel groups at the same time (www.shwe.org.).

The construction of pipeline on the Indian side will also expose the North East to further militarization. With 5 km. reserve on both sides of the pipeline for security reasons, establishment of military infrastructurės on such a vast tract of land is a matter of serious concern for the peoples of the North East given the poor human rights record of the Indian army and paramilitary forces. Frequent clashes between the security forces and the insurgent groups resulting in several collateral damages can be expected. It is perceived that movement of insurgents from either side of the pipeline will be stalled. Subsequently, activities of the insurgents groups will be checked to a great extent. But the pipeline if constructed as it is presently conceived will also cause serious administrative inconveniences due to artificial barriers thrown up by the pipeline. Restriction in free transportation is likely to affect the economic transaction and social intercourse among the peoples. The gas pipeline has the potential of igniting communal frenzy and ethnic polarization with serious repercussions. For instance, the Chakmas and the Brus of Mizoram have the possibility of forming an autonomous political unit much to the displeasure of the Mizos with the pipeline becoming the ethnic boundary line between communities. Human displacement and question of proper rehabilitation in addition to environmental threat would constitute some of the problems generated by the gas pipeline.

The Rail Link: [De]Railing the North East?

Apart from the Trans-Asian Highways sponsored by the International Financial Institutions, the GoI has recently initiated a new railway scheme in pursuit of India's LEP. The rail link scheme proposed by the Ministry of External Affairs (MEA) is part of the

Mekong Ganga Cooperation (MGC) Project. The scheme, which is in its nascent stage, envisages bringing the Asian countries closer to each other for ensuring more interactive economic cooperation. Keeping this aspiration in view, India and Myanmar signed a memorandum of understanding (MoU) on July 29, 2004 under which India would make available a line credit of US dollar 56 million to Yangon authorities to facilitate them to build a modern utility along the North Western and Central flank of that country. The Rail India Technical and Economic Services (RITES), an ancillary of the Indian Railways had already completed the drawing up of a preliminary feasibility survey to build a broad-gauge track between Moreh in Manipur and Segyi in Myanmar with an estimated cost of INR13.39 billion. In conjunction with this plan, Prime Minister Manmohan Singh and the Railway Minister Lalu Prasad Yadav had laid the foundation stone of the railway line from Jiribam to Tupul in Manipur's Tamenglong district in November 2004. The Indian Railways had also initiated the preliminary task to extend the broad gauge track from Jiribam in Southwest Manipur and the state's lone railhead to Moreh via Tupul and Imphal in phase manner (*The Telegraph,* April 20, 2006).

While the importance of such transport facilities cannot be denied, apprehension looms large on the unforeseen consequences likely to emerge from such a developmental project. Firstly, in the absence of a viable market structure and trading infrastructure, construction of highways and extension of railways will not augment much to alleviate the existing predicament. The North East will be reduced to a mere transit point or a corridor route in the whole scheme of things. Transformation of the region from the 'local' to the 'global' will not entail any guarantee for development as already depicted by Myanmar unless the local economy is restructured. And economic gain, if there could be any, would be neutralised by the surplus migrant population that shall arrive with the coming of highways and railways. Impending demographic pressure of the migrant population will undoubtedly result in shrinking of social and economic space of the indigenous peoples. The North East will experience intensified immigrant influx from mainland India in addition to aggravation of existing social problems including AIDS, prostitution, illegal arms-trade, illicit drug smuggling and human trafficking. The fragile local economy already in the grip of the outsiders will ultimately crumble and consequently, the indigenous peoples of the region have a chance of becoming beggars in their own land. Ultimately, the land and its distinct identity will perish. Secondly, the most immediate danger lies in further militarisation of the already militarised North East. Heavy deployment of security forces along the highways and railways will become highly inevitable given the prevalence of conflict situation in the region. Illegal detention, involuntary disappearance, arrest without warrant, undesirable frisking, summary execution, staged encounter, torture and rape can be expected on an unprecedented scale if past experiences are any indication. The army officers and the central leaders will find a more suitable ground to justify the continual extension of the Armed Forces (Special Powers) Act, 1958 (AFSPA) while much new inhuman legislation may be forthcoming. In this way, the security forces will be better equipped to launch counter-insurgency operations with higher rate of success and of course the insurgency problem may be eventually minimised through excessive physical liquidation if necessary or through coercive negotiation if possible. An alarming aspect of the whole exercise is the price peoples of the North East have to eventually pay.

India's Myanmar Policy: A Case of Political Promiscuity

Inconsistencies in Indian foreign policy remain exposed when India reversed its policy towards Myanmar in the post-Cold War era. Thirst for alternative energy sources, strategic competition with China and internal security obsession wove together into a policy that in a way exhibits a marked betrayal of the very principle India has purportedly cherished for so many decades. Initial support for democracy movement got gradually supplanted with active diplomatic engagement towards the military junta. In the process, India has virtually abandoned democracy, the very basis of its own existence on the pretext of promoting 'national interests' which in reality is the interests of the Indian industrial class. Any form of maintaining formal diplomatic relations with the military junta amounts to recognising the regime and this is not without numerous implications. Extending recognition to Yangon conspicuously defies the logic of claiming to be the largest democracy in the world. Recognition also implies endorsement of the policies adopted by the junta. Viewed thus, India has directly or indirectly become a party to the atrocious military regime, which perpetrates human rights violation against the Myanmarese people. Therefore, India deserves equal condemnation for patronising and legitimising the military dictatorship of Yangon at the cost of democracy and human rights. By aligning with the dictators, India has neutralised the mounting international pressure built up over one and a half decade against the military junta for restoration of democracy in Myanmar. India's hypocrisy and double standards become stark in its relentless opposition to the military regime in Pakistan.

Making a deal on gas pipeline involves the danger of further entrenchment of the military regime in Myanmar. A strong apprehension lies in the fact that the position of the Myanmarese generals would be strengthened considerably by the profit generated from the sale of gas, which will be used for buying military hardwares. Such a case has the potential of causing more suffering and hardship for the common people of Myanmar. General speculation got substantiated when the military regime came forward with demands to expel Myanmarese refugees and to crackdown on the pro-democracy activists taking shelter in India.

Past experience indicates the propensity of India to give more and more concessions to Myanmar in order to secure its interests in the Eastern front. The geo-political position of Myanmar enables it to exploit the strategic rivalry between China and India to its own advantage. In such a situation, India cannot afford to give further concession to Myanmar, as it will not yield any positive result for the simple fact that the competition between the two Asian giants is there to stay as long as they remain neighbours. India has already stepped into the diplomatic quagmire of Myanmar without realising the impending self-defeat. Both India and China are bound to lose the battle for strategic dominance with Myanmar assuming the role of the 'Laughing Third' holding the scale and alternately weighing in favour of the one or the other as it deems expedient to extract optimum benefit from both sides. In this context, it is significant to note that India's softness towards Myanmar in spite of the latter's extractive character reflects political bankruptcy of the Indian policy framers. It also nevertheless questions the professed independence of the Indian foreign policy. India needs to rethink its policy towards Myanmar, as the policy of constructive engagement has not resulted in a single democratic reform by the military regime. A far-sighted foreign policy demands India to snap all diplomatic ties with the despotic military junta by applying the same yardstick with which it denounces the military of Pakistan.

Dissecting India's LEP: A Post-Mortem Report

An interesting aspect, which captures the imagination of the people, is New Delhi's attitude towards the North East. The notion of North East as a 'frontier' has dominated the mindset of Indian ruling elites for a long time and there seems no end to such a legacy inherited from the colonial past. Even the introduction of the LEP could not effectuate any qualitative shift to the outlook of Indian political leadership. In spite of the new policy initiative, economic integration of the North East with mainland India remains a far-fetched dream. Development in the last one decade has not shown any meaningful step to transform the frontier concept of the North East. Earlier, the concept of frontier denoted an area that needs to be defended militarily (Konthoujam 2006b: 47). Now it has been extended to encompass an economic connotation of frontier as an area that should be exploited economically. The possibility of the North East to be used only as a transit point or as corridor lends authenticity to such an argument. Because, one can hardly see any tangible development of trading infrastructure in the region except for the construction of roads and highways. On the contrary, the centre is all set to exploit the hydroelectric potential of the North East.

The operational aspect of India's LEP in the context of the North East seems heavily confined to development of surface transport infrastructures like highways and railways. Once considered a landlocked region, the power that be in New Delhi had sought excuses for the transport bottleneck of the North East to its topographical features as an inaccessible terrain. But the onset of globalization since the early Nineties has led to falsification of such a traditional notion. The logic behind such a paradox infers that the Central Government had deliberately kept the region backward on one pretext or the other. It is only when the Indian corporate class began to realise the importance of the North East that the Government of India started acting on their behalf in collaboration with the multinational corporations (MNCs). However, in the absence of any concrete policy framework committed to bringing about substantial economic development in the North East, the peoples of this region can hardly expect a qualitative change in their existence.

India's LEP is fraught with the state-centric notion of viewing any developmental project in the North East from the security paradigm. The military implications inherent in any of these projects—be it the Tipaimukh High Dam, the Border Trade, the Trans-Asian Highways, the Trans-continental Railways or the Shwe Gas Pipeline—reflect the persistence of a colonial mindset. It is colonial in a sense that the developmental projects which are purportedly undertaken in the name of effecting economic upliftment is overshadowed by the underlying logic of militarization. The notion of development is used as a mere pretext for deployment of more military personnel and structures. Legitimacy to conduct military operations is also derived from the concept of development that asserts peace as a necessary pre-condition for development. Maintenance of peace and order makes it imperative for the state to use force. Hence, developmentalism has been a powerful justificatory doctrine of state violence against the civil population. The concept of development is employed to conceal the real intent of military operations designed to subdue the armed resistance movements in the North East. This truth substantiates the assertion of the North East as a 'frontier periphery' that needs to be defended militarily. If this is the case, it will not be false to hold the view that the North East region never formed a part of the mainstream imagination of Indian nationhood.

The Indian ruling elites tried to conceal the real picture of deploying security forces in the North East by inventing an 'illusion'. This illusion got articulated in the expression commonly made by political leaders and army officers in the public platform or the mass media—Insurgency is due to economic backwardness and that economic development has been stalled because of insurgency'. A sort of vicious circularity is implied in the statement but a deeper analysis will prove it to be a strategy to mislead the people so as to justify the perpetual military presence and their activities in the North East. Because, empirical observation reveals that insurgency is basically neither an economic problem nor economic development is stalled solely due to the existence of insurgency. It can be argued that if economic backwardness, regional imbalance, lack of infrastructural development, unemployment and poverty were considered as the prime factors responsible for the emergence of insurgency in the North East, Arunachal Pradesh would have topped the list for having the highest number of insurgent outfits which is not the case in reality. The same can be said of the state of Mizoram where relative peace exists at the moment as an exception. But the economic logic of insurgency as espoused by the Indian leaders fails to operate in Manipur, which has witnessed the existence of more than twenty armed groups although the state is economically more advanced than either Arunachal Pradesh or Mizoram. Besides, Assam ranks first in terms of economic development, yet it has several armed insurgent groups. Here, how would the Indian leaders explain the proliferation of insurgent outfits in Manipur and non-proliferation in Mizoram or Arunachal Pradesh if economic underdevelopment plays the most decisive role in the rise of insurgency movements in the North East?

The lack of a consistent policy of the Indian government to deal with insurgency is reflected in its paradoxical approach to solve the problem. An economic approach rather than a militaristic one should have been adopted to resolve the crisis if the central government believed it was the case of economic discontentment. Ironically, however, the Indian state fails to respond to the peripheral reaction with proper accommodation within the bounds of developmentalism instead of militarism. And this demonstrates a wilful negligence on the part of the Indian government to solve the problem besetting the North East for the last many decades. In the final analysis, it can be concluded that the existence of armed groups in the North East serves the Indian interest to justify the presence of its military in the region in a larger strategy to defend the mainland. Therefore, the notion of North East as a 'buffer zone' or a 'military defence shield' still holds true even today. This is further corroborated by the simple fact that AFSPA is still enforced in areas like Mizoram and Arunachal Pradesh where armed conflict is virtually non-existent.

The indigenous peoples of the North East have nothing to expect from India's LEP, as the prospect of economic benefits likely to be associated with it is still fuzzy. Certain informed quarters have observed that despite the rise in the overall volume of trade between India and Myanmar, trade through the Moreh-Tamu route has been declining over the years (Yumnam 2005: 77). The border trade posts on the Indian side is also said to be lacking in infrastructure and supportive institutional structure. Owing to such an absence of appropriate domestic preparedness, border trade has not shown any significant stride even after the signing of border trade agreement about a decade back. This is not unexpected since economic development of the North East never figured prominently in the evolution of this policy. Observation coming from analyst indicated that security considerations far outweigh economic considerations as far as the Indo-Myanmar border trade is concerned (Konsam 2005b: 92). Besides, the security overtone involved in any of the projects associated with the LEP seemed highly incompatible with the prospect of gain the common people are expected to derive from it.

The implementation of India's LEP exhibits a tendency to reduce the North East to a mere corridor to Southeast Asia. A glaring example can be found in the case of the Shwe Gas Pipeline project. So far, there is no visibility of installing any gas plant in the North East where the pipeline shall have to pass through. Paradoxically the cost of the gas pipeline shall have to be borne by the peoples of this region in terms of environmental destruction, demographic dislocation and human rights violation. Worse still, the gas from the developing gas fields of Tripura and Assam will also be transported through the pipeline to Kolkata. This is nothing less than colonial exploitation of a backward area by a metropolitan power. Similar is the case with the Asian Highways or the Trans-Asian Railways that are being considered as the backbone of continental LEP. Unless there are structural changes in the mode of production of the North East economy, the region will only remain a 'transit point' or rather a mere bridge in the execution of future trans-national trade. Reading between the lines, the only things the North East can expect from India's LEP are economic exploitation, demographic transfiguration, environmental destruction, obliteration of cultural identity, intensified political subjugation and extensive militarization.

REFERENCES

Arif, Nazeeb. 2006. 'The North East: Political Hub for International Business'. *The North-East Window,* Volume-II, Issue 11, April 30.

Baruah, Sanjib. 2004. *Between South and Southeast Asia: North East India and the Look East Policy.* Guwahati: CENISEAS.

Chakma, Suhas. 2003. *Time Out of Hand: An Analysis of the Statement at the United Nations Working Group on the Draft Declaration on the Rights of Indigenous Peoples*. New Delhi: AITPN.

Kangujam, Sanatomba. 2005. 'India's Look East Policy: The Unfolding Dynamics', *Alternative Frames*. Vol. 1, Issue I, October-December.

Khan, Sharier. 2005. 'Delhi May Accept Dhaka's Terms', *The Daily Star*.

Konsam, Ibo Singh. 2005a. 'Insurgency in North East India and the Myanmar Connection' in S.K. Agnihotra (eds.). *Perspective of Security and Development in North East India*. New Delhi: Concept Publishing Company.

———. 2005b. 'Indo-Myanmar Border Trade: Imperatives and Present Status' in Gurudas Das, *Indo-Myanmar Border Trade: Status Problems and Potential*. New Delhi: Akansha Publishing House.

Konthoujam, Indrakumar. 2005a. 'Mapping India's Look East Policy: Shifting Alignment', *Alternative Frames*. Vol. I, Issue I, October-December.

———. 2006b. 'Imagining the North East through India's Look East Policy: Towards a Contextual Understanding', *Alternative Frames*, Vol. II, Issue II, January-March.

Langpoklakpam, Suraj Singh. 2006. *Movement for Democracy in Myanmar*. New Delhi: Akansha Publishing House.

Ministry of External Affairs, Government of India. 1993. *Annual Report, 1992-93*. New Delhi.

Oinam, Bhagat. 2005. 'Manipur' in Mayumi Murayama (eds.). *Sub-Regional Relations in the Eastern South Asia: With Special focus on India's North Eastern Region*. Tokyo: Yugengaisha Tohkohsha.

Ramachandran, Sudha. 2005a. 'Indian Troops Poised to Enter Myanmar'. *Asia Times Online*.

———. 2006b. 'Myanmar on Laughing Gas'. *Asia Times Online*

Strategic Digest. 2004. Vol. 34, No. I, November.

Shan Herald Agency, 22 April 2006. Sino-Burma Pipeline will set of more Relocation <http://www.shwe.org/news/newsarchive/2006_04_01_archive.html>

The Other Media & Shwe Gas Project Campaign Committee India. *Shwe Gas Pipeline Project-Implications on India and Burma. (place and year of publication).*

The Telegraph, 2006. Guwahati, 21 March.

The Telegraph, 2005. Guwahati, 16 December.

The Telegraph, 2006. Guwahati, 8 March.

The Telegraph, 2006. Guwahati, 29 April.

The Telegraph, 2006. Guwahati, 13 June.

The Telegraph. 2006. Guwahati, 3 June.

The Telegraph, 2006. Guwahati, 20 April.

'The Shwe Gas Movement'. <http://www.shwe.org/issue/abuses>

Yumnam, Amar 2005. 'Indo-Myanmar Trade through Moreh: Status and Assessment' in Gurudas Das, *Indo-Myanmar Border Trade: Status, Problems and Potentials*, New Delhi: Akansha Publishing House.

12

Look East Policy: Its Gaze and Danger in the North East

HANJABAM GYANENDRO SHARMA

State foreign policy is often shaped by consideration of varied interests. Taking cue from this point, India's Look East Policy can be considered as a tendency of reshaping its foreign policy in accordance with the global turn of capitalism. Formulation of LEP reflects the need to review India's geo-political position in the ongoing global configurations in general and in the South East Asian region in particular. Introduction of the phenomenon of Post-Fordism in India became visible when Structural Adjustment Programmes were initiated in the beginning of 1990s. LEP is another initiative on the lines of the new wave primarily aimed at the introduction of economic 'liberalization' with the urge for market expansion in the North East region. Political economy of LEP can thus be located in the attempt to redefine India's relation to South East Asia in the context of globalization.

The paper focuses on the mapping of the North East as a visible territory in the globalspace through LEP. T' is is an investigation of the policies that India is formulating with a view to make the 'local' a 'global space'; a move for active participation in the growing trade with the South Asian countries. The paper explores the context of LEP as an emergence of a new global imagining at the 'local', which is represented by the North East. Apart from making an attempt to locate LEP in the building of the 'global', the paper also directs the discussion towards an interrogation of the cultural shift that LEP is aiming at and the possible tension associated with the shift, its cultural and political forms.

Ordering the Navigation of LEP

Political perspective of the new initiative called LEP can be recovered from the vents, which subsequently led to a necessity to redefine India's position in the newly emerging global political economic 'order'. Collapse of the Soviet Union and consequent departure from the socialist 'order' led to a situation where there was a move towards global participation in the making of a neo-liberal 'order' as a new mode of governance and relations among the governments. The US became the main architect. A new world order was visualized with finance capital accorded a central role in the process. The forces exerted by IMF-WB have been successful in persuading other states to adjust themselves to the American framework and as a result many states began to inquire into the prospects of institutionalizing the American initiative. Many of these moves already found success in revaluating and redefining respective foreign as well as domestic policies *vis-à-vis* the changing global politico-economic scenario. India, being no exception, has not only started following the prescriptions of the IMF-WB but also has invented a 'void' in its traditional economic regime. Following the directions of the IMF-WB on the one hand and demands of domestic 'capitalists' on the other, India's foreign policy makers feel the need of undoing the earlier objectives of both domestic and foreign policies, though not completely. The balance of payment crisis in July 1991 is one such case that induced the Government of India to authorize the claim that India needs a shift to a liberalized, privatized and globalised economy. Introduction of Structural Adjustment Programmes in 1991 by the Narasimha Rao government gave the ground to formulate the LEP in 1992.

LEP inherits both political and economic implications of the larger policy framework associated with Liberalization, Privatization and Globalization. Politically LEP is an approach to avoid possible confrontations with neighbouring countries like China. It is a new agenda of reformulating *panchsheel,* which, in the contemporary context where India has established its importance as an economic player and as a useful partner in the South Asian and South East Asian region, needs to be revalidated both to balance China and insert India's role in the strengthening of economic ties particularly with the South Asian region. After SAARC fell short of expectations, the region realized the problems and difficulties in achieving the stipulated objectives. With India's intention to play a dominant role increasingly on the wane, it started looking towards East with a view to open the incentives as well as to capture the opportunities.

Despite many factors involved in the making of the initiative, a few can be mentioned to give a picture of the political navigation of Look East Policy. India's IT (Information Technology) capacity, which is another key factor in framing new ties between India and Southeast Asian countries is one example. Taking into consideration India's growing GDP which is currently standing at 6.5 and the huge amount of energy resources required to meet the domestic growth-engine, it needed an economically and politically visible appearance in the region to tap the opportunity coming out of successful ties with South East Asian economies. For instance, ever increasing demand of natural gas in India that by 2010 may stand at a staggering 400 million standard cubic metres a day necessitates to form viable political and economic ties with South East Asian economies to fill this gap.

The prospect of having cordial ties with South Asian societies can also be considered in the light of the historical linkages that India and the these societies share especially in religion, culture and architecture. Though the political navigation of colonialism produces the mapping of a fragmented geo-political space of historically connected cultural landscape of India and South Asian societies, the shared values and beliefs put testimony to the fact that there is a strong possibility to remake the ties. In the post colonial phase, Cold War politics starts remapping the geo-political space of the world territory on the basis of bloc formation and this subsequently leads to further fragmentation of both the ties within the region and between India and the region. As India kept aloof from South East Asian politics due to its commitment to Non-Alignment policy, the distance became pronounced among the societies, including India's in relation to the former.

The Code: LEP Presented

Cultural logic of economic domination, which is more appropriate to describe the present global scenario of formation of hegemony and counter-hegemony, exhibits another perspective of examining LEP by situating it in the contemporary experience of capitalism. It is a well-established practicc since the period of formal colonialism down to contemporary period of imperialist imaginations that culture inscribes legitimacy for political intervention as well as the very ideological space of imperialism, thus formalizing the inscription that subsequently practices imperialism as an invisible exercise. The notion of political domination by the use of military force no longer holds ground. With the rise of neo-imperialism the pattern and techniques of colonialism has changed substantially. Hegemonic formation of hyper superpowers like USA or emerging superpowers like China and India can be considered as a political decoding of imperial imaginings of culture and its possibility of being inscribed in economic opportunities. American 'popular cultures', Cola drinks, media and 'knowledge' formation in various specialized disciplines can be cited as the best examples in this regard. Though debates around the role of popular culture and 'knowledge' in the hegemonic and counter hegemonic formations are not dealt in the paper, understandings in the field have already built up to an acknowledgeable level.

LEP can reveal the emergence of a cultural 'locale' in the attempt to globalize the cultural landscape drawn between India and Eastern societies. It further generates a proposal that LEP is not merely an opportunity package to be shared across the boundaries; rather, it is a search for a compatible strategy to enable the 'Global' to operate in the landscape given above. From the experience of globalization, one can show that LEP constitutes another cultural logic complementary to the phenomenon of late capitalism in the world. Inherent with the logic, the North East will appear as a mere possibility in the imperial imagining of the Economic giants of the west and Asia.

Further examining the mode of cultural operation the paper draws on 'culture', which operates in a historical context as a representation of both discontinuity and continuity of the context. Culture generates meaning and permeates into the exercise of materiality that is manifested in various discourses of knowledge in the form of human sciences, art, literature, film, and other forms of popular culture. Culture is both an embodiment of knowledge and values embodied in meanings associated with the discourse of knowledge. It is clearly manifested in objects of knowledge and attainment of subjectivity. Following Tomlinson, culture is predicated on a discontinuous space and reflects distinctiveness of societies. However, territoriality of culture has been largely deterritorialised as narrated by the experience of globalization. The invented global space that is produced as spatio-temporal relations by globalization has presented huge displacements of the earlier form of territoriality of culture. As a result culture becomes mobile and territory is no more a fixed reference.

LEP captures the political imagining of 'Reterritorialization' of the North East in the global space. The region is reinvented to make it visible in the global space. The visibility is founded by giving an account of the factors responsible for the chronic underdevelopment that the region has been experiencing since British colonial rule. The account, put in the neo-liberal vocabulary, is directed towards linking its underdevelopment to the 'landlocked position', the outcome being unavailability of opportunities and incentives arising out of 'tested' neoliberal governance and methods of development. Thus the invented global space gives a gaze over the region and the attempt to make it visible necessarily produce an image of the region a politically 'reterritorialised' North East which is visible to the neo-liberal methods of development. It shows that LEP is more than an economic project. It is also an attempt that seeks to involve a political reinvention of the North East.

At the same time, the visibility is arranged by 'deterritorializing' the cultural particularities so that mobile formation of culture that is globally pushed forward is enabled to articulate a project of its own operation. The arrangement is inscribed in LEP and from this fact one can judge that the privileged position resulting from the territorial remapping of the region that is visible to the vocabulary of the gaze of LEP is actually deterritorialized in the global space. It marks certain features worth considering. While the North East is arranged a visible order by reinventing it in particular political shape that is compatible to the changing situations in the South Asia and the world at large the very attempt to image the visibility is characterized by contradictions and resistance. While many keep waiting for its implementation, the expectations may not be at par with the challenges it poses and, of course, the implosion of LEP in the region will tell the fortune of the project. Paradoxical logic of 'gazing' and 'imagining' the North East is thus an anxiety of the people in the region of which the paper can be cited as a partial reflection, and this is purely attributable to the intrusion of the LEP project.

Decoding in the North East: LEP Unmasked

The North East along the historical, cultural and political arrangements of civilizations in the rest of India is prominently present in a different order, though not essentializing its distinctiveness. Though it seemingly informs of the civilizational unity, the historical experiences of communities in the region tell a different story when one looks at the context in which they encounter with many forces, colonialism, for example. North East was significantly reshaped in the encounters it had with the colonial modernity. It was reinvented in different forms with various devices legitimated during the colonial rule till the first half of the twentieth century. It had experienced unprecedented ranges of conflicts within the 'encounter' and this still continues even today with anxieties and hangovers even after the British had left them many decades ago. The LEP, as pointed out earlier, is another project to reinvent the North East in a new form that would subject both to validations and contestation in itself. We will discuss it in the light of the cultural contestation, taking place in the region.

The origin of the Indian cultural influence on the indigenous way of life in the region can be traced from the Mughal period while Western culture came with the advent of British imperialism in the region. In Assam, Manipur and Tripura, where Hinduism had a deep root it was less pronounced. In the other four states, viz., Nagaland, Mizoram, Meghalaya, Western culture as propounded and promoted by Christianity is predominant. Even then the younger generations of the region are equally under the heavy spell of Western culture characterised by Western popular music and Hollywood lifestyle. Religious affiliation to two distinct and alien religions Hinduism and Christianity has created a line of division, which has resulted in various kinds of conflicts among the peoples of North East.

The LEP will enhance the present trend of popular culture in the North East that exhibits narrative experiences of 'deterritorialization process'. The homogenization process of globalization that is aimed at bringing about a 'single space' certainly puts the question before the indigenous lifestyles of how to construct their identity and cultures *vis-à-vis* global (read American) culture. The phenomenon of deterritorialization occurs simultaneously with reterritorialization process. Reterritorialization process involves reinscription and reinsertion of new cultural articulations into a particular cultural domain entirely different from the arriving global pastry made up of different tastes and meanings.

The strong undercurrents of cultural forces have permeated as well as assimilated with the popular culture in the North East. The cultural intrusion from India and the West has brought about not only dissension but also enmity among the peoples of the North East. As such, the simultaneous mobile formation of global culture and Indianization has put a threat to the hopes of safeguarding the distinct cultural identities of the region.

If one examines the nature of the contestations and the practices of the experiences of being a part of the dominant forces on the one hand and a subjugated but resisting side on the other, the imperialism can be foregrounded in culture. In many cases, colonial domination operates along with cultural imperialism. And cultural imperialism lingers on for a long time even after the decolonization of the colonies. In the post-colonial period, cultural imperialism takes a totally different form and needs to be considered on a different plane. If one observes the proceedings and undercurrents in the North East, one realizes that demographic restructuring or reengineering (read huge influx of outsiders into the region) is playing a pivotal role in superimposing the Hindu Indian cultures. Cultural obliteration of the indigenous culture and the subsequent assimilation into the Hindu Indian cultures is projected towards a negation to separate nationality of being an Indian and identity of being a native possible. However, weathering away of the reality of the 'nation' (Indian nation) in the North East is made to admit prominence of political practice of 'resistance' underlying many 'national efforts' in the region.

Obliteration and subsequent assimilation of territorialized cultures into the mobile global space and culture have become an effective but subtle tool to negate the aspirations for being involved in a distinctive 'national discourse' as defined in the movements seen in the region. Physical presence of inscribed outsiders, inauguration of megacultural manufacturers in the form of electronic media (particularly Doordarshan and All India Radio) and popular Hindi and Hollywood movies and music, installation of digital and terrestrial traffic system display the cultural presence of 'forgetting' supplanted by adaptations to new images. It also provides a possibility of the retrieval enterprises in the form of 'counter memory' in that the possessed self is interrogated with a new vision and recognition of the unbridgeable gap between the present identity which is largely shaped by the dominant articulations and the visualized memory but not essentially implying a return to 'traditions'. 'Counter memory' emerges as a form of resistance against both forgetting and adaptations in the contemporary political practices of experiences in the region. For instance, an armed opposition group had banned the screening of Hindi movies and telecasting of Hindi channels in satellite TV in Manipur. Similar moves to desist from screening Hindi movies were also seen in Assam. The possibility of encompassing anti-globalization dimensions into the present liberation movement just like the Zapatista model of movement as in Mexico cannot be ruled out.

Apart from the forms of contestation mentioned above there are some other conflicts that will emerge in the context of LEP operation. Inability to provide a major portion of the occupied cultural experiences to the formation of alien cultural values is bound to give rise to a fundamentalist and conservative politics in the North East and as a result desire for democratic engagement with the differences already present in the political arsenal of the various communities in the region may be renounced and may further give way to disorientation of the entire political order of the region to a worse direction. Such a scenario is seen in the case of many parts of the world, especially in the Middle East, India and in the United States.

India's LEP will further generate an array of marginalizations linked to the economic development which is predicated to the neoliberal methods and understandings. Prior to the Structural Adjustment Programmes (SAP) the North East was subservient to the capitalist structure of the Indian economy. The SAPs failed to fully tap the resources in the region due to many factors ranging from law and order to capital insipidity of the mega companies operating in the core economy. The North East was not viably present in the core economy and this is the reason why infrastructure initiatives were not taken into consideration when development is defined in the region. It is no doubt that the middle class which has proximity with the State and a small 'group' of capitalists in the region may enjoy the benefits from the much-hyped India's LEP. The large populace of the North East region may be dislocated socially and economically. The current trend of 'retreatist behaviour' in the region particularly in Manipur can be considered to be closely associated with the peripheralization process and such phenomenon may strike hard to the economically vulnerable sections of the society.

An examination of the relations between the weaker sections, having no or very little access to productive infrastructure, and the possible effects of LEP raises new questions. The availability of huge consumer goods and items with the full operationalization of LEP may usher the economically weaker sections of our society into retreatist behaviour. Retreatist behaviour is a social phenomenon which manifests a crisis between the low purchasing power and rising wants and needs seen in consumerism. Such phenomenon bears more psychological implications in the North East that has already been a conflict zone.

The high-pitched form of consumerism, a LEP phenomenon, will endanger the North East by exposing it to a situation where there is tension in the wants which, in order to balance global consumer tastes, images, needs and meanings, consequently compels it to desire things which are actually absent. This is not a novel experience as we have already observed it in the case of Marshall Island that talks about excessive consumption of liquor and high rate of suicide. With the full operationalization of India's LEP, the abundant availability of consumerist items and goods in the North East region is more or less certain which would in most cases serve the interest of these MNCs.

In conclusion, LEP needs to be targeted taking into consideration of cultural inscription embedded in the policy imperatives by affirmatively judging that it is a project of formation, implantation of the 'global' at the local. Going further from this understanding one may put LEP in a schematic fashion that it is a project grounded not on localization of the 'global' but on building of the 'global' at the local. In this context, Globalization could rather be seen in the way the global is produced in different forms and different layers, or precisely, globalization is the invention of many 'global'. The question therefore is how much we are a part of the making of the 'global' on us and what our own position will be in inventing our 'local' to be the 'global' when we talk about Look East Policy in the North East.

REFERENCES

Appadurai, A. 1991. 'Global Ethnoscapes: Notes and Queries for a Transnational Anthropology' in R.G. Fox (ed.). *Recapturing Anthropology: Working in the Present*, Santa Fe; School of American Research.

Christian, McMurray and Smith Roy, 2001. *Diseases of Globalization: Socio-Economic Transitions and Health.* UK: Earthscan Publication.

Christophe Jaffrelot, 2003. 'India's Look East Policy: Asianist Strategy in Perspective', *India*, Vol. II, No. 2, April.

Clifford, James. 1997. *Routes: Travel and Translation in the Late 20th Century*. Cambridge: Harvard University Press.

'Cultural-Imperialism' http://en.wikidpedia.org/wiki/cultural-imperialism

Harvey, David. 1989. *The Condition of Postmodernity*. Oxford Publication: Blackwell Publishers.

Kumar, Anand. 2005. India-Myanmar Gas Pipeline Through Bangladesh: Pipe Dream. Source <http://www.saag.org/papers13/paper1216.html>.

Merton, RK and D Chirot. 1986. *Social Change in the Modern Era*. San Deigo: Harcourt Brace Jovanovich.

Robertson, R. 1992. *Globalization: Social Theory and Global Culture*. London: Sage Publication.

Strassoldo, R. 1992. 'Globalism and Localism: Theoretical Reflections and Some Evidence' in Z Mlinar (ed.). *Globalization and Territorial Identities*. Aldershot: Avebury.

13

India's Look East Policy and the Political: An Interrogation into the Survey of the 'Global' in Manipur

HIDAM PREMANANDA

This essay is a general engagement with the idea of development, which is frequently referred to in its relation to the notion of security. Despite various existing perceptions on what constitutes development, it is crucial to raise certain fundamental issues on Look East Policy (LEP) by relating it to the context of security. An interesting part of the general engagement with the debates around the issue lies with the attempts to find connection between development and security *vis-à-vis* the application of LEP in Manipur. The connection can be retrieved from the historical configurations underpinning the emergence of Association for South East Asian Nations (ASEAN) characterised by various ideological underpinnings and lines of divisions across the region—in Southeast Asia during the 'Cold War'. The question of development, so prominently embodied in the ASEAN doctrines, and the full-fledged economic integration through LEP visualized in Southeast Asia by 2012 clearly show an understanding on the need to institute a corrective norm in the relations among the countries.

The implications of the perceptions are instituted in such a way that it can ensure establishment of a link between development and security. Political preoccupation of security continues to be intensively considered a basic condition for national reconstruction. The reverse is not less significant than the former to say that security is governed more efficiently when development is well regulated. This provides a ground for interrogation. The essay presents an overview of the historical articulation of regionalism in Southeast Asia to comprehend the Indo-ASEAN partnership of which Look East Policy is one such embodiment that is intensively built from various layers. It seeks to register an interrogation of the essentialization of perceptions inscribed within the survey of the 'global' in Manipur. The interrogation revolves round the ways in which LEP will contribute to the production of fragmented subjectivities in Manipur located in its search for the conditions governing security and development. Fragmentation of the collective experience in terms of ethnicity, community, language, culture and gender has found rarefied articulation in the 'global'.

Incitement: ASEAN/LEP

Britain's involvement in Southeast Asia had a specific political meaning in the context of its imperial ventures during the early twentieth century. British imperial experiences in Malaya, Burma, Singapore, and Thailand reflected the obsessions of nineteenth century imperial mapping of the region. These experiences have produced their own trajectories in the contemporary history of the region. The cardinal importance of Southeast Asia, which was considered to constitute a chain of imperial defense, was pretty much recognised by the colonial presence during the time (Welfare 2006: 14). Historical evolution of Southeast Asia itself is easily available to the imperial imaginings and that it was mapped from the colonial political economy and military strategy could also be retrieved from the survey of the history of the Southeast Asian countries. Furthermore, the context of political assertion, amid different political and ideological eruptions of the 1960s, only laid claims over the implication of the need for integration among the newly independent states in the region. The implication of the integration can be understood by taking into account the nature of political conditions prevailing at the point of time where the association that we know today as ASEAN emerged.

At the end of the first half of the twentieth century, the historic verities of South Asia were beginning to assert themselves for political independence. Burma was impossible to be denied of independence, Thailand had already slipped out of the imperial control in 1930s, Malaya got independence by 1957, Malaysia in 1967, Singapore ended its relation with the empire in 1965, the Indo-China territories finally became independent state of Laos, Cambodia, North and South Vietnam, the Dutch were compelled to leave Indonesia in 1949, and Philippines got independence in 1946. However, the environment that emerged after political independence gave new challenges due to prevailing political and ideological currents of the period. Emergence of Japan as an economic powerhouse produced various pressures in the region. Final replacement of British hegemony by the United States with the outbreak of Vietnam War and Chinese communist influence gave enormous alarm to the ruling elites of the newly independent states. The external pressure of domination and attempts to repeal hegemonic images of old powers by newly emerging power structures were potentially threatening to the sustenance of new found independence in the region. The internal feuds, rivalries, and disputes among the newly independent states only served to weaken the region further internationally. For example, Burma and Thailand experienced new twists and turns in the last five decades. Indonesian confrontation with Malaysia and internecine strife and genocide in Vietnam and Cambodia immensely heightened the anxiety over security and integrity of the states. This was the situation in the beginning of the second half of the twentieth century that characterised the political impression of the whole of Southeast Asia. By the beginning of the 1960s political leadership of the region started to articulate a strategy for addressing the issues in international relations among the newly independent states. The failed strategy of the British Empire to bring the region under direct control of the Empire got revived in the form of a new political initiative under the leadership of Thanat Khoman, the Thai Foreign Minister (Sadhu 1992: xvii).

At the same time, other political leaders like Malayan Prime Minister Tunkul Abdul Rahaman and the President of the Philippines Carlos. P Garcia also initiated similar moves and finally, reached an agreement on a proposal for a Southeast Asian Friendship and Economic Treaty in 1959. In 1961, Malaya, Philippines and Thailand formed the Association of Southeast Asia (ASA). Keeping in mind the diplomatic positions and the relations of the three original members with other external powers, the intent of the ASA could not serve the purpose of the formation. Thailand and the

Philippines were allies of the United States while Malaya was tied to Britain in the Anglo-Malayan treaty. Thanat took the initiative to organise a meeting of foreign ministers at Bang Sean, a coastal resort at Bangkok. Later, the Meeting came out with the Bangkok Declaration of 8th August, 1967. The Declaration called for the establishment of the Association of Southeast Asian Nations (ASEAN). Adam Malik, the Indonesian Foreign Minister suggested the title of the Association. The objectives of ASEAN were described as acceleration of economic growth, social progress, and cultural development in the region through joint endeavors in the spirit of equality and partnership in order to strengthen the foundations of a prosperous and peaceful community of Southeast Asian Nations; the promotion of regional peace, and stability through abiding respects for justice and active collaboration and mutual assistance in the economic, social and cultural arena, technical and scientific, administrative matters. It rigorously foregrounded the need for expansion of trade and transport and communications; the promotion of Southeast Asian Studies.

A brief look at the statistics of recent years shows positive signs of prosperity. Between 1993 and 1996 exports between ASEAN countries expanded from US$ 43 billion to almost US$ 80 billion in 1996, representing an annual growth of some 28 per cent. In 1996, of 28.6 million tourist arrivals in ASEAN, 40 per cent came from within ASEAN. ASEAN has become a major economic player with Gross Domestic Product of US$ 737 billion and a total of US$ 720 billion. In 2002 EU was ASEAN's second largest export market and third largest trading partner after the USA and Japan. Perhaps, however, the most important general political development in the recent years has been the declaration of ASEAN Concord II at a meeting in Bali in 2003. It was declared that political and security cooperation, economic and socio-cultural cooperation would be constituted as the three major pillars for durable peace, stability and shared prosperity (Welfare 2006: 25).

Indian Involvement in the ASEAN enterprise for economic cooperation was mooted in 1991 with the formulation of Look East Policy. China, South Korea and ASEAN countries have emerged as significant entities among India's most dynamic trade partners in the world. Starting as a sectoral dialogue partner of ASEAN in 1992, India became a full dialogue partner in 1995. In 2003, India signed a Framework Agreement for Comprehensive Economic

Cooperation involving Free Trade Agreements to be implemented over a ten-year period. India's Framework Agreement with ASEAN is complemented by other bilateral and sub-regional attempts towards economic cooperation including bilateral agreements with Thailand and Singapore with sub-regional initiatives such as BIMST-EC and Mekong-Ganga Cooperation (MGC).

It has been recognised that a combination of fourteen of the largest and fastest growing economies of Asia—East Asia and Japan, China, India, Korea (JACIK) trade bloc—is a potential third pole of the world economy. A total population of 3 billion or half of the world population will have gross national income of US$ 16 trillion, much larger than either NAFTA or EU. JACIK's exports will add up to US$ 1.66 trillion compared to US$ 1.48 trillion of NAFTA. The combined official reserves of the JACIK economies at US$ 1.6 are more than US$ 2 trillion. Regional Trade Agreement in JACIK countries could produce efficiency gains worth US$ 147 billion. Because of this potentiality involved in the creation of institutional capacity of integrating the Southeast Asian economies with Indian economy, 'regionalism' became a highly valued enterprise in the last decade. With a US$ 700 billion economy growing at 7-8 per cent per annum, an even faster growth rate and sizeable (300 million strong) middle class, India has to direct its attention towards East. Recent studies indicate that India is poised to emerge the third largest economy in the world by 2032. Another study by IMF finds India poised to sustain about 7 per cent growth rates for over next 30-40 years with very few downside risks (IMF 2004: 118). According to IMF, India is contributing nearly 10 per cent of the global growth and 20 per cent of Asian growth (IMF 2005: 36-37).

Apart from these, the share of East Asia as a trade partner in India's trade is increasingly more important compared to the EU or the United States. India's trade with China grew by nearly 75 per cent in 2004 to surpass US$ 13 billion. Trade with Korea stood at 48 per cent in 2003. ASEAN-India trade has grown by over 30 per cent over the past couple of years and is projected to cross US$ 30 billion by 2007. Keeping a view on the prospects of aligning with the tariff structures of the Southeast Asia India has been autonomously engaging in tariff reduction since 1991. In the Budget 2005-06, the peak tariffs were brought down from 20 per cent to 15 per cent. Because of economic growth and ambitious unilateral trade liberalization, India's imports have grown by 27 per cent a year on average over the past three years and crossed US$ 100 billion in 2004-05. India is evolving FTAs with ASEAN and +3 countries. India signed a Framework Agreement on Comprehensive Economic Cooperation with ASEAN at the Bali Summit involving FTAs to be implemented in ten years. This is complimented by bilateral agreements signed with Thailand and Singapore (RIS Discussion Paper). India's strengths in software and services R&D, engineering and designing, and high quality manufacturing have acquired global dimension, for instance, Samsung's R&D Centre in India, recently announced successful development of hybrid mobile phones. China's Huawei Technologies employs hundreds of engineers in Bangalore; Hyundai uses its Indian operations as an outsourcing base for compact cars; Toyota is outsourcing engines from its Indian plant for Southeast Asian markets. The production networks also include those being developed by Indian enterprises. For instance, Daewoo Trucks has become linked with the production chain of Tata Motors with its acquisition by the latter. Several Indian companies have also begun to take advantage of cheaper manufacturing costs for hardware in China and other East Asian countries by rationalising their production (RIS Discussion Paper 1). The trend is more likely to be strengthened with the implementation of LEP. The changing demographic profile currently experienced by the Southeast Asian countries seems complimentary with India's increasing young middle-class working population. Look East Policy has implanted the channel of combating the demographic challenges of these countries by giving access to the working population of the country through IT and other service sector industries.

An Interrogation: LEP/the Political

The link between security and development can be seen as a gradual application of the technology to regulate other sectors of social life that finally count as 'Governmentality' in Foucault's theoretical framework (Gordon and Miller 1991; Lemke 2001: 190-207; Dean 1999). It is a concept that seeks to explain the process of normalization in the relation between the objects to be governed and the rationality of applying the technology of government/ governance in such a way that a series of institutions, which develop in the process of installing the relation, are used as sources of knowledge. Consequently, justification of the practices and application of the technology to other domains of life including personal life follows. It is, in brief, a technology of self-regulation adopted by individuals involved and thus developing a particular subjectivity fixed onto it. The interrogation in this section will focus on how governmentalising of security and development transforms the *'political'* into the production of fragmented subjectivities in Manipur.

Technology of regulation is deeply inscribed in the contemporary liberal development models. Interestingly, rise of contemporary 'market centred' development creates a regime based on mobility of capital, in marked contrast to the general assumption that it involves less regulation compared to earlier or other non-liberal models of development. There is an increasing concern, or perhaps even wider concerns, to regulate the mobility of capitals on a non-territorialised space. The entire spectrum of integrationist school of development holds credence to show the link between security and development. However, amid the optimism, which is expected to come out of the initiatives between the ASEAN and JACIK, there are still some questions that need to be directed at the larger policy framework, that is, Look East Policy. Though there are signs of prosperity among the members of ASEAN and growing concerns of strengthening the initiatives under the political leadership of the countries, actual application of the project in the North East and Manipur, in particular, is not possible without giving rise to the interrogations concerning the issue of the 'political'.

The rationality behind the formulation of economic and cultural landscapes of LEP directs the expectations around the Project towards an integration of the people of Manipur to the global matrix. A rigorous thrust, mainly at the political level of the project, seeks to register credence to the expectation that LEP is opening an opportunity for access to other parts of the world. Claims are relentlessly made of unavailability of other options. As such, interactions and openings with the outside world otherwise is deemed impossible. Though not in conformity with the nature of diplomatic initiation deemed integral to the formulation of the policy, it will be illogical to deny the subsequent intensification of 'political occupation' experienced by the people. The *'political'* may be understood in terms of 'enabled articulation' grounded on the experiences as a field of encountering the formation of a particular political subjectivity. The term is rather used as a suggestive formulation. However, a brief discussion on the notion of 'political space' can be compared with the current term that is the 'political' as Ernesto Laclau and Chantal Mouffe (1985) engage with it in *Hegemony and Socialist Strategy*. The term 'enabled articulation' or simply 'political occupation' experienced may be understood in the way political concerns are articulated on the part of both the resistance movement and the Government on the one hand and expansion of a 'space' which is politically defined with references to the terms of discourse constructed as 'civil society' on the other. The two have jointly developed a regime of experiences. This regime is preoccupied with diverse and contradictory emphases on questions of law, nation, development, security, peace, violence, 'order' and identity. That the *'political'* is in the process of transformation becomes more vivid in terms of the locations of the references, which are produced by the very transformation of the *'political'*. The transformation shows the presence of diverse trajectories in Manipur—imperial structure instituted within the 'national formation' of the 'Indian' in Manipur, parallel nationalist articulations, development with explicit reference to 'security', and identity as representation. A survey of the 'global' in the political landscape of the development agenda inscribed in LEP has further invented new political positions that will consequently result in a serious elaboration of the nature of the occupation. As a result, cultivation of the 'political' may be more pronounced than ever before in that experiences will be elaborated as a field of enhanced intervention, contestation, divisions and intensified articulations and disarticulations.

The incitement behind the formulation of the LEP may proffer several other avenues to navigate the possible ways of applying it alongside the much-vaunted economic integration. However, one of the issues involved in it is whether the incitement of the glamour built up around LEP will be in accord with the contemporary political rendering of the kind of experiences that the people have been undergoing at present. The issue is particularly significant in terms of the enormity of political convulsions experienced in the entire period of about last six decades in Manipur. This is an issue that would certainly redefine the 'political' of which contemporary experiences narrate in multiple dimensions.

The logic behind the installation of 'global' is thus closely related with issues pertaining to means and ways to control the 'political'.

It implies an essentialization of a norm aimed to be instituted at the level of governmentality. Thus LEP can be seen as a project to identify the vantage point of resisting a formation of a particular political subjectivity that is incompatible with the objective of the project. It is a project defined to target the points of application, an initiative to control the experiences and govern the regime of possible experiences. However, the occupation it tries to displace and the field it aims to control is on that regime which has long been constituted by doubles. This is not to be confused with contradictions or an incompatible presence of two differences: so that the mark is drawn as the space between absence and presence of the constitutions of an identity; for example, the diffusion in recognising the self. It has been already mapped as a surface of experiences marked by a series of fragmented articulations. The doubles have an evasive pattern of existence. A close examination on these micro events, which are not visibly presented to the basic gaze of surveillance, exhibits the fact that it is an irruption in articulating one's experience. In other words, a gradual process of appropriating one's self in different discourses presented to the way one has to exercise the self or the formulation of the rules of governing the subjectivity one is experiencing with has consequently threatened 'daily life' itself. It is far more difficult to represent in the midst of experiences in the entire period starting from the middle of the twentieth century. While its disaggregation can be made visible and tangible, the positive substance of what is being defended tends to reduce itself to non-recognised oddities, a victim of violence and a shattered self. Inability to articulate the representation of the daily life is one of the most concrete outcomes of the nature of 'political occupation' manifested in the events fit to the ongoing conflict between occupying the domain of experiences and resisting the experience itself. Security ceases to be a fixed reference when there is a conflict between the occupation and the resistance of experiences. Thus development, which is projected in the policy, may produce further fragmentation of experiences. Security is bound to be interrogated and contested more intensely.

Emergence of an 'innocent subject' in both the private and public rules of governing one's self is an example of the prominence of a particular political subjectivity lingering inside the very crisis of daily life in contemporary Manipuri society. The rise of innocent subject as a form of political subjectivity can be traced from two conditions of the emergence of a subjectivity: one, by involving the individual into a series of events that in relation to the position of the subject, for example citizen, rebel, criminal or anti-national or terrorist, or civilian, forms an intelligible field of participation of which the subject speaks, practice and bears the marker. Two, by representing the self into the exercise of that subject position as a visible character, which is recognised, validated and also face opposition at the same time, or contestations from outside the discourse of the events and the participation. However, the contemporary 'political' in Manipur rather produces a break in spite of the conditions that are present. Consequently, these two conditions have formally established a separation of experience and its representation. It can be further inquired by locating the political subjectivity into the separation of the experience and representation.

Sequestrating the experience of the self from being represented both at private and public field is related to a gradual development of a regime of surveillance which itself tells the very evidence of a conflict in daily life. It is a separation of the events and the articulation of the experiences. The crisis of daily life in contemporary Manipur speaks of a gradual deletion of events from experiences. Experiences are embodied into different but often conflicting meanings and consequently an event becomes a moment of unparticipated game where its disappearance begins. It does not mean that the event is meaningless but rather implies a condition of disappearing itself from being represented. That is how experiences cannot be represented in the exercise of the rules of governing one's self within the surveillance. An interesting point in this regard is the fact that disciplinary surveillance does not originate from external forces only, for example, the State and the National movement. It has its origin within the individuals too. It is here that the 'innocent subject' rises. It rises because events are unconstrained from representation. Disappearance of events from the intelligibility of the discourse, of which the events bear the mark and articulate, takes a form of political subjectivity, which is fragmented, disarticulated, disjuncted, disengaged and unrepresented. This subject is the 'innocent subject.' Innocence is thus an alarming crisis of the 'political'.

Production of disengaged subjectivities is made to be a condition of governing development while ensuring security in the process. The Look East Policy will further intensify the crises of historical contingencies. The crisis of political subjectivity in Manipur will further support for more forms of disarticulations. The survey of the global in the state is a challenge both to control and resist experiences. Subversive politics behind the construction of the security map on the non-territorialised space in complicity with the intricacies of possible reclamation of new 'political' will expose the underlying tendencies of LEP that one can see it as a condition of hybrid articulations/disarticulations in contemporary Manipuri society. The challenge is again only the 'political' and its subsequent crises.

REFERENCES

Dean, Mitchell. 1999. *Governmentality.* London: Sage Publication.

Foucault, M.. 1991. 'Governmentality' in Burchell, Gordon and Miller,(eds.). *The Foucault Effect: Studies in Governmentality.* The University of Chicago Press.

IMF Working Paper (04/118). 2005. 'Is India becoming an Engine of Global Growth?' in *World Economic Outlook,* IMF, September.

Khoman, Thanat. 1992. 'ASEAN: Conceptions and Evolutions' in KS Shadhu (ed.). *The ASEAN Reader.* Singapore: Institute of Southeast Asian Studies.

Laclau, Ernesto and Chantal Mouffe. 1985. *Hegemony and Socialist Strategy.* London: Verso.

Lemke, Thomas. 2001. 'The Birth of Bio-politics: Michel Foucault's lecture at the College de France on Neo-liberal_Governmentaity'. *Economy and Society,* Volume 30, May, Number 2.

RIS, *Discussion Papers,* 100 'Towards a broader Asian Community: Agenda for East Summit'.

RIS, *Discussion Papers,* 100.

Welfare, Paul J. J. 2006. *Integration in Asia and Europe.* Heidelberg Springer.

Index